Real Reading 2

Creating an Authentic Reading Experience
David Wiese

Lynn Bonesteel
Series Editor

Paul Nation
Series Consultant

PEARSON
Longman

Real Reading 2: Creating an Authentic Reading Experience

Pearson Education, 10 Bank Street, White Plains, NY 10606

Staff credits: The people who made up the **Real Reading 2** team, representing editorial, production, design, and manufacturing, are Nancy Flaggman, Ann France, Dana Klinek, Amy McCormick, Joan Poole, Robert Ruvo, Debbie Sistino, and Jennifer Stem.

Cover art: Shutterstock.com
Text composition: TSI Graphics
Text font: Helvetica Neue
Illustrations: TSI Graphics—pages 13, 153, 177, 184, 194; Gary Torrisi—pages 35, 37, 125

Library of Congress Cataloging-in-Publication Data

Bonesteel, Lynn.
  Real reading : creating an authentic reading experience / Lynn Bonesteel.
      p. cm.
  Includes index.
  ISBN-10: 0-13-606654-2 (Level 1)
  ISBN-10: 0-13-814627-6 (Level 2)
  ISBN-10: 0-13-714443-1 (Level 3)
  ISBN-10: 0-13-502771-3 (Level 4)
  [etc.]
  1. English language--Textbooks for foreign speakers. 2. Reading comprehension.
  3. Vocabulary. I. Title.
  PE1128.B6243 2010
  428.6'4--dc22

                                                    2010017172

PEARSON LONGMAN ON THE **WEB**

Pearsonlongman.com offers online resources for teachers. Access our Companion Websites, our online catalog, and our local offices around the world.

Visit us at **pearsonlongman.com**.

ISBN 10: 0-13-814627-6
ISBN 13: 978-0-13-814627-6

Printed in the United States of America
1 2 3 4 5 6 7 8 9 10—V011—15 14 13 12 11 10

CONTENTS

Acknowledgments...v

Introduction vi

The Real Reading Unit viii

Scope and Sequence xiv

References..xviii

UNIT 1 **The Truth About Shyness**..............................1
CHAPTER 1 Why Are We Shy? 2
CHAPTER 2 It's All an Act...8

UNIT 2 **The Good Guys in Sports**..........................15
CHAPTER 3 A Tall Order...16
CHAPTER 4 Hull City Tigers Discussion Board 23

UNIT 3 **It's Not Easy Being Green**.........................30
CHAPTER 5 A Cleaner Way to Shop?.......................31
CHAPTER 6 Green Airplanes....................................37
Fluency Practice 1 45

UNIT 4 **Strange Travels**.......................................51
CHAPTER 7 The World's Strangest Hotels 52
CHAPTER 8 Small Town, Strange Festival................58

UNIT 5 **The Food We Love**....................................68
CHAPTER 9 What Is American Food?.......................69
CHAPTER 10 Why Chilies Are Hot............................77

UNIT 6 **Music**...84
CHAPTER 11 All About Music 85
CHAPTER 12 Can't Name That Tune?......................92
Fluency Practice 2 101

UNIT 7 **The Movie Business**...107

    CHAPTER 13 Famous Flops 108

    CHAPTER 14 Sleeper Hits...................................115

UNIT 8 **All in the Family**...124

    CHAPTER 15 Rebel with a Cause......................125

    CHAPTER 16 About *The Nurture Assumption* 132

UNIT 9 **Haiku**...140

    CHAPTER 17 The Haiku Master.........................141

    CHAPTER 18 So You Want to Write Haiku?.........147

    Fluency Practice 3 154

UNIT 10 **Big Buildings** 160

    CHAPTER 19 Race for the Sky 161

    CHAPTER 20 Anybody Want to Buy a Stadium? 167

UNIT 11 **Body Language: The Science of Pheromones** .. 177

    CHAPTER 21 Pheromone Perfume 178

    CHAPTER 22 The Language of Pheromones 186

UNIT 12 **High Seas, High Tech**..............................196

    CHAPTER 23 The Chronometer.........................197

    CHAPTER 24 The Treasure of the SS *Central America*...203

    Fluency Practice 4 210

Unit 3 Quiz: How Green Are You? 215

New Words 216

Vocabulary Practice 1–12 218

Fluency Progress Charts 230

Fluency Practice Answer Key 231

Pronunciation Table 233

Vocabulary Index 234

Credits..237

MP3 Audio Tracking Guide 238

Acknowledgments

I would like to extend my sincere gratitude to all those at Pearson who contributed advice, expertise, and hard work to this project. Special thanks to Debbie Sistino for her mentorship, to Series Editor Lynn Bonesteel for her creative genius, to Senior Editors Joan Poole and Dana Klinek for their constant support, and to Associate Managing Editor Robert Ruvo, Senior Art Director Ann France, and Photo Research Manager Aerin Csigay for creating a beautifully designed and illustrated book.

I would also like to thank Paul Nation, whose conception of an authentic reading experience was the inspiration for this series, Alice Savage, whose good humor and creativity made the *Real Reading* collaboration a pleasure, and John Beaumont, who introduced me to so many of the above people.

Finally, I would like to thank my parents Ken and Julie, my lovely wife Gessi, and my family and friends for their unconditional love and support over so many years.

David Wiese

Reviewers

William Brazda, Long Beach City College, Long Beach, CA; **Abigail Brown**, University of Hawaii, Honolulu, HI; **David Dahnke**, North Harris Community College, Houston, TX; **Scott Fisher**, Sungshin Women's University, Seoul, Korea; **Roberta Hodges**, Sonoma State American Language Institute, Sonoma, CA; **Kate Johnson**, Union County College Institute For Intensive English, Elizabeth, NJ; **Thomas Justice**, North Shore Community College, Danvers, MA; **Michael McCollister**, Feng Chia University, Taiching, Taiwan; **Myra Medina**, Miami-Dade Community College, Miami, FL; **Lesley Morgan**, West Virginia University, Morgantown, WV; **Angela Parrino**, Hunter College, New York, NY; **Christine Sharpe**, Howard Community College, Columbia, MD; **Christine Tierney**, Houston Community College, Houston, TX; **Kerry Vrabel**, GateWay Community College, Phoenix, AZ.

INTRODUCTION

Real Reading 2 is the second book in a four-level (beginning, low intermediate, intermediate, and high intermediate) intensive reading series for learners of English. The books in the series feature high-interest readings that have been carefully written or adapted from authentic sources to allow effective comprehension by learners at each level. The aim is for learners to be able to engage with the content in a meaningful and authentic way, as readers do in their native language. For example, learners who use *Real Reading* will be able to read to learn or feel something new, to evaluate information and ideas, to experience or share an emotion, to see something from a new perspective, or simply to get pleasure from reading in English. High-interest topics include superstitions, shyness, neuroscience, sports, magic, and technology, among others.

> THE *REAL READING* APPROACH

To allow for effective comprehension, the vocabulary in the readings in the *Real Reading* series has been controlled so that 95-98 percent of the words are likely to be known by a typical learner at each level. The vocabulary choices were based on analyses of the General Service Word List (GSL) (Michael West, 1953), the Academic Word List (AWL) (Averil Coxhead, 2000), and the Billuroğlu-Neufeld List (BNL) (Ali Billuroğlu and Steve Neufeld, 2007).

Research has shown that as they read a text, good readers employ a variety of skills.[1] Thus, essential reading skills, such as predicting, skimming, making inferences, and understanding text references, are presented, practiced, and recycled in each level of *Real Reading*, with level-appropriate explanations and practice. The goal is for learners to become autonomous readers in English; the reading skills are the tools that will help learners achieve this goal.

Vocabulary development skills and strategies are prominently featured in every chapter in *Real Reading*. The importance of vocabulary size to reading comprehension and fluency has been well documented in the research on both first and second language acquisition.[2] Thus, in the *Real Reading* series, learners are given extensive practice in applying level-appropriate skills and strategies to their acquisition of the target words in each chapter. This practice serves two purposes: First, because the target words have been selected from among the most frequent words in general and academic English, learners who use the books are exposed to the words that they will encounter most frequently in English texts. Second, through repeated practice with vocabulary skills and learning strategies, learners will acquire the tools they need to continue expanding their vocabulary long after completing the books in the series.

---

[1] Nation, I.S.P. *Learning Vocabulary in Another Language.* Cambridge, England: Cambridge University Press. 2001.

[2] Nation, I.S.P. *Teaching Vocabulary: Strategies and Techniques.* Boston, MA: Heinle, Cengage Learning. 2008.

VOCABULARY: FROM RESEARCH TO PRACTICE
By Paul Nation

Real Reading puts several well-established vocabulary-based principles into practice.

1. There is the idea that meaning-focused input should contain a small amount of unknown vocabulary but that this amount should be limited so that the learners can read for understanding without being overburdened by a large number of unknown words. Research suggests that somewhere around two percent of the running words in a text may be initially unknown and still allow a reasonable level of comprehension. If the number of unknown words is too large, then the learners cannot participate in an authentic reading experience. That is, they cannot read the text and react in the same way as a native speaker would. The texts in *Real Reading* have been developed so that learners are likely to gain a high level of comprehension while encountering some new words that they can begin to learn.

2. The activities in *Real Reading*, along with the texts, provide learners with the opportunity to thoughtfully process the unknown vocabulary that they encounter. In most of the exercises, the contexts for the target words are different from the contexts provided in the texts. This helps stretch the meaning of the new words and makes them more memorable. The various exercises also require the target words to be used in ways that will help learning.

3. *Real Reading* includes a systematic approach to the development of important vocabulary learning strategies. The ultimate goal of instructed vocabulary learning should be to help learners become autonomous language learners. An important step in this process is gaining control of effective vocabulary learning strategies, such as using word cards, using word parts, and using a dictionary. *Real Reading* includes vocabulary strategies in every unit. The strategies are broken down into their components, practiced and recycled in the vocabulary practice pages at the back of the books.

4. The sequencing of the vocabulary in *Real Reading* has been carefully designed so that the new items will not interfere with each other. That is, presenting the target words together with new vocabulary that belongs to the same lexical set or consists of opposites or synonyms greatly increases the difficulty of vocabulary learning. It is much more helpful if the unknown vocabulary fits together in ways that are similar to the ways the words occur in the texts.

5. Finally, a well-balanced language course provides four major kinds of opportunities for vocabulary learning. A unique feature of *Real Reading* is its use of these research-based principles. First, there is the opportunity to learn through *meaning-focused input*, where the learners' attention is focused on the message of what they are reading or listening to. Second, there is an opportunity to learn through *meaning-focused output*, where the learners are intent on conveying messages. Third, there is the opportunity to learn through *language-focused learning*, where learners give deliberate attention to language features. Fourth, there is the opportunity to *develop fluency* with what is already known. In a variety of ways, the *Real Reading* textbooks provide these opportunities. Their main focus is on deliberate learning through conscious attention to vocabulary, and through the use of specially designed exercises.

THE *REAL READING* UNIT

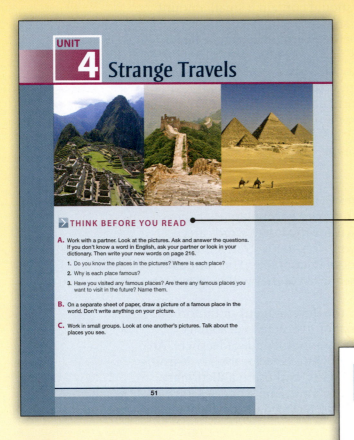

THINK BEFORE YOU READ

Each unit begins with a captivating opener that introduces students to the unit theme, elicits vocabulary relevant to the theme, and includes discussion questions to activate students' prior knowledge and stimulate interest.

PREPARE TO READ
This section previews words and phrases that students will encounter in the reading. Students reflect on what they already know and then answer questions about the topic.

READING SKILLS Every unit has one or two reading skills, which include previewing and predicting; understanding topics, main ideas, and details; and understanding cause and effect, among others.

READ The readings feature a wide variety of high-interest, contemporary topics, including business, science and nature, music and the visual arts, culture and society, sports and exercise, and health and nutrition, as well as a variety of genres, including newspaper and magazine articles, blogs, Web sites, newsletters, travel logs, personal essays, poetry, and short stories. Vocabulary is tightly controlled at each level, and target words are recycled from one chapter to the next within a unit, from unit to unit, and from one level to the next.

Reading Skill: Previewing and Predicting

Before you read something, first get a general idea about the topic and type of text by *previewing*. To preview, read the title and any headings. Look at any pictures. Think about what you already know about the topic. Also think about what kind of text it is—for example, a story, an article, or an e-mail. For a short text, read the first and last sentence of every paragraph. Try to guess, or *predict*, what the reading will be about.

C. Preview the newspaper article "A Cleaner Way to Shop?" Then answer the questions.

1. What is the main idea of the reading?
   a. Online shopping costs more than shopping in a store.
   b. Online shopping is bad for the environment.
   c. You should not buy things online.

2. What helped you figure out the main idea?
   a. the picture
   b. the first sentence of the first paragraph
   c. the last sentence of the first paragraph

READ

Read "A Cleaner Way to Shop?" Underline the sentence that gives the main idea of the reading.

A Cleaner Way to Shop?

Need to buy something? Why go to a store? Buy it on the Internet! Need it now? Why wait? Ask for next-day **delivery**! Each day, more and more people try online shopping.
[5] In fact, online sales have **doubled** in the last ten years. But not everyone is excited. Some scientists now say that online shopping is bad for the **environment**.
   People are surprised to hear this. "They [10] think, 'I don't need to drive, and the business doesn't need to build a store, so there will be less pollution,'" says Nuria Prost, an environmental scientist. "But it is not so simple. In [15] fact, online shopping is **wasteful**. It also adds to air pollution."
   In truth, the Internet is not always as good a friend [20] to the environment as it seems. For example, most people thought that the Internet would help offices use less paper and other [25] **materials**. But paper use increased by 33 percent between 1986 and 1997. "[Online shopping]

could have similarly negative effects," says Nevil Cohen, a professor of environmental science.
   Part of the problem is what people are [30] buying these days. In the past, people bought things on the Internet that did not **require** much packing material, such as books and clothing. But now people also shop online for large, heavy products such as televisions, [35] computers, and furniture. These products need to be packed in large amounts of plastic and paper. This creates a lot of waste.
   Another problem caused by online shopping is air pollution. When **customers** [40] buy products and ask for next-day delivery, companies often have to send them by air. Airplanes use much more **fuel** than cars and produce more carbon dioxide.[1] When people buy a lot of different things from different [45] online businesses, this creates even more travel by airplanes.
   Online product returns are also a problem. For example, an online shoe store may **allow** customers to return shoes for free if they [50] are the wrong size. This doubles the packing materials and number of airplane trips required to sell one pair of shoes.
   "If people want to protect the environment, they need to think before they shop," says [55] Prost. "People need to ask themselves: Is this exactly what I want? Do I really need it tomorrow, or can I wait?" Online stores can also **charge** customers for returns. This may make people shop more carefully. "Online [60] shopping is fast and easy," says Prost, "but we can't forget the negative effect it has on the environment."

[1] **carbon dioxide:** the gas produced when people or animals breathe out or when carbon is burned in air, which may make the Earth warmer

Vocabulary Check

Write the boldfaced word from the reading next to the correct definition. Use the correct form of the word.

1. _____ = a substance such as coal, gas, or oil that can be burned to produce heat or energy
2. _____ = to need something
3. _____ = the act of bringing something (e.g., a letter or package) to a particular place or person
4. _____ = things such as wood, plastic, paper, etc., that are used for making or doing something
5. _____ = to give someone permission to do something
6. _____ = using more of something than is needed
7. _____ = someone who buys things from a store or company
8. _____ = the land, water, and air in which people, animals, and plants live
9. _____ = to become twice as large, or twice as much
10. _____ = to ask for a particular amount of money for a service or something you are selling

32   UNIT 3 ■ It's Not Easy Being Green

CHAPTER 5 ■ A Cleaner Way to Shop?   33

VOCABULARY CHECK This section gives students an opportunity to focus on the meaning of the target vocabulary before completing the comprehension activities.

THE *REAL READING* UNIT (continued)

READING GOAL The reading goal gives students a purpose for rereading the text before completing the comprehension activities. Reading goals include completing a graphic organizer, giving an oral or written summary of a text, retelling a story, identifying the writer's point of view, and giving an opinion on the content of a text, among others.

COMPREHENSION CHECK
Engaging and varied exercises help students achieve the reading goal. Target vocabulary is recycled, giving students additional exposure to the high frequency words and expressions.

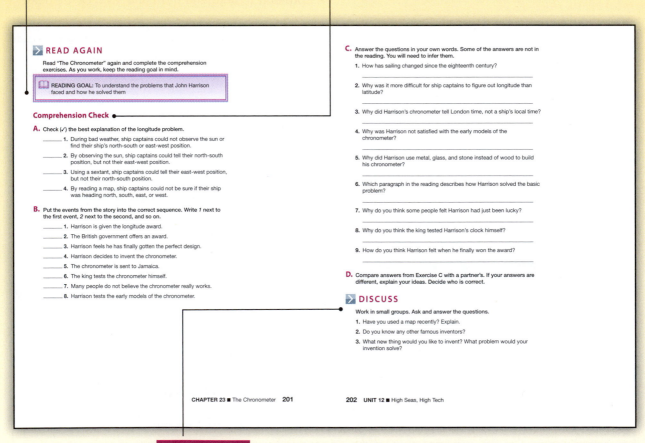

READ AGAIN

Read "The Chronometer" again and complete the comprehension exercises. As you work, keep the reading goal in mind.

> **READING GOAL:** To understand the problems that John Harrison faced and how he solved them

Comprehension Check

A. Check (✓) the best explanation of the longitude problem.

_____ 1. During bad weather, ship captains could not observe the sun or find their ship's north-south or east-west position.

_____ 2. By observing the sun, ship captains could tell their north-south position, but not their east-west position.

_____ 3. Using a sextant, ship captains could tell their east-west position, but not their north-south position.

_____ 4. By reading a map, ship captains could not be sure if their ship was heading north, south, east, or west.

B. Put the events from the story into the correct sequence. Write *1* next to the first event, *2* next to the second, and so on.

_____ 1. Harrison is given the longitude award.

_____ 2. The British government offers an award.

_____ 3. Harrison feels he has finally gotten the perfect design.

_____ 4. Harrison decides to invent the chronometer.

_____ 5. The chronometer is sent to Jamaica.

_____ 6. The king tests the chronometer himself.

_____ 7. Many people do not believe the chronometer really works.

_____ 8. Harrison tests the early models of the chronometer.

C. Answer the questions in your own words. Some of the answers are not in the reading. You will need to infer them.

1. How has sailing changed since the eighteenth century?
_____

2. Why was it more difficult for ship captains to figure out longitude than latitude?
_____

3. Why did Harrison's chronometer tell London time, not a ship's local time?
_____

4. Why was Harrison not satisfied with the early models of the chronometer?
_____

5. Why did Harrison use metal, glass, and stone instead of wood to build his chronometer?
_____

6. Which paragraph in the reading describes how Harrison solved the basic problem?
_____

7. Why do you think some people felt Harrison had just been lucky?
_____

8. Why do you think the king tested Harrison's clock himself?
_____

9. How do you think Harrison felt when he finally won the award?
_____

D. Compare answers from Exercise C with a partner's. If your answers are different, explain your ideas. Decide who is correct.

DISCUSS

Work in small groups. Ask and answer the questions.

1. Have you used a map recently? Explain.

2. Do you know any other famous inventors?

3. What new thing would you like to invent? What problem would your invention solve?

DISCUSS A variety of activities for small group or pair work encourages students to use vocabulary from the current unit as well as previous units.

VOCABULARY SKILL BUILDING

This section offers presentation and practice with skills such as identifying parts of speech, learning and using derived forms of target words, learning common affixes and roots, and recognizing common collocations, among others.

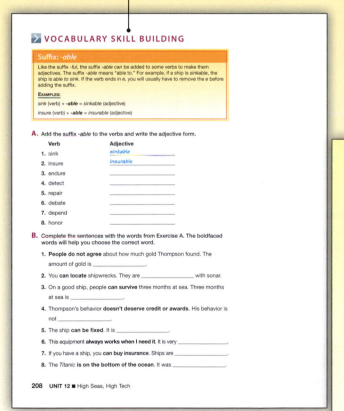

VOCABULARY SKILL BUILDING

Suffix: -able

Like the suffix -ful, the suffix -able can be added to some verbs to make them adjectives. The suffix -able means "able to." For example, if a ship is sinkable, the ship is able to sink. If the verb ends in e, you will usually have to remove the e before adding the suffix.

EXAMPLES:

sink (verb) + -able = sinkable (adjective)

insure (verb) + -able = insurable (adjective)

A. Add the suffix -able to the verbs and write the adjective form.

Verb	Adjective
1. sink	sinkable
2. insure	insurable
3. endure	
4. detect	
5. repair	
6. debate	
7. depend	
8. honor	

B. Complete the sentences with the words from Exercise A. The boldfaced words will help you choose the correct word.

1. **People do not agree** about how much gold Thompson found. The amount of gold is _____.

2. You **can locate** shipwrecks. They are _____ with sonar.

3. On a good ship, people **can survive** three months at sea. Three months at sea is _____.

4. Thompson's behavior **doesn't deserve credit or awards.** His behavior is not _____.

5. The ship **can be fixed.** It is _____.

6. This equipment **always works when I need it.** It is very _____.

7. If you have a ship, you **can buy insurance.** Ships are _____.

8. The Titanic **is on the bottom of the ocean.** It was _____.

208   UNIT 12 ■ High Seas, High Tech

LEARN THE VOCABULARY

This final section of each unit challenges students to practice strategies and techniques outlined by Paul Nation that will help them to acquire not only the target vocabulary but also vocabulary beyond the text. Activities include learning from word cards, guessing meaning from context, discovering core meaning, using a dictionary, and learning word parts, among others.

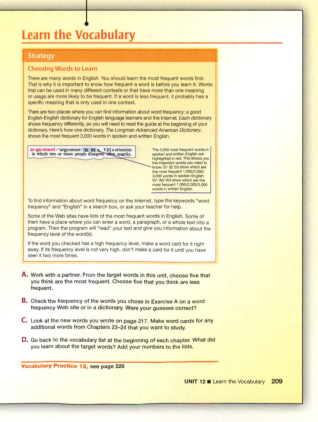

Learn the Vocabulary

Strategy

Choosing Words to Learn

There are many words in English. You should learn the most frequent words first. That is why it is important to know how frequent a word is before you learn it. Words that can be used in many different contexts or that have more than one meaning or usage are more likely to be frequent. If a word is less frequent, it probably has a specific meaning that is only used in one context.

There are two places where you can find information about word frequency: a good English-English dictionary for English language learners and the Internet. Each dictionary shows frequency differently, so you will need to read the guide at the beginning of your dictionary. Here's how one dictionary, The Longman Advanced American Dictionary, shows the most frequent 3,000 words in spoken and written English.

ar-gu-ment /ˈɑrgyəmənt/ n. W1 S1 a situation in which two or more people disagree, often angrily.

The 3,000 most frequent words in spoken and written English are highlighted in red. This shows you the important words you need to know. S1 S2 S3 show which are the most frequent 1,000/2,000/3,000 words in spoken English. W1 W2 W3 show which are the most frequent 1,000/2,000/3,000 words in written English.

To find information about word frequency on the Internet, type the keywords "word frequency" and "English" in a search box, or ask your teacher for help.

Some of the Web sites have lists of the most frequent words in English. Some of them have a place where you can enter a word, a paragraph, or a whole text into a program. Then the program will "read" your text and give you information about the frequency level of the word(s).

If the word you checked has a high frequency level, make a word card for it right away. If its frequency level is not very high, don't make a card for it until you have seen it two more times.

A. Work with a partner. From the target words in this unit, choose five that you think are the most frequent. Choose five that you think are less frequent.

B. Check the frequency of the words you chose in Exercise A on a word frequency Web site or in a dictionary. Were your guesses correct?

C. Look at the new words you wrote on page 217. Make word cards for any additional words from Chapters 23–24 that you want to study.

D. Go back to the vocabulary list at the beginning of each chapter. What did you learn about the target words? Add your numbers to the lists.

Vocabulary Practice 12, see page 229

UNIT 12 ■ Learn the Vocabulary   209

THE *REAL READING* UNIT (continued)

FLUENCY PRACTICE

Four fluency practice sections address learners' extensive reading needs. Learners practice fluency strategies, read passages, check comprehension, and calculate their reading times. Fluency progress charts are provided at the back of the book for students to record their reading times and Comprehension Check scores.

VOCABULARY PRACTICE

These pages appear at the back of the book and reinforce understanding of the target vocabulary, vocabulary skills, and vocabulary learning strategies.

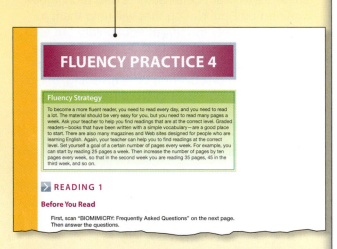

FLUENCY PRACTICE 4

Fluency Strategy

To become a more fluent reader, you need to read every day, and you need to read a lot. The material should be very easy for you, but you need to read many pages a week. Ask your teacher to help you find readings that are at the correct level. Graded readers—books that have been written with a simple vocabulary—are a good place to start. There are also many magazines and Web sites designed for people who are learning English. Again, your teacher can help you to find readings at the correct level. Set yourself a goal of a certain number of pages every week. For example, you can start by reading 25 pages a week. Then increase the number of pages by ten pages every week, so that in the second week you are reading 35 pages, 45 in the third week, and so on.

▶ **READING 1**

Before You Read

First, scan "BIOMIMICRY: Frequently Asked Questions" on the next page. Then answer the questions.

FLUENCY PRACTICE 4

	Words per Minute	
	First Try	**Second Try**
Reading 1		
Reading 2		
Comprehension Check Score _____%		

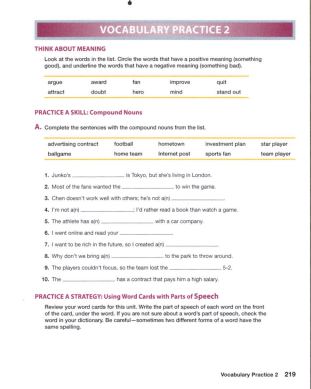

VOCABULARY PRACTICE 2

THINK ABOUT MEANING

Look at the words in the list. Circle the words that have a positive meaning (something good), and underline the words that have a negative meaning (something bad).

argue	award	fan	improve	quit
attract	doubt	hero	mind	stand out

PRACTICE A SKILL: Compound Nouns

A. Complete the sentences with the compound nouns from the list.

advertising contract	football	hometown	investment plan	star player
ballgame	home team	Internet post	sports fan	team player

1. Junko's _____ is Tokyo, but she's living in London.
2. Most of the fans wanted the _____ to win the game.
3. Chen doesn't work well with others; he's not a(n) _____
4. I'm not a(n) _____; I'd rather read a book than watch a game.
5. The athlete has a(n) _____ with a car company.
6. I went online and read your _____
7. I want to be rich in the future, so I created a(n) _____
8. Why don't we bring a(n) _____ to the park to throw around.
9. The players couldn't focus, so the team lost the _____ 5-2.
10. The _____ has a contract that pays him a high salary.

PRACTICE A STRATEGY: Using Word Cards with Parts of Speech

Review your word cards for this unit. Write the part of speech of each word on the front of the card, under the word. If you are not sure about a word's part of speech, check the word in your dictionary. Be careful—sometimes two different forms of a word have the same spelling.

Vocabulary Practice 2   219

- **MP3 Audio CD-ROM:** Each level has a bound-in MP3 Audio CD-ROM with recordings of all target vocabulary and readings.

- **Teacher's Manual:** The online Teacher's Manual provides a model lesson plan and includes the Student Book Answer Key. The Teacher's Manual is available at www.pearsonlongman.com/realreading.

- **Tests:** The Online Tests consist of a reading passage followed by comprehension, vocabulary, and vocabulary skill questions for each unit. An answer key is included. The Tests are available at www.pearsonlongman.com/realreading.

HOW TO USE THE LESSON PLAN

Overview of Unit Format

Each unit of Real Reading 1 consists of two thematically related chapters. Compelling readings in a variety of genres have been carefully written or adapted from authentic sources and feature a principled approach to vocabulary development.

- Chapters consist of pre-reading and post-reading activities, including a reading skill, a reading goal, comprehension questions, and discussion activities.
- Reading and vocabulary skill building and vocabulary learning strategies based on Paul Nation's research help students become more confident and successful in preparation for academic reading and reading on standardized tests.

Suggested Methods of Instruction

This lesson plan can serve as a generic guide for any chapter in the student book.

- Suggested methods for delivering instruction for each section or activity in a chapter are presented.
- Alternative ways to handle each activity are provided under the heading
  Variations. These options allow instructors to vary the way they treat the same activity from chapter to chapter and in so doing to identify the methods that work best for a specific class or individual students.

Think Before You Read

The activities in this section are designed to prepare students for the topics, themes, and key vocabulary in the readings.

A. and B. *(approximately 10 minutes)*

1. Give students a few minutes to read the discussion questions. Answer any questions.
2. Have students form pairs to discuss their answers. Tell them they will report at least one of their answers to the class.

After 10 minutes, ask several students to share their answers.

Variations

- After students have discussed the questions, ask them to write for 1–3 minutes in answer to the questions. Have students exchange their writing with a partner or group member and compare their ideas.
- Ask students to answer the discussion questions in writing at home. Have them read their partner's or group members' answers in class and discuss their answers.
- Assign one discussion question per pair or small group. Have each pair or group discuss the question and report their ideas to the class.
- Choose one discussion question and have each student do a one-minute freewrite to expand ideas generated from the discussion. The students' writing can be passed around the class or reviewed in small groups to encourage further feedback and discussion. The activity may also serve as a closure to the discussion.

Real Reading Teacher's Guide   **1**

NAME: _____   DATE: _____   SCORE: ____ /40

UNIT 1
TEST
Synchronized Swimming

It's part swimming, part gymnastics, and part dance. It's synchronized swimming, one of the more unusual sports in the Olympic Games. Many people love to watch it. The swimmers move their bodies in and out, forward and back, on the surface and under water. They move in perfect time with each other and the music.

Synchronized swimming was first called "water ballet." It's easy to see why. It's like ballet. And like ballet, it seems easy, but it isn't. The swimmers seem natural and relaxed, but they have to train for a long time. Many exercises are done under water, so they have to hold their breath for as long as two minutes. It takes a lot of strength, power, and energy.

Synchronized swimming first began in Europe in the 1890s. At that time, swimmers often trained outside, in rivers or in lakes. The first synchronized swimmers were men. But by the middle of the 20th century, most synchronized swimmers were women. Swimmers sometimes performed in the theater, where they swam in large water tanks on the stage! Later, some Hollywood musicals used synchronized swimmers. The actress Esther Williams starred in movies such as *Bathing Beauty* in 1944 and *Million Dollar Mermaid* in 1952.

Synchronized swimming became an Olympic sport in 1984. In the Olympic Games, swimmers work in teams of nine athletes, or in pairs. They show their skills by doing special movements above and below the water. They do not touch the bottom of the pool. Instead, they move their hands like flippers and kick their feet. This helps them stay up in the water. Like all Olympic athletes, they work very hard. Their dream is the same: to win a medal for their country in the Olympic Games.

Part 1

Comprehension

Circle the letter of the correct answer to complete each sentence.

1. In the Olympics, synchronized swimming is done _____.
   a. on land   b. to music   c. by one person
2. According to the article, synchronized swimming looks _____.
   a. easy   b. difficult   c. dangerous
3. Swimmers have to hold their breath because they need to _____.
   a. be underwater b. train outside   c. swim on the surface
4. Synchronized swimming was first done by _____.
   a. children   b. men   c. women
5. In the early part of the twentieth century, people watched synchronized swimming _____.
   a. in the Olympics   b. in the theater   c. at the beach
6. In the Olympics, the swimmers cannot _____.
   a. kick their feet b. move their hands   c. touch the bottom

   Total: ____ / 6

© 2011 by Pearson Education, Inc. Duplication for classroom use is permitted.

SCOPE AND SEQUENCE

Unit	Chapter	Reading Skill
1 The Truth About Shyness	**1** Why Are We Shy?	Understanding the Topic and Main Idea
	2 It's All an Act	Understanding Pronouns
2 The Good Guys in Sports	**3** A Tall Order	Understanding Sequence
	4 Hull City Tigers Discussion Board	Making Inferences
3 It's Not Easy Being Green	**5** A Cleaner Way to Shop?	Previewing and Predicting
	6 Green Airplanes	
Fluency Practice 1	**Reading 1** Aquatic Exercise	
	Reading 2 Michael Phelps: Keys to Success	
4 Strange Travels	**7** The World's Strangest Hotels	Visualizing
	8 Small Town, Strange Festival	Using a Graphic Organizer
5 The Food We Love	**9** What Is American Food?	
	10 Why Chilies Are Hot	Understanding Cause and Effect
6 Music	**11** All About Music	Understanding Examples
	12 Can't Name That Tune?	
Fluency Practice 2	**Reading 1** Dangerous Dining	
	Reading 2 Wild Treasures	

Vocabulary Skill	Vocabulary Strategy
Nouns, Verbs, Adjectives, and Adverbs	Making Word Cards
Compound Nouns	Using Word Cards: Compounds and Example Sentences
Suffixes: *-ful, -ment*	Using a Dictionary
Suffixes: *-ation, -ition, -sion, -ion*	Using a Dictionary: Stressing the Correct Syllable
Suffix: *-y*	Word Cards: Changing Order and Grouping
Adjective Forms of Verbs: *-ing, -ed*	Figuring Out Meaning from Context

SCOPE AND SEQUENCE

Unit	Chapter	Reading Skill
7 The Movie Business	**13** Famous Flops	Understanding Figurative Language
	14 Sleeper Hits	Identifying Key Details
8 All in the Family	**15** Rebel with a Cause	Comparing and Contrasting
	16 About *The Nurture Assumption*	
9 Haiku	**17** The Haiku Master	Scanning
	18 So You Want to Write Haiku?	Following Steps in a Process
Fluency Practice 3	**Reading 1** Folktales	
	Reading 2 Anansi Tales	
10 Big Buildings	**19** Race for the Sky	Recognizing Text References
	20 Anybody Want to Buy a Stadium?	
11 Body Language: The Science of Pheromones	**21** Pheromone Perfume	Distinguishing Facts from Opinions
	22 The Language of Pheromones	Summarizing
12 High Seas, High Tech	**23** The Chronometer	Identifying Problems and Solutions
	24 The Treasure of the SS *Central America*	
Fluency Practice 4	**Reading 1** BIOMIMICRY: Frequently Asked Questions	
	Reading 2 Swarm Intelligence	

Vocabulary Skill	Vocabulary Strategy
Understanding Word Meaning	Finding the Core Meaning of Words
Word Families	Choosing Which Words to Study
Prefix: *over-*	Adding a Picture for Example Sentences
Collocation Patterns	Using Word Parts to Figure Out Meaning
Knowing the Meanings of Roots	The Keyword Technique
Suffix: *-able*	Choosing Words to Learn

References

Allen, J. (1999, July 27). *This 'witch' boasting wicked marketing brew.* CNN. Retrieved August 1, 2009, from: http://www.cnn.com/SHOWBIZ/Movies/9907/27/blair.witch/

Are pheromones a secret weapon for dating? (2005, December 9). ABC News. Retrieved February 20, 2009, from http://abcnews.go.com/2020/Health/story?id=1386825

Benson, E. (2002, October). A pheromone by any other name. *American Psychological Association: Monitor on Psychology*, 33(9), 48.

Christensen, T. (2006, November 28). Corvallis company riding trend of tortilla popularity. *Missoulian.*

Dumars, D. (2000, March 7). *Writer-director David Twohy on his sleeper sci-fi success.* Retrieved January 30, 2009, from: http://www.mania.com/pitch-black-writerdirector-david-twohy-his-sleeper-scifi-success_article_19722.html

Global warming; Chilies. (2008, December 20). *The Economist*, 59–60.

Harris, J.R. (1998). *The nurture assumption.* New York: Touchstone.

Hass, R. (Ed.) (1996). The essential haiku: Versions of Basho, Buson, & Issa. New York: Harper Collins.

Hoon, G. (2009, May 5). *Three steps to a better future.* Speech: Department for Transport. Retrieved July 1, 2009, from: http://www.iacwashington.org/speeches/GeoffHoonIACspeechMay09.pdf

Itano, N. (2008, July 21). As Olympic glow fades, Athens questions $15 billion cost. *Christian Science Monitor*, 4–5.

Miller, B. (2007, July 9). *Boeing unveils 'green' aircraft.* ABC Radio News. Retrieved July 15, 2009, from http://www.abc.net.au/worldtoday/content/2007/s1973371.htm

Sulloway, F.J. (1996). *Born to rebel.* New York: Pantheon.

Tash, J. (2009, March 31). *Ocean side salsa maker rings up sales.* San Diego News Network: http://www.sdnn.com

Technomic top 500 annual report details slowdown in chain restaurant growth rates. (2009, March 30). Business wire: Technomic.

Williams, S. (2006, January 18). *Online shopping and its impact on the environment.* Gotham Gazette. Retrieved October 30, 2009, from: http://www.gothamgazette.com/article/environment/20060118/7/1721

Xiaoying, H. (2008). *Concerns about post-games use of Olympic stadiums.* Retrieved May 4, 2009, from http://www.china.org.cn/olympics/news/2008-09/02/content_16375196.htm

The Truth About Shyness

> THINK BEFORE YOU READ

A. Work with a partner. Look at the picture. Ask and answer the questions. If you don't know a word in English, ask your partner or look in your dictionary. Then write your new words on page 216.

1. What do you see in the picture? Point to the things you see and name them in English.

2. How do you think the woman is feeling? How can you tell?

B. Work with a partner. Ask and answer the questions.

1. Read the definition for *shy*. Are you a shy person? Explain.

> **shy** /ʃaɪ/ (**adj.**) = nervous and embarrassed about meeting and speaking to other people, especially people you do not know

2. Why might shyness keep people from saying and doing what they want to do?

Why Are We Shy?

> PREPARE TO READ

A. Look at the words (and phrases) in the list. Write the number(s) next to each word to show what you know. You may be able to write more than one number next to some of the words. You will study all of these words in this chapter.

    1. I can use the word in a sentence.

    2. I know <u>one meaning</u> of the word.

    3. I know <u>more than one meaning</u> of the word.

    4. I know how to pronounce the word.

B. Work with a partner. Ask and answer the questions. If you don't know a word in English, ask your partner or look in your dictionary. Then write your new words on page 216.

    1. What are some possible reasons for shyness?

    2. Are people born shy, or do they become shy as they grow up?

_____ acquire

_____ anxious

_____ blame

_____ failure

_____ genetic

_____ get over

_____ increase

_____ remarkable

_____ shy

_____ succeed

Reading Skill: Understanding the Topic and Main Idea

When you read something, think about the topic and the main idea:
- The topic is the person, place, or thing that the reading is about. The title of the reading often tells you the topic.
- The main idea is the author's most important idea about the topic. To find the main idea, ask yourself, "What is the writer trying to tell me about the topic?" Sometimes the first or last sentence in a paragraph will help you understand the main idea.

C. Read the first paragraph of the article "Why Are We Shy?" on the next page. Then answer the questions.

1. What is the topic of the reading?
   a. people
   b. shyness
   c. scientists

2. Based on paragraph 1, what is the main idea of the reading?
   a. Close to 50 percent of people are shy.
   b. Shyness is becoming more and more common.
   c. Scientists have some interesting ideas about why people are shy.

 **READ**

First, look at the picture. Why might shyness increase because of the Internet? Then read "Why Are We Shy?" on the next page to find out. Underline the answers to the questions from Exercise B.

Why Are We Shy?

1 Are you **shy**? If you are, you are not alone. In fact, close to 50 percent of people are shy. Almost 80 percent of people feel shy at some point in their lives. These days, shyness 5 is becoming more and more common. Now, scientists are trying to understand shyness. They have some interesting ideas about why people are shy.

Is it possible to be born shy? Many 10 scientists say yes. They say 15 to 20 percent of babies behave shyly. These babies are a little quieter and more watchful than other babies. Interestingly, these shy babies usually have shy parents. As a result, scientists think that some 15 shyness is **genetic**.

Family size might cause people to be shy as well. Scientists at Harvard University studied shy children. They found that 66 percent of them had older brothers and sisters. The 20 scientists said that these children were often bullied[1] by their older brothers and sisters. As a result, they became shy. At the same time, children with no brothers and sisters may be shy as well. Growing up alone, they often play 25 by themselves. They are not able to **acquire** the same social skills as children from big families.

You may also be shy because of where you were born. When scientists studied 30 shyness in different countries, they found remarkable differences. In Japan, most people said they were shy. But in Israel, only one in three people said so. What explains the difference? One scientist says the 35 Japanese and Israelis have different opinions of **failure**. In Japan, when people do not **succeed**, they feel bad about themselves. They **blame** themselves for their failure. In Israel, the opposite is true. Israelis often 40 blame failure on outside reasons, such as family, teachers, friends, or bad luck. In Israel, freedom of opinion and risk taking[2] are strongly supported. This may be why Israelis worry less about failure and are 45 less shy.

Technology could be another cause of shyness. As more and more people use the Internet, they spend less time outside, talking to people. As a result, they lose practice at 50 conversation. Speaking to new people face to face can make them feel **anxious**. Scientists think this may be why the number of shy people in America has **increased** by 10 percent in recent years.

55 For shy people, it can be difficult to make friends, speak in class, and even get a good job. But scientists say you can **get over** your shyness. They suggest trying new things and practicing conversation. And don't forget—if 60 you are shy, you are not the only one.

---

[1] **bullied:** hurt or frightened by someone bigger or stronger
[2] **risk taking:** doing something even though there is a chance that something bad will happen

Vocabulary Check

Complete the sentences with the boldfaced words from the reading.

1. Something that has a bad final result is a(n) _____.

2. When you do something and you _____, you have a good final result.

3. If a problem stops you from doing something, you want to

   _____ it, or learn to control the problem.

4. When you _____ another person, you say that person is

   responsible for something bad.

5. If something is _____ , it surprises you and you want to

   tell people about it.

6. Students often feel _____ before an important test.

7. If you have a good job and earn a lot of money, you can

   _____ a big house and a nice car.

8. If it is difficult for you to meet and speak to new people, you may be a(n)

   _____ person.

9. When something has _____ , it has become larger in

   number or amount.

10. Something that is _____ is passed down to you from your

    parents.

> READ AGAIN

Read "Why Are We Shy?" again and complete the comprehension
exercises. As you work, keep the reading goal in mind.

> READING GOAL: To identify some of the possible causes of shyness

Comprehension Check

A. Read the statements about shyness. Check (✓) the statements that are
true according to the reading.

_____ 1. There are fewer shy people now than there were in the past.

_____ 2. Shy parents often have shy children.

_____ 3. Most Israeli people are shy.

_____ 4. Many shy people have older brothers and sisters.

_____ 5. Children from big families often acquire social skills at home.

_____ 6. Genetics, family size, and birthplace may all cause shyness.

_____ 7. Shyness can cause serious problems.

_____ 8. If you are shy now, you will be shy forever.

B. Complete the outline of the reading. Don't look back at the reading.

Topic: _____ *Shyness* _____

  I. Shyness = common

    A. Almost 50% of people are shy

    B. _____% of people feel shy at some point

    C. These days shyness is becoming more common

    D. _____ are studying shyness

Main idea: Scientists have interesting _____ about why people are shy

  II. 1st idea about why people are shy = _____

    A. 15 to 20% of _____ behave shyly

    B. Shy babies usually have shy _____

  III. 2nd idea about why people are shy = _____

    A. Most shy children have _____ brothers/sisters

    B. Children with no brothers/sisters don't _____ social skills at home

  IV. 3rd idea about why people are shy = where you are _____

    A. In _____, most people say they are shy

    B. In _____, only one in three people say they are shy

    C. People in these countries have different opinions of _____

  V. 4th idea about why people are shy = _____

    A. People who use the Internet lose practice at face-to-face

    _____

    B. Shyness has _____ by 10% in America in recent years

  VI. Conclusion: For shy people, it can be difficult to make friends,

    _____ in class, get a good job

    A. Scientists say people can _____ their shyness

    B. They can practice conversation and try new things

C. Now look back at the reading. Check your answers from Exercise B. Correct any mistakes.

> DISCUSS

Work in small groups. Ask and answer the questions.

1. Did anything in the reading about shyness surprise you? Explain.

2. Do you think shyness is common in your home country? Explain.

3. Other than practicing conversation and trying new things, what else can people do to get over their shyness?

> VOCABULARY SKILL BUILDING

Nouns, Verbs, Adjectives, and Adverbs

To use a word correctly, you need to know its part of speech. *Nouns, verbs, adjectives*, and *adverbs* are the most common parts of speech in English.

Nouns are words for people, places, things, and ideas. The word *scientist* is a noun.

Verbs describe actions, experiences, or states. The words *say* and *believe* are verbs. Some words can be **both nouns and verbs**. The word *cause* can be both a noun (*a cause of shyness*) and a verb (*What causes shyness?*).

Adjectives describe nouns. The words *big* and *surprising* are adjectives.

Adverbs describe verbs and adjectives, or they can describe an entire sentence. The word *usually* is an adverb. Adding *-ly* to an adjective forms many adverbs, as in *surprisingly* and *shyly*.

Are the underlined words nouns, verbs, adjectives, or adverbs? Write *N* for noun, *V* for verb, *ADJ* for adjective, and *ADV* for adverb.

_____ 1. My parents are <u>shy</u> and so am I.

_____ 2. Shyness is <u>increasingly</u> common.

_____ 3. There has been an <u>increase</u> in shyness.

_____ 4. I often feel <u>anxious</u> when I speak in class.

_____ 5. I told the doctor about my <u>anxiety</u>.

_____ 6. Scientists think shyness is <u>genetic</u>.

_____ 7. I <u>succeeded</u> in getting over my shyness.

_____ 8. Judy is shy, but she's had a lot of <u>success</u> in life.

_____ 9. Shyness is <u>remarkably</u> difficult to get over.

_____ 10. He <u>blames</u> himself for his problems.

_____ 11. Shyness may be genetic, or you may <u>acquire</u> it during your life.

_____ 12. Most people <u>successfully</u> get over their shyness if they try.

It's All an Act

> PREPARE TO READ

A. Look at the words (and phrases) in the list. Write the number(s) next to each word to show what you know. You may be able to write more than one number next to some of the words. You will study all of these words in this chapter.

    1. I can use the word in a sentence.

    2. I know <u>one meaning</u> of the word.

    3. I know <u>more than one meaning</u> of the word.

    4. I know how to pronounce the word.

B. Work with a partner. Look at the pictures. Ask and answer the questions. If you don't know a word in English, ask your partner or look in your dictionary. Then write your new words on page 216.

    1. Who are the people in the pictures?

    2. Do you think they are shy people? Why or why not?

    3. What are good jobs for shy people to do? Why?

    4. For shy people, what jobs would be difficult to do? Why?

_____ break out of

_____ coach

_____ crowded

_____ frequently

_____ imaginary

_____ in common

_____ in control

_____ perform

_____ scared

_____ star

C. Read the first two sentences of the magazine article "It's All an Act." Underline the pronoun. What noun(s) does it replace?

 READ

Read "It's All an Act." Underline any pronouns.

It's All an Act

1   Julia Roberts, Nicole Kidman, Tom Cruise, Robert De Niro, and Johnny Depp have something **in common**. They are all movie **stars**, and very successful. But remarkably,
5   they have all described themselves as shy. Movie stars have to **perform** in front of many people, so it seems strange for famous actors to be shy. But, "The fact is," says Roger Moore, who once played James Bond,[1] "most
10 actors are shy people." Could there be a connection between acting and being shy?

Shy people **frequently** like to pretend to be someone else. This, of course, is the same thing actors do at their work. Acting **coach**
15 John Harmon says, "The best actors are usually shy children. They play alone and pretend to be kings, queens, and their favorite animals. Over time, they learn to act in this way." Shy people and actors may feel more comfortable
20 in an **imaginary** world than in the real one. As Nicole Kidman once said, "As a teenager, I was like, 'I hate who I am, I hate how I look, I hate how I feel.' Theater was a place where I could go and just be somebody else." These
25 days, Kidman feels much better about herself and her acting ability. Even so, she still finds herself feeling shy. "I don't like walking into a **crowded** restaurant by myself; I don't like going to a party by myself," she explains. And
30 as strange as it seems, Kidman is not alone.

In fact, many actors worry more about everyday conversation than they do about performing. "I find it hard to talk to people," says Daniel Radcliffe, the star of the Harry
35 Potter[2] movies. Like many shy people, Radcliffe sometimes worries about what to say during a conversation. When acting, of course, this is not a problem. "Actors like acting because they know what to say; the words are already
40 written for them," says Harmon. "They feel **in control** and more comfortable.

For many actors, acting is a way to get over their shyness. "I started [acting] when I was in college because I was shy and
45 thought it would be a good way to **break out of** that," says actor Catherine Bell, who has starred in various popular television shows. Like Bell, some actors get over their shyness after many years of acting. But for
50 most actors, the shyness never completely goes away. "I'm still a little shy," says Julia Roberts, "but now I'm not **scared** of a thing!"

---

[1] **James Bond:** a fictional British spy in books by Ian Fleming and in movies based on these books
[2] **Harry Potter movies:** a fantasy series based on books by British writer J.K. Rowling

Vocabulary Check

A. Write the boldfaced word from the reading next to the correct definition.

1. _____ = very full of people or things

2. _____ = very often or many times

3. _____ = to change the way you live or behave

4. _____ = to show a special ability, such as acting or playing music, in front of other people

5. _____ = someone who trains a person in a sport or special ability

6. _____ = able to remain calm

B. Complete the sentences with the boldfaced words from the reading.

1. Magazines have stories about well-known movie _____, such as Brad Pitt and Nicole Kidman.

2. The young actor felt _____ before her performance, but once she was in control she did a great job.

3. Juan and Seiko have many things _____: They are both tall, shy, and love scary movies.

4. Harry Potter and James Bond are not real people; they are _____ characters from movies.

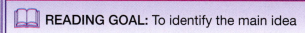 **READ AGAIN**

Read "It's All an Act" again and complete the comprehension exercises on the next page. As you work, keep the reading goal in mind.

> **READING GOAL:** To identify the main idea

Comprehension Check

A. Check (✓) the main idea of the reading.

_____ **1.** Acting is one of many different ways you can get over your shyness.

_____ **2.** There might be a connection between being shy and being an actor.

_____ **3.** Actors are shy, so they pretend to be someone else.

_____ **4.** Shy actors often feel anxious before they perform.

B. Study the boldfaced pronouns. Circle the letter of the word or phrase the pronoun replaces. You will need to look at the reading again. The numbers in parentheses are the paragraphs where you can find the sentences.

1. But remarkably, **they** have all described themselves as shy. (1)
   a. many people
   b. actors who played James Bond
   c. Julia Roberts, Nicole Kidman, Tom Cruise, Robert De Niro, and Johnny Depp
   d. most actors

2. **This**, of course, is the same thing actors do at their work. (2)
   a. pretending to be someone else
   b. being shy
   c. performing in front of many people
   d. being a coach

3. "Over time, **they** learn to act in this way." (2)
   a. kings, queens, or their favorite animals
   b. the best actors
   c. acting coaches
   d. Nicole Kidman and John Harmon

4. And as strange as **it** seems, Kidman is not alone. (2)
   a. the fact that Kidman feels much better about herself
   b. the fact that Kidman feels better about her acting ability
   c. the fact that Kidman still finds herself feeling shy
   d. the fact that Kidman is a successful actress

(continued on next page)

5. When acting, of course, **this** is not a problem. (3)

    a. being Harry Potter

    b. going to the theater

    c. feeling in control

    d. worrying about what to say

6. "I started [acting] when I was in college because I was shy and thought it would be a good way to break out of **that**." (4)

    a. being in college

    b. being shy

    c. acting

    d. conversation

C. These sentences are not in the reading, but they could be added. Write the number of the paragraph where you could add each sentence.

    _____ **1.** In an imaginary world of superheroes or princesses, they don't worry about real life.

    _____ **2.** Similarly, actor Rip Torn says, "I think most actors are shy people, I really do."

    _____ **3.** He worries the most when he is talking to people his own age.

    _____ **4.** In fact, their movies make hundreds of millions of dollars in profit.

    _____ **5.** The college acting classes helped her lose her feelings of shyness.

> DISCUSS

Work in small groups. Ask and answer the questions.

1. Do you know all or some of the actors in the reading? Do you think it is true that most actors are shy?

2. When you were a child, did you ever pretend to be someone else? Who? What did you do?

3. Have you ever performed in a play at school? Describe it.

Learn the Vocabulary

Strategy

Making Word Cards

Word cards are a very good way to learn vocabulary. It is easy to make and use them. Just follow these steps:

- Write the new word on one side of a small (4 x 6) index card.

- On the other side of the card, write the translation in your native language, draw a picture of the word, or write the definition in English. See the example below of a word card with *shyness* in Korean.

- Write the word's part of speech—noun, verb, adjective, or adverb—on the front of the word card, to the right of the word. If the word can be more than one part of speech, include all parts of speech on the card.

- Review your cards at least once a day. When you review, look at one side of the card, and try to remember the information on the other side.

- Say the English word out loud and spell it.

Every day, make a few new cards for the words you want to learn that day and review all of your cards. Never throw any cards away.

shyness (n.)

수줍음

A. Make cards for the words from Chapters 1–2 that were new to you when you started the unit. Include target words and words that you wrote on page 216. Make sure you spell the new words correctly!

B. Work with a partner. Take one of your partner's cards and show him or her the back side of it (the side with the translation, drawing, or definition on it). You look at the front side of the card. Your partner will say and spell the word in English. If your partner makes a mistake, correct him or her. Then your partner will do the same with one of your cards. Continue until you review all of the cards.

C. Go back to the vocabulary list at the beginning of each chapter. What did you learn about the target words? Add your numbers to the lists.

Vocabulary Practice 1, see page 218

UNIT 2

The Good Guys in Sports

> THINK BEFORE YOU READ

A. Work with a partner. Look at the picture. Ask and answer the questions. If you don't know a word in English, ask your partner or look in your dictionary. Then write your new words on page 216.

    1. Who is the man in the picture and what is he doing?

    2. What else do you see in the picture? Point to the things you see and name them in English.

B. Work with a partner. Imagine you work for a news magazine. Choose "The Sports Star of the Year." Rank the following from *1* (most important) to *5* (least important), based on your opinion. Compare your choices.

    _____ **1.** He/She wins many important games.

    _____ **2.** He/She always follows the rules of the game.

    _____ **3.** He/She does good things to help other people.

    _____ **4.** He/She is good-looking.

    _____ **5.** He/She always plays well.

A Tall Order

> PREPARE TO READ

A. Look at the words in the list. Write the number(s) next to each word to show what you know. You may be able to write more than one number next to some of the words. You will study all of these words in this chapter.

   1. I can use the word in a sentence.

   2. I know <u>one meaning</u> of the word.

   3. I know <u>more than one meaning</u> of the word.

   4. I know how to pronounce the word.

B. Work with a partner. Look at the picture. Ask and answer the questions. If you don't know a word in English, ask your partner or look in your dictionary. Then write your new words on page 216.

   1. What sport does the man play?

   2. Do you have a favorite sport? Why is it your favorite?

   3. Do you have a favorite sports star? Why is this person your favorite?

   4. What is the meaning of the unit title "The Good Guys in Sports"? Who are the bad guys in sports?

_____ afford

_____ argue

_____ athlete

_____ award

_____ doubt

_____ hero

_____ improve

_____ quit

_____ reach

_____ salary

_____ treat

To understand the order, or *sequence*, of events that happen in a reading, pay attention to sequence words. They will help you understand the reading. Also, look for dates and age clues.

EXAMPLES:

Common sequence words:

a few years later	over time
at first	soon
at the time	then
for weeks	when

Sample dates and age clues:

13 years old	by 1997
at age 40	in 1985

C. Read the first three paragraphs of the awards brochure "A Tall Order" on the next page and circle the sequence words, dates, and age clues. Then check (✓) the event that happened first.

_____ **1.** Dikembe went to the United States.

_____ **2.** Dikembe cut his face.

_____ **3.** Dikembe started to practice seriously.

 READ

First, look at the picture. Why might a sports star like Dikembe raise money? Then read "A Tall Order" on the next page to find out. Circle sequence words, dates, and age clues as you read Dikembe's life story.

A Tall Order

He is a true basketball **hero**. His full name is Dikembe Mutombo Mpolondo Mukamba Jean-Jacques Wamutombo. Friends call him "Deke." He once hoped to be called Dr. Mutombo. But life gave him another way to help people: as an **athlete**.

A Mind for Medicine, a Body for Basketball

Dikembe was born in 1966 in the African town of Kinshasa, in Zaire, now known as the Democratic Republic of the Congo. The first time he touched a basketball was 1979. He was thirteen years old. At the time, Dikembe was 7 feet tall and still growing. In his first game, he fell and cut his face. He decided he hated basketball. Dikembe told his parents he wanted to **quit**. For weeks, they **argued**. His parents said he had the perfect body for basketball. They told him to keep playing. Dikembe said he was more interested in studying medicine.

But Dikembe realized basketball could pay for his education. He then started to practice seriously. A few years later, in 1985, Georgetown University in Washington, D.C., gave him a scholarship.[1] Soon, Dikembe was on a plane traveling to the United States.

A Difficult New Life

Life was not easy for Dikembe in the United States at first. He had learned eight different languages in Africa. But English wasn't one of them. Also, he couldn't **afford** to call his family in Africa. He often felt sad and lonely. So he filled his time with work. During the day, he studied English in Georgetown's ESL program. At night and on weekends, he practiced basketball.

But Dikembe never imagined he would play in the National Basketball Association (N.B.A.), the professional men's basketball league in North America.

He **doubted** his ability. Basketball was new to him. He often made mistakes while playing. Dikembe's coaches told him to be patient. Over time, he **improved**. When he graduated in 1991, he was invited to play in the N.B.A. Dikembe was delighted.[2] With his long arms, he became an expert in defense.[3] He won Defensive Player of the Year **awards** in 1995 and 1996.

Dikembe's Big Promise

By 1997, Dikembe was a famous athlete with a high **salary**. Then one morning he received a phone call that changed his life. His mother had died in Africa. Suddenly ill, she hadn't been able to **reach** a hospital. Dikembe bitterly[4] remembered his dream of becoming a doctor. He made a promise: He would build a hospital in his hometown of Kinshasa.

It took Dikembe years to save the money. In 2006, at age forty, he became the oldest player in the N.B.A. Each year his knees hurt more, and his salary went down. At times, he wanted to quit. But he never forgot his promise.

In 2007, his sixteenth year in the N.B.A., his dream finally came true. A new hospital opened in his hometown. It had space for thousands of patients. "If I was a doctor for the rest of my life, I could never **treat** this many people," he said. Because of Dikembe, life is better for many people now. That is why Dikembe is a real hero. He found his own way to care for others.

---

[1] **scholarship:** money given to someone by an educational organization to help pay for that person's education

[2] **delighted:** very pleased and happy

[3] **defense:** the practice of preventing the other team from scoring points

[4] **bitterly:** done in a way that shows feelings of great sadness or anger

Vocabulary Check

Complete the diary entry with the boldfaced words from the reading.

Amy's Basketball Diary

November 24, 2010

Three years ago, I wasn't a good player. But then I practiced and I
(1)_____. Now I play well. The only problem is I can't
(2)_____ the basket, even when I jump as high as I can.

Learning to play basketball was difficult for me. I often
(3)_____ myself—I thought I couldn't succeed.
Sometimes, I wanted to (4)_____ and never play again.

My parents didn't want me to be a(n) (5)_____. They
said playing sports was a waste of time. They wanted me to study
all day. We always (6)_____ about that. But then I
got a basketball scholarship from my university—now my parents
are happy!

One time I hurt my foot really badly during a game. The doctor in
my hometown couldn't (7)_____ me, so I had to go to
a hospital in the city.

My favorite basketball player is Tamika Catchings. She is my
(8)_____. I want to be just like her. She wins lots of
(9)_____, including WNBA Defensive Player of the Year.
I want to go see her play one day, but I can't (10)_____
a ticket right now. They are so expensive! Oh well, maybe I'll see her
in the future, when I have a job and a good (11)_____.

READ AGAIN

Read "A Tall Order" again and complete the comprehension exercises. As you work, keep the reading goal in mind.

> 📖 **READING GOAL:** To understand important events in the life of Dikembe Mutombo

Comprehension Check

A. Work with a partner. Put the events into the correct sequence. Write *1* next to the first event, *2* next to the second, and so on.

_____ **1.** Dikembe's mother died.

_____ **2.** Georgetown University offered Dikembe a scholarship.

_____ **3.** Dikembe won awards for his great defense.

_____ **4.** A new hospital opened in Kinshasa.

_____ **5.** Dikembe fell and cut his face.

_____ **6.** Dikembe started to practice basketball seriously.

_____ **7.** Dikembe started learning English at Georgetown.

_____ **8.** An N.B.A. team invited Dikembe to play.

B. There are ten mistakes (including the example) in the summary of Dikembe's story. Find the mistakes and correct them. The first one is done for you. When you finish, look at the reading again to check your answers.

(1) Kinshasa

Dikembe was born in ~~Washington, D.C~~, in what is today called the Democratic

Republic of the Congo. He played basketball for the first time when he was

thirteen years old. At first, he loved basketball. He hoped to become a basketball

coach. Then one day he realized basketball could pay for his education.

Dikembe went to the United States to play basketball, and life was easy for

him at first. He could afford to call his family in Africa, and he didn't speak English.

When Dikembe went to the N.B.A. in 1991, he became famous for his

defense. He won two scholarships for defense in 1995 and 1996.

But then one day in 1997 Dikembe's father died. Dikembe felt very sad. He

decided to build a university in his hometown. He saved money for months.

Over time, his arms started to hurt from playing, and his salary went down. Then

finally, his dream came true in 2007.

C. Work in small groups. Your teacher will give each group a number. Each group will act out a different part of a play called *The Dikembe Mutombo Story*. Find your group's part of the play below:

1. Dikembe plays basketball for the first time but doesn't like it.

2. Dikembe receives a scholarship and leaves home.

3. Dikembe experiences a new life in the United States.

4. Dikembe becomes a successful N.B.A. player and wins awards.

5. Dikembe learns that his mother has died.

6. The new hospital opens in Dikembe's hometown.

D. With your partners, follow these steps to prepare for your acting:

- Decide what happens in your part of the play.

- Decide which character each student in your group will play (for example, one student is Dikembe, another student is his coach, and so on).

- Write what you will say on pieces of paper.

- Together practice reading your lines. Try to remember what you will say.

E. Watch the other groups act out their parts of the story. Do they present the details correctly?

> DISCUSS

Work in small groups. Look up the word *charity* in your dictionaries. Then ask and answer the questions.

1. Have you ever given your time or money to charity? What did you do?

2. Do you know some other famous people who have given a lot of money to charity? If so, name them.

3. Why do famous people give money to charity? Do they really do it to help others? Explain your opinion.

▸ VOCABULARY SKILL BUILDING

> ### Compound Nouns
>
> Nouns often go together with other nouns to make compound nouns. In compound nouns, the first noun describes the following noun. Some are written as one word, as in *basketball*. Some are written as two words, as in *tennis player*. If you are not sure if a compound noun is one or two words, check a dictionary. If it is not listed, check each of the words separately. If you don't find it under either listing, then it may be very new or uncommon.

A. Work with a partner. Combine the words in Column 1 with the words in Column 2 to form one-word or two-word compound nouns. You can put the words in Column 1 before or after the words in Column 2, and you can use most words more than once. Write the compound nouns in the correct column in the chart.

Column 1

ball
home
player
sports

Column 2

foot   star
hero   team
plate   town
soccer

One word	Two words
football	*soccer player*

B. Complete the sentences with the compound nouns from the chart.

1. Dikembe's _____ is Kinshasa, in the Democratic Republic of the Congo.

2. In most countries except the United States, soccer is called _____.

3. The baseball player ran from third base to _____ and scored a run.

4. If you are a _____, you work well as a member of a group.

5. Usually, the _____ on a team gets the highest salary.

6. Baseball and football are _____; you can't play them by yourself.

CHAPTER 4

Hull City Tigers Discussion Board

> PREPARE TO READ

A. Look at the words (and phrases) in the list. Write the number(s) next to each word to show what you know. You may be able to write more than one number next to some of the words. You will study all of these words in this chapter.

1. I can use the word in a sentence.

2. I know <u>one meaning</u> of the word.

3. I know <u>more than one meaning</u> of the word.

4. I know how to pronounce the word.

B. Work with a partner. Ask and answer the questions. If you don't know a word in English, ask your partner or look in your dictionary. Then write your new words on page 216.

1. Look at the picture. What type of clothing are the men wearing? What sport do they play?

2. Are there any professional sports teams in your hometown? If so, name them.

3. What are the most famous sports teams in your home country? What are the most famous sports teams in the world?

_____ advertising

_____ attract

_____ contract

_____ fan

_____ focus

_____ investment

_____ mind

_____ positive

_____ post

_____ stand out

Reading Skill: Making Inferences

Sometimes a writer does not say everything directly in the text. Instead, the reader has to think about the information in the text and make his or her own conclusion based on that information. That conclusion is called an *inference*. An inference is stronger than a guess. A guess might be correct or incorrect. An inference is probably correct because it is based on real information in the text.

EXAMPLE:

The game just ended. Leah and her teammates are all smiling.

↓

Inference: Leah's team won the game.

C. Read the first paragraph of the "Hull City Tigers Discussion Board" on the next page. Check (✓) the inference that you can make based on the information in that first paragraph.

_____ **1.** Hull City won last night's game.

_____ **2.** Hull City lost last night's game.

_____ **3.** Everyone expected Hull City to win the game.

> READ

Read the "Hull City Tigers Discussion Board." Was your inference in Exercise C correct?

HULL CITY TIGERS DISCUSSION BOARD

1   Hello Tigers **fans**! What a week for Hull[1] football! I hope you were able to watch last night's game. The whole team played well. I think we surprised a lot of people. This is a really good start to our first year in the Premier League![2]

It's time to think about our future. People in Hull may love the Tigers, but 5 how can we **attract** fans from other places? Winning more games will help, but there is another thing we could do—we could change our jerseys.[3]

I love the Tigers' jerseys as much as the next fan. I'm proud to wear the orange and black, especially when we're playing so well! And I don't **mind** the **advertising** on our jerseys. Almost every football team does the same thing.

10   Well, one team in Spain is actually doing something different. As you may know, FC Barcelona[4] is giving money to UNICEF[5] in order to wear the UNICEF logo[6] on its jerseys. And I think the Tigers should do the same thing, or something similar. Let me explain.

1 **Hull:** a city near the North Sea in Northern England

2 **the Premier League:** a group of England's top football teams that play games against each other

3 **jersey:** a shirt worn as part of a sports uniform

4 **FC Barcelona:** a football team from Barcelona, Spain

5 **UNICEF:** an organization created by the United Nations that gives food, clothing, and medicine to poor children

6 **logo:** a small design that is the official sign of a company or organization

By giving money to UNICEF, FC Barcelona helps other people. But the team also helps itself. UNICEF
15 is a charity. It helps poor children. Everyone has a **positive** opinion of UNICEF. The UNICEF logo
connects FC Barcelona to that positive feeling. It makes FC Barcelona **stand out** in a really good way.
The team can attract new fans in other countries. Stores will sell more of the team's jerseys. Basically, it's
an **investment**. By giving a little money to UNICEF, the team will make more money than it would
without this investment.

20 So, the Tigers should make the same investment. We could be the first English team to do so. If more
people like the team, more people will want to visit Hull. This will help our city as well.

In 2010, the Tigers' advertising **contract** with Karoo[7] will end. Our team can live without the
advertising money. Why don't we give money to a charity and wear its logo? What's your opinion,
Tigers fans?

Post your comments below!

COMMENTS

↓ Posted 10/9 11:01 AM	
• **Mike T**	Karoo pays the team a lot of money. The money can go toward a star player's salary. Although giving to charity is nice, it's not a smart investment right now.

↓ Posted 10/9 11:15 AM	
• **Footy Fan**	I think it's a good idea. Some people have a bad opinion of Hull. This could change people's ideas about the city.

↓ Posted 10/9 11:32 AM	
• **Nebb**	FC Barcelona has way more money than we do. FCB can afford this; we can't. It would be a mistake.

↓ Posted 10/9 12:06 PM	
• **Tiger012**	If the Tigers have extra money, they should lower ticket prices!!!

↓ Posted 10/9 12:15 PM	
• **Emma B**	It's a good idea, but we should give money to a local charity. How about Dove House? It offers free medical care in Hull.

↓ Posted 10/9 12:42 PM	
• **HC2000**	People will only buy Tigers' jerseys if the team is winning games. We should just **focus** on improving the team.

↓ Posted 10/9 12:52 PM	
• **Louis K**	I agree with Emma B, but I think it should be a global charity. UNICEF is known around the world. Dove House isn't. The Tigers are already popular in Hull. We need to make fans in new places. A global charity would help us do that.

Post new comment:

---

[7] **Karoo:** a company that provides Internet service in Hull, England

Vocabulary Check

Write the boldfaced word from the reading next to the correct picture or definition.

1. _____ =
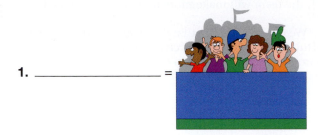

2. _____ =

3. _____ =

4. _____ =

5. _____ =

6. _____ = a written agreement that says what people must do for one another

7. _____ = when you give money to a bank, business, etc., in order to make more money in the future

8. _____ = good, useful; not negative

9. _____ = to put a message on the Internet so that other people can read it

10. _____ = to feel annoyed about something

> READ AGAIN

Read the "Hull City Tigers Discussion Board" again and complete the comprehension exercises. As you work, keep the reading goal in mind.

> 📖 **READING GOAL:** To make inferences based on the information given

Comprehension Check

A. Circle the letter of the correct answer to complete each sentence.

1. The writer is probably a _____.
   a. player on FC Barcelona
   b. worker at UNICEF
   c. fan of the Tigers

2. _____ pays to put its logo on the Tigers' jersey.
   a. UNICEF
   b. Dove House
   c. Karoo

3. Hull's football team is called the Tigers because of its _____.
   a. long history in the Premier League
   b. jersey colors
   c. star players

4. The writer wants the Tigers to pay a charity because _____.
   a. he knows many poor people
   b. it is an investment in the team's future
   c. he doesn't like advertising on jerseys

5. FC Barcelona is probably _____ the Tigers.
   a. more popular than
   b. as popular as
   c. less popular than

6. Mike T's opinion is similar to _____.
   a. Footy Fan's
   b. HC2000's
   c. Louis K's

7. Emma B's opinion is similar to _____.
   a. Nebb's
   b. Tiger012's
   c. Footy Fan's

B. Which person would probably make each comment? Write the first letter of the person's name next to each comment.

Footy Fan (F)	HC2000 (H)	Louis K (L)
Nebb (N)	Tiger012 (T)	Emma B (E)

_____ **1.** FC Barcelona spent over 380 million euros ($560 million) last year!

_____ **2.** People buy FC Barcelona jerseys because the team wins a lot of games.

_____ **3.** It is important for people to have a positive opinion of our city.

_____ **4.** There is a global charity called Oxfam—Hull should wear its logo.

_____ **5.** I can't afford to pay 25 pounds ($40) for a seat!

_____ **6.** Among our local charities, Dove House stands out.

> DISCUSS

Work in small groups. Read each statement. Write _A_ if you agree with it or _D_ if you disagree with it. Explain your ideas and opinions.

_____ **1.** Internet posts usually say positive things.

_____ **2.** Having a professional sports team is good for a city.

_____ **3.** Professional sports teams should give money to charity.

_____ **4.** Star players' salaries are usually too high.

_____ **5.** Fans don't mind when sports stars have advertising on their jerseys.

_____ **6.** Most young people can afford tickets to watch professional sports.

Learning the Vocabulary

A. Add possible compounds to the front and example sentences to the back of each of the cards that you made for Unit 1.

B. Make cards for the words from Chapters 3–4 that were new to you when you started the unit. Include target words and words that you wrote on page 216. Write possible compounds and an example sentence for each word.

C. Work with a partner. Quiz each other on all of your cards (Units 1 and 2). If you can't remember a word, your partner will read the example sentence on the card but will say "blank" in place of the word. If you still can't remember the word, put that card to one side. Then have your partner quiz you on that card again after you finish all of your other cards.

EXAMPLE:

Student A: If you practice every day, you will _____ your English.
Student B: Improve!
Student A: Yes. That's correct.

D. Go back to the vocabulary list at the beginning of each chapter. What did you learn about the target words? Add your numbers to the lists.

Vocabulary Practice 2, see page 219

It's Not Easy Being Green

> THINK BEFORE YOU READ

A. Work with a partner. Look at the picture. Ask and answer the questions. If you don't know a word in English, ask your partner or look in your dictionary. Then write your new words on page 216.

1. What do you see in the picture? Point to the things you see and name them in English.

2. What problem does this picture show?

3. Who and what does this problem affect?

4. What does it mean to "be green?" What can people do to be green?

B. Do you create a lot of pollution? Take the quiz on page 215 to find out.

A Cleaner Way to Shop?

> PREPARE TO READ

A. Look at the words in the list. Write the number(s) next to each word to show what you know. You may be able to write more than one number next to some of the words. You will study all of these words in this chapter.

1. I can use the word in a sentence.

2. I know <u>one meaning</u> of the word.

3. I know <u>more than one meaning</u> of the word.

4. I know how to pronounce the word.

B. Work with a partner. Look at the picture. Ask and answer the questions. If you don't know a word in English, ask your partner or look in your dictionary. Then write your new words on page 216.

1. What is the man in the picture doing?

2. Have you ever bought anything on the Internet? If so, what did you buy?

3. What are some advantages and disadvantages of online shopping?

4. Which do you think creates more pollution: buying something in a store or buying it online?

_____ allow

_____ charge

_____ customer

_____ delivery

_____ double

_____ environment

_____ fuel

_____ materials

_____ require

_____ wasteful

Reading Skill: Previewing and Predicting

Before you read something, first get a general idea about the topic and type of text by *previewing*. To preview, read the title and any headings. Look at any pictures. Think about what you already know about the topic. Also think about what kind of text it is—for example, a story, an article, or an e-mail. For a short text, read the first and last sentence of every paragraph. Try to guess, or *predict*, what the reading will be about.

C. Preview the newspaper article "A Cleaner Way to Shop?" Then answer the questions.

1. What is the main idea of the reading?
   a. Online shopping costs more than shopping in a store.
   b. Online shopping is bad for the environment.
   c. You should not buy things online.

2. What helped you figure out the main idea?
   a. the picture
   b. the first sentence of the first paragraph
   c. the last sentence of the first paragraph

 **READ**

Read "A Cleaner Way to Shop?" Underline the sentence that gives the main idea of the reading.

A Cleaner Way to Shop?

Need to buy something? Why go to a store? Buy it on the Internet! Need it now? Why wait? Ask for next-day **delivery!** Each day, more and more people try online shopping.
5 In fact, online sales have **doubled** in the last ten years. But not everyone is excited. Some scientists now say that online shopping is bad for the **environment**.

People are surprised to hear this. "They
10 think, 'I don't need to drive, and the business doesn't need to build a store, so there will be less pollution,'" says Nuria Prost, an environmental scientist. "But it is not so simple. In
15 fact, online shopping is **wasteful**. It also adds to air pollution."

In truth, the Internet is not always as good a friend
20 to the environment as it seems. For example, most people thought that the Internet would help offices use less paper and other
25 **materials**. But paper use increased by 33 percent between 1986 and 1997. "[Online shopping]

could have similarly negative effects," says Nevil Cohen, a professor of environmental science.

Part of the problem is what people are buying these days. In the past, people bought things on the Internet that did not **require** much packing material, such as books and clothing. But now people also shop online for large, heavy products such as televisions, computers, and furniture. These products need to be packed in large amounts of plastic and paper. This creates a lot of waste.

Another problem caused by online shopping is air pollution. When **customers** buy products and ask for next-day delivery, companies often have to send them by air. Airplanes use much more **fuel** than cars and produce more carbon dioxide.[1] When people buy a lot of different things from different online businesses, this creates even more travel by airplanes.

Online product returns are also a problem. For example, an online shoe store may **allow** customers to return shoes for free if they are the wrong size. This doubles the packing materials and number of airplane trips required to sell one pair of shoes.

"If people want to protect the environment, they need to think before they shop," says Prost. "People need to ask themselves: Is this exactly what I want? Do I really need it tomorrow, or can I wait?" Online stores can also **charge** customers for returns. This may make people shop more carefully. "Online shopping is fast and easy," says Prost, "but we can't forget the negative effect it has on the environment."

---

[1] **carbon dioxide:** the gas produced when people or animals breathe out or when carbon is burned in air, which may make the Earth warmer

Vocabulary Check

Write the boldfaced word from the reading next to the correct definition. Use the correct form of the word.

1. _____ = a substance such as coal, gas, or oil that can be burned to produce heat or energy

2. _____ = to need something

3. _____ = the act of bringing something (e.g., a letter or package) to a particular place or person

4. _____ = things such as wood, plastic, paper, etc., that are used for making or doing something

5. _____ = to give someone permission to do something

6. _____ = using more of something than is needed

7. _____ = someone who buys things from a store or company

8. _____ = the land, water, and air in which people, animals, and plants live

9. _____ = to become twice as large, or twice as much

10. _____ = to ask for a particular amount of money for a service or something you are selling

Read "A Cleaner Way to Shop?" again and complete the comprehension exercises. As you work, keep the reading goal in mind.

> 📖 **READING GOAL:** To identify three reasons why online shopping is bad for the environment

Comprehension Check

A. Read the statements about the reading. Write *T* (true) or *F* (false). If it is not possible to tell, write *?*.

_____*T*_____ **1.** Online shopping is becoming more popular, but it is also wasteful.

_____ **2.** Most customers know that online shopping is bad for the environment.

_____ **3.** Most of the products customers buy online are big and weigh a lot.

_____ **4.** The delivery of heavy products requires a lot of materials.

_____ **5.** An airplane creates more pollution than a car.

_____ **6.** "Next day delivery" is helpful for the environment.

_____ **7.** When online stores charge a fee for returns, customers shop more carefully.

_____ **8.** Nuria Prost tells shoppers *not* to buy products on the Internet.

B. Answer the questions. Try not to look back at the reading.

1. What problem does online shopping cause?

_____

2. What are some reasons for the problem? List three.

_____

_____

_____

C. Now look back at the reading. Check your answers from Exercise B. Correct any mistakes.

> DISCUSS

A. Work with a partner. You and your partner are customers who need to buy some type of television or radio. First, decide about the questions.

1. What type of television or radio do you need to buy?

2. Why do you need to buy this product?

B. Decide who is A and who is B. Then role-play. Use some of the target words from page 31 in your discussion.

A: You want to buy the product online. Explain your opinion to B.

B: You don't want to buy the product online. You prefer to drive to a store. Explain your opinion to A.

VOCABULARY SKILL BUILDING

Suffixes: -ful, -ment

Adding a suffix to a word often changes its part of speech. For example, you can add the suffix *-ful* to some nouns and verbs to make them adjectives. You can add the suffix *-ment* to some verbs to make them nouns.

EXAMPLES:

waste (noun/verb) + ***-ful*** = *wasteful* (adjective)

require (verb) + ***-ment*** = *requirement* (noun)

A. Add the suffix *-ful* or *-ment* to create new forms of the words.

Word	Adjective	Noun
require (verb)		*requirement*
advertise (verb)		
doubt (noun or verb)		
invest (verb)		
improve (verb)		
success (noun)		
treat (verb)		

B. Complete the sentences with the words you wrote in the chart. The boldfaced words will help you choose the correct word.

1. I don't want to **give you money** to start an online store. It's not a good business _____.

2. Han's new computer is **better** than his old one. It is a big _____.

3. If pollution makes people sick, they need to **see a doctor**. They need medical _____.

4. Susanna's Internet business is **doing well**. It is very _____.

5. My grandparents may buy a few things online, but **I don't think so**. It is _____ they like online shopping.

6. You should **tell customers about your business**. Why don't you make a(n) _____?

Green Airplanes

GATE 30 - 66

> PREPARE TO READ

A. Look at the words (and phrases) in the list. Write the number(s) next to each word to show what you know. You may be able to write more than one number next to some of the words. You will study all of these words in this chapter.

1. I can use the word in a sentence.

2. I know <u>one meaning</u> of the word.

3. I know <u>more than one meaning</u> of the word.

4. I know how to pronounce the word.

B. Work with a partner. Look at the picture. Ask and answer the questions. If you don't know a word in English, ask your partner or look in your dictionary. Then write your new words on page 216.

1. Who are the people in the picture? Where are they? Point to the things you see and say the words in English.

2. In what ways do you think air transport will be different in the future?

_____ benefit

_____ complain

_____ extra

_____ generation

_____ luggage

_____ made up of

_____ passenger

_____ regular

_____ satisfied

_____ shape

C. Preview the magazine article "Green Airplanes." Then check (✓) the questions that you think the reading will answer.

_____ **1.** What are some of the problems with new airplanes?

_____ **2.** Where can people learn how to fly an airplane?

_____ **3.** What kind of fuel will future airplanes use?

_____ **4.** What will future airplanes look like?

_____ **5.** Will future airplanes crash more often than today's planes?

_____ **6.** Why is it dangerous to travel by airplane?

 **READ**

Read "Green Airplanes." Underline the answers to the questions that you checked (✓) in Exercise C.

Green Airplanes

1   The next **generation** of airplanes has arrived. They have bigger seats. Their windows are larger. They have more space for **luggage**. And they are coming to an airport near you.

5   These new airplanes, such as the Boeing 787 Dreamliner or Bombardier CSeries, are more comfortable for **passengers**. They also **benefit** the environment. By using less fuel, they will create less pollution. Airline companies are

10 excited, but scientists wonder if the airplanes' designers could do even more.

    The secret to using less fuel is less weight. Therefore, these new planes are made of light materials. They are mostly **made up of**

15 carbon fiber,[1] a very light but strong plastic. Unlike older planes, they do not contain much heavy metal. As a result, they require 20 to 25 percent less fuel than similarly sized older planes.

20   By using less fuel, these new airplanes will create less pollution. Because of this, Boeing and Bombardier like to describe their new products as "green airplanes." In a speech in front of 15,000 workers, Boeing president

25 Scott Carson called the Dreamliner the most environmentally friendly[2] aircraft ever built.

    Some people, however, are still not **satisfied**. They say that the new airplanes only produce 20 percent less pollution. "We need

30 to go further than that," says transport expert

---

[1] **carbon fiber:** a human-made material consisting of thin pieces of carbon glued together that is very strong for its weight

[2] **environmentally friendly:** not harmful to the environment

Geoff Hoon. Experts like Hoon hope airplanes will one day use only biofuel.[3] Unlike **regular** fuel, made from oil, biofuel is made from plants like corn or sugarcane.[4] Scientists believe
35 that the use of biofuel will produce less air pollution. Studies show that biofuel produces half the carbon dioxide of oil-based fuel.

Some scientists also **complain** about the new airplanes' design. Although they weigh
40 less, the Dreamliner and CSeries still look like regular planes. And for the last fifty years, the design of airplanes hasn't changed much.

Scientists say that creating planes with a new shape could save much more weight and fuel.
45 One idea is to make planes that look like a very large single wing. Another is to create planes in the **shape** of a flying saucer.[5] The round shape of a flying saucer, scientists say, would use half the fuel of modern planes.

50 If you fly on an airplane soon, it won't be a flying saucer, but it may be a new Dreamliner or CSeries. If so, enjoy the **extra** room and big windows. Just don't forget about the air outside.

[3] **biofuel:** fuel produced from plant materials, such as corn, or from organic waste, such as animal waste

[4] **sugarcane:** a tall tropical plant from which sugar is obtained

[5] **flying saucer:** a type of aircraft shaped like a plate that some people believe carries creatures from another world

Vocabulary Check

Complete the sentences with the boldfaced words from the reading.

1. I have everything I want in life. I feel completely _____.

2. I lost my pen; do you have a(n) _____ one I can borrow?

3. Exercising can _____ your health; it helps you lose weight and live longer.

4. She made a cake in the _____ of an airplane for her son's birthday party.

5. The _____ seats in the airplane cost $800. If you want a first-class seat, you will have to pay $1,200 extra.

6. Many cars today waste a lot of fuel, but the next _____ of cars will use less fuel.

7. The bus driver told the _____ to sit down while the bus was moving.

8. Carbon dioxide is a gas that is _____ carbon and oxygen.

9. My flight was late, and my luggage was lost. I'm going to _____ to the airline company.

10. I usually pack only one small bag when I travel. I don't like to carry a lot of _____.

Read "Green Airplanes" again and complete the comprehension exercises. As you work, keep the reading goal in mind.

> 📖 **READING GOAL:** To understand the design of new airplanes and two different opinions about this design

Comprehension Check

A. Circle the letter of the correct answer to complete each sentence.

1. The new generation of airplanes can carry more _____.
   a. luggage
   b. passengers
   c. biofuel

2. Carbon fiber is beneficial because it _____ less than heavy metal.
   a. costs
   b. breaks
   c. weighs

3. Airline companies are excited about the new airplanes because they _____.
   a. look like very large single wings
   b. use less fuel
   c. cost more to build

4. The Dreamliner is a "green" airplane because it _____.
   a. is very comfortable
   b. produces less air pollution than older airplanes
   c. uses biofuel instead of regular fuel

5. Some _____ are not happy with the new generation of airplanes.
   a. Boeing workers
   b. passengers
   c. transport experts

6. If their design changes, future airplanes may not need _____ in order to fly.
   a. two wings
   b. fuel
   c. carbon fiber

B. Complete the summary of "Green Airplanes." Do not look back at the reading. There is more than one way to complete some of the sentences. You do not need to use the same words as in the reading, but make sure the meaning is the same.

New airplanes such as the Boeing Dreamliner are made of special

(1) _____, such as carbon fiber. This reduces the airplanes'

(2) _____. Because of this, they use about 20 to 25 percent

less (3) _____, and they produce 20 percent less air

(4) _____. Passengers will like the airplanes because they

are comfortable and have large (5) _____.

But some people are not (6) _____ with these new

airplanes. They want airplanes to use (7) _____, which is

made from plants. They also want to change the (8) _____

of airplanes. One suggestion is to create a plane in the shape of a

(9) _____. In the future, airplanes may look very

(10) _____ from the way they look today.

C. Work with a partner. Compare your summaries. Are they similar? If your answers are different, look back at the reading.

> DISCUSS

Work in small groups. Ask and answer the questions.

1. In what ways can technology help the environment?

2. Do you agree with the title of this unit, "It's Not Easy Being Green"? Why or why not?

3. If you learn that a company produces a lot of pollution, will you stop buying its products? Why or why not?

4. Do you think people in your home country do a good job of protecting the environment? What things could they do differently?

Learn the Vocabulary

Using a Dictionary

You can find a lot of useful information about how to use a word in a monolingual (English–English) dictionary. Here are some of the things you can find in an entry for a word:

- division of the word into syllables (each part that contains a vowel sound)
- pronunciation and stress (the part of the word with the most emphasis)
- part of speech (e.g., noun, verb, adjective, adverb, preposition)
- meanings, with the most common meaning listed first
- example sentences that show how to use the word
- grammar patterns and collocations (e.g., words that are often used with the word, or word partners)
- other words in the same word family (or different forms of the word)
- where the word comes from (or the word's origin)

When you make word cards, you do not need to make the same type of card for each new word you learn. For example, for some words, you may only need a definition. For other words, you may need to write the pronunciation and the definition on your card, especially if it's a word that you don't use in speaking because you have trouble pronouncing it. For other words, you may want to add information about how the word is used; for example, by writing example sentences on your card.

A. Look at the two dictionary entries on the next page. Then read the descriptions of the parts of an entry below. Identify the part that each arrow (→) is pointing to. Write the number in the space next to the arrow.

1. how to pronounce the word

2. the word's part of speech (noun, verb, etc.)

3. the most common meaning of the word

4. the second most common meaning of the word

5. an example of the word in a sentence

6. how a word is often used with another word (e.g., a collocation, or word partner)

7. other forms of the word or members of the word's family

8. the word's origin

a. _____

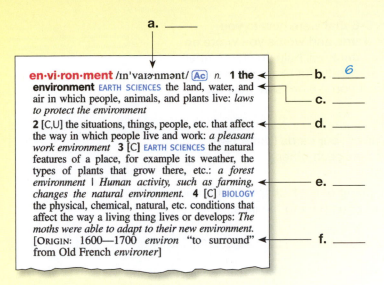

en·vi·ron·ment /ɪnˈvaɪərnmənt/ (Ac) *n.* **1 the** environment EARTH SCIENCES the land, water, and air in which people, animals, and plants live: *laws to protect the environment*
2 [C,U] the situations, things, people, etc. that affect the way in which people live and work: *a pleasant work environment* **3** [C] EARTH SCIENCES the natural features of a place, for example its weather, the types of plants that grow there, etc.: *a forest environment* | *Human activity, such as farming, changes the natural environment.* **4** [C] BIOLOGY the physical, chemical, natural, etc. conditions that affect the way a living thing lives or develops: *The moths were able to adapt to their new environment.* [ORIGIN: 1600—1700 *environ* "to surround" from Old French *environer*]

b. _6_
c. _____
d. _____
e. _____
f. _____

g. _____

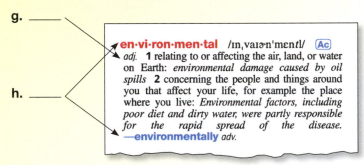

en·vi·ron·men·tal /ɪnˌvaɪərnˈmɛntl/ (Ac) *adj.* **1** relating to or affecting the air, land, or water on Earth: *environmental damage caused by oil spills* **2** concerning the people and things around you that affect your life, for example the place where you live: *Environmental factors, including poor diet and dirty water, were partly responsible for the rapid spread of the disease.* —**environmentally** *adv.*

h. _____

B. Look up the boldfaced words in an English–English dictionary. Answer the questions.

1. What part(s) of speech is *extra*?

   _____

2. What other words are in the same family as *benefit*? Write them here.

   _____

3. How many meanings does your dictionary give for the adjective *regular*?

   _____

4. What noun is often used after *customer* as part of a compound noun?

   _____

5. How many example sentences are there for the verb *complain*?

   _____

C. Make cards for the words from Chapters 5–6 that were new to you when you started the unit. Include target words and words you wrote on page 216. Include any information that you think will help you remember the meaning and the correct way to use the word. For example, write the two most common meanings of the word. If you are not sure how the word is used, add example sentences.

D. Work with a partner. Quiz each other on all of your cards (Units 1–3). (See page 29 for explanations of ways to quiz each other.)

E. Go back to the vocabulary list at the beginning of each chapter. What did you learn about the target words? Add your numbers to the lists.

Vocabulary Practice 3, see page 220.

FLUENCY PRACTICE 1

 **READING 1**

Before You Read

Preview the reading on the next page. Answer the questions. Circle the letter of the correct answer.

1. What is "aquatic exercise"?
   a. exercise you do with a coach
   b. exercise you do in the water
   c. exercise you do at home

2. Who can do aquatic exercise?
   a. professional athletes
   b. people who have been hurt in an accident
   c. everyone

Read

A. Read "Aquatic Exercise." Time yourself. Write your start and end times and your total reading time. Then calculate your reading speed (words per minute) and write it in the progress chart on page 230.

Start time: _____ **End time:** _____ **Total time:** _____ (in seconds)

Reading speed:
381 words ÷ _____ (total time in seconds) x 60 = _____ words per minute

Aquatic Exercise

1   Do you worry about your health? Have you tried to run or walk for exercise and then quit? If you answered yes, you should try a new type of exercise: aquatic exercise. Aquatic exercise
5 is like exercise on land, but you do it in a swimming pool. For example, you can run, walk, or even do a mind-body practice, such as yoga.
    More and more people are trying aquatic exercise. In the United States, the number has
10 grown by 25 percent in recent years. People in other countries are also doing aquatic exercise more frequently.
    Aquatic exercise has many benefits. First of all, it feels easier than exercising on land.
15 Why? You weigh about 90 percent less in the pool. It is also better for your knees than running or walking.
    Aquatic exercise feels easy, but you still burn calories. Water is 1,000 times thicker and heavier
20 than air. To move through the water, your body has to work four times as hard. As a result, in the same amount of time, you can burn more calories in the pool than in the gym. That's because it takes more energy to move in the water.

25   But what if you are scared of the water? No problem! There is nothing to worry about. Aquatic exercise is safe and easy to learn. It doesn't require any special skills. For most kinds of aquatic exercise, you don't even need
30 to know how to swim.
    In fact, most people say they feel more relaxed in the water. They stop thinking about the things that make them anxious. They feel in control of their bodies. The cool,
35 quiet environment makes them feel good. And because they feel so good, they will probably exercise more.
    Aquatic exercise is for everyone. You can do it at any age. It can even help people who
40 have been hurt in accidents. With aquatic exercise, they can move in ways they cannot on land. For example, some people who cannot walk on land can walk and even run in the water.
45   So are you looking for a fun new way to improve your health? Why not try aquatic exercise? Join the millions of people who are burning calories while keeping cool in the pool.

B. Read "Aquatic Exercise" again, a little faster this time. Write your start and end times and your total reading time. Then calculate your reading speed (words per minute) and write it in the progress chart on page 230.

Start time: _____ **End time:** _____ **Total time:** _____ (in seconds)

Reading speed:
381 words ÷ _____ (total time in seconds) x 60 = _____ words per minute

Comprehension Check

A. Circle the letter of the correct answer to complete each sentence.

1. Aquatic exercise is _____.
   a. becoming more popular
   b. difficult to learn
   c. not safe for older people

2. One problem with running is _____.
   a. it doesn't burn calories
   b. your body works four times as hard as in the water
   c. it can hurt your knees

3. Your body is lighter in the water than on land, so _____.
   a. it feels easier to exercise in the pool
   b. small children shouldn't try aquatic exercise
   c. you lose more weight when you exercise on land

4. When you do aquatic exercise, you don't need _____.
   a. to know how to swim
   b. a swimming pool
   c. energy

5. Most people who try aquatic exercise say it makes them feel _____.
   a. anxious
   b. focused
   c. calm

6. Sometimes people who can't walk on land can _____.
   a. run in the water
   b. walk in the gym
   c. weigh more in the water

B. Answer the questions. Try not to look back at the reading.

1. What is aquatic exercise?
   a. Who does it? _____
   b. Where do they do it? _____
   c. What do they do? _____

2. What are some advantages of aquatic exercise? List three.

   _____

   _____

   _____

C. Check your answers for the comprehension questions in the Answer Key on page 231. Then calculate your score and write it on the progress chart on page 230.

   _____ (my number correct) ÷10 x 100 = _____%

▶ READING 2

Before You Read

What characteristics does a person need to be an Olympic[1] swimmer? Write your ideas on the lines below.

_____

_____

_____

_____

_____

Read

A. Read "Michael Phelps: Keys to Success" on the next page. Time yourself. Write your start and end times and your total reading time. Then calculate your reading speed (words per minute) and write it in the progress chart on page 230.

Start time: _____   **End time:** _____   **Total time:** _____ (in seconds)

Reading speed:
529 words ÷ _____ (total time in seconds) x 60 = _____ words per minute

---

[1] **Olympic:** related to the Olympics, an international sports event that happens every four years

Michael Phelps: Keys to Success

1   Swimmer Michael Phelps has had a lot of success. He was a star of the 2008 Beijing Olympics. He has won awards all over the world. How does he do it? There are two keys

5 to Phelps's success. One is that he is a great athlete. The other is that he learned always to think positively.

    It helps, of course, that Phelps has the perfect body for swimming. He is tall: 6 foot 4

10 (1.93 meters). He has long arms. He also has remarkably big feet. What's more, his feet are very flat. In many ways, they look like the flippers certain sea animals, such as seals and dolphins, use to move through water.

15   These big, flat feet are a real benefit to Phelps in the water. Phelps uses a special move called the dolphin kick when he swims. If our feet leave the water when we are swimming, we swim more slowly. With the dolphin kick, a

20 swimmer's feet never leave the water. Dolphins swim the same way as Phelps, and they are some of the fastest animals in the ocean.

    But it takes more than big feet to win in the Olympics. To become the best swimmer of his

25 generation, Phelps needed a happy and healthy way of thinking.

    Phelps learned to think positively as a child. School was not easy for him. Phelps was very tall. In ways, he felt different from other

30 children. His classmates often bullied him. He had problems with teachers as well. One teacher told him he would never succeed as a swimmer. But Phelps never doubted himself. Each day, he went to the pool to practice.

35   Phelps also learned that failure is part of sports. No athlete can win 100 percent of the time. Phelps realized this at a young age. After losing a swimming race, Phelps would try to think positively. Instead of wanting to quit, he

40 would try to identify his mistakes. He would also try to find something to feel satisfied about. He learned not to blame others for his problems. With this positive view, he was able to improve each year.

45   As an Olympic athlete, Phelps uses positive thinking to help him focus. From the moment a race begins, Phelps thinks only about winning. He forgets everything else in his life. As a result, he never feels anxious in

50 the pool. "Swimming is normal for me," he says. "I'm relaxed. I'm comfortable. It's my home." Experts say this ability to stay calm in important moments is something most star athletes have in common.

55   Now Phelps is very famous. He has new problems to worry about. Fans follow him everywhere he goes. Thousands of articles are written about him in magazines and on the Internet. Some of these articles tell the

60 truth, others do not. Phelps is learning that it is not so easy to be famous. But he doesn't want success to change him. He says that he's the same kind of guy he was before all this happened.

65   To his fans, Phelps is a real hero. He shows how hard work can create success. He also reminds sports fans of the power of positive thinking.

B. Read "Michael Phelps: Keys to Success" again, a little faster this time. Write your start and end times and your total reading time. Then calculate your reading speed (words per minute) and write it in the progress chart on page 230.

Start time: _____   End time: _____   Total time: _____ (in seconds)

Reading speed:
529 words ÷ _____ (total time in seconds) x 60 = _____ words per minute

C. Go back to the list of characteristics you wrote on page 48. Put checkmarks (✓) next to any of the characteristics on your list that were mentioned in the reading, Then add any new characteristics you learned about in the article.

Comprehension Check

A. Read the statements about the reading. Write *T* (true) or *F* (false).

_____ **1.** Michael Phelps is one of the fastest swimmers in the world.

_____ **2.** Phelps has large feet.

_____ **3.** A teacher once told Phelps he couldn't succeed as a swimmer.

_____ **4.** Phelps has never lost a swimming contest.

_____ **5.** Swimming is stressful for Phelps.

_____ **6.** Anyone can swim as fast as Phelps if they think positively and practice.

B. Complete the summary of the reading with the words in the list. Try not to look back at the reading.

anxious	failures	kick	success
body	feet	positively	swimmer

Michael Phelps is a (1) _____. He has had a lot of

(2) _____. There are two reasons for this. First, he has the

perfect (3) _____ for swimming. He has big, flat

(4) _____ that look like flippers. This allows him to do a

special move called the dolphin (5) _____. The other reason

for Phelps's success is he thinks (6) _____. He always tries

to learn from his (7) _____. When he swims, he doesn't feel

(8) _____. He only focuses on winning. In short, Phelps has

the perfect body and mind for his sport.

C. Check your answers for the comprehension questions in the Answer Key on page 231. Then calculate your score and write it in the progress chart on page 230.

_____ (my number correct) ÷ 14 x 100 = _____%

4 Strange Travels

▷ THINK BEFORE YOU READ

A. Work with a partner. Look at the pictures. Ask and answer the questions. If you don't know a word in English, ask your partner or look in your dictionary. Then write your new words on page 216.

  1. Do you know the places in the pictures? Where is each place?

  2. Why is each place famous?

  3. Have you visited any famous places? Are there any famous places you want to visit in the future? Name them.

B. On a separate sheet of paper, draw a picture of a famous place in the world. Don't write anything on your picture.

C. Work in small groups. Look at one another's pictures. Talk about the places you see.

The World's Strangest Hotels

a.   b.   c.

> PREPARE TO READ

A. Look at the words (and phrases) in the list. Write the number(s) next to each word to show what you know. You may be able to write more than one number next to some of the words. You will study all of these words in this chapter.

1. I can use the word in a sentence.

2. I know <u>one meaning</u> of the word.

3. I know <u>more than one meaning</u> of the word.

4. I know how to pronounce the word.

B. Work with a partner. Look at the pictures. Ask and answer the questions. If you don't know a word in English, ask your partner or look in your dictionary. Then write your new words on page 216.

1. What do you see in these pictures of strange hotels?

2. Which hotels would or wouldn't you like to visit? Why?

_____ check out

_____ converted

_____ entirely

_____ extreme

_____ originally

_____ prison

_____ provide

_____ reserve

_____ theme

_____ towers

_____ unique

Reading Skill: Visualizing

When you read, it is helpful to make a picture in your head of what the writer is explaining or describing. This is called *visualizing*. When you visualize, pay attention to important or unusual details. Later, the picture in your head will help you remember the person, place, or thing that you read about.

C. Read the first two paragraphs of the Web site "The World's Strangest Hotels" on the next page. How do you visualize a capsule hotel? Which picture on page 52 shows one? Write the letter of that photo next to paragraph 2.

D. Preview the Web site on the next page. Then look at the photograph below. Which underlined heading in the site describes the photograph? Write the heading below the photo.

 READ

Read "The World's Strangest Hotels" on the next page. Pay attention to the examples and details that help you visualize each hotel. Then write the letter of the photo on page 52 next to the paragraph that describes it.

_____

The World's Strangest Hotels

1 Maybe you want a **unique** vacation. Maybe you want to save money. Maybe you want to be romantic. Or maybe you don't want a boring hotel room. If so, try one of these
5 strange hotels!

Capsule[1] Hotels, Japan: These unusual hotels are common in big Japanese cities. They have unusually small rooms. In fact, there is only enough space to sleep! Each
10 capsule is less than 2 square meters (21.52 square feet). Inside, you'll find a bed, a light, an alarm clock, and maybe a small TV and radio. There is a separate safe box outside the capsule for your luggage. The
15 benefit? The capsules cost less than $20 a night, while a regular hotel room in Tokyo can cost as much as $300 a night.

If sleeping in a capsule is not for you, consider these other hotels:

20 Hostel Celica, Slovenia: This **converted** hotel in downtown Ljubljana, Slovenia, used to be a **prison**! Now, it has twenty rooms and a modern art **theme**. In some rooms, colorful paintings cover the walls. The doors
25 and windows still have metal bars on them. You'll be safe at night for sure! And unlike being in a real prison, you can **check out** whenever you want.

Jumbo Hostel, Sweden: You've probably
30 slept on a plane before. Why not do it again, but in comfort? This hotel is a converted 747 airplane. It has twenty-five rooms, each with a TV. As in a regular airplane, you keep your luggage in a box by the ceiling. The best
35 room of all is the cockpit[2]—but be sure to bring your favorite copilot.[3]

Converted hotels are great if you want to try something different. But for a real adventure, try one of these hotels in **extreme** locations.
40 Ariau Amazon **Towers**, Brazil: Every part of this hotel—including the pool—is near the top of a tree. You can watch monkeys and birds play outside your window. Walk among the trees and feel the warm sun on your face.
45 Enjoy the sound of the Amazon River 100 feet below you.

Hôtel de Glace, Canada: This unique hotel is made up **entirely** of ice—even the furniture! You'll be given a special sleeping bag to keep
50 warm. Each year, artists re-create the hotel, using 15,000 tons[4] of snow and ice. Many details are handmade. Be sure to see the chandelier;[5] it's a true work of art! **Reserve** a room soon, before this year's ice hotel
55 disappears.

Jules' Undersea Lodge,[6] Florida: This is the granddaddy[7] of strange hotels. **Originally** a research station, it is now an underwater hotel. It can only be reached by scuba
60 diving.[8] Don't worry; there are classes for first-time divers. Once there, the hotel **provides** everything you need. Enjoy dinner at the bottom of the ocean! Watch fish pass by your window! The only problem: It may be
65 hard to send a postcard.

---

[1] **capsule:** a small container

[2] **cockpit:** the part of the airplane where the pilot sits

[3] **copilot:** a person who helps the main pilot (the person at the controls) fly an airplane

[4] **ton:** a unit of weight equal to 2,000 pounds

[5] **chandelier:** a frame that holds lights or candles and hangs from the ceiling

[6] **lodge:** a building where people can stay for a short time, especially to do a particular activity

[7] **granddaddy:** the oldest, first, or best example of something

[8] **scuba diving:** the sport of swimming under water while breathing from a container of air on your back

Vocabulary Check

Circle the letter of the correct answer to complete each sentence. The boldfaced words are the target words.

1. The church **towers** near our hotel are very _____.
   - **a.** tall
   - **b.** flat
   - **c.** wide

2. When you **check out** of a hotel, you _____.
   - **a.** go to sleep
   - **b.** leave your bag in your room
   - **c.** pay the bill and leave

3. The hotel was **originally** a prison. Prisoners lived there _____.
   - **a.** in the beginning
   - **b.** in the middle
   - **c.** in the end

4. The hotel restaurant is _____, so I should **reserve** a table for us.
   - **a.** quiet
   - **b.** crowded
   - **c.** expensive

5. The hotel is **entirely** full. There are _____ empty rooms.
   - **a.** many
   - **b.** few
   - **c.** no

6. When the weather is **extreme**, for example, _____, we don't like to travel.
   - **a.** on a sunny day
   - **b.** during a big storm
   - **c.** when it's cloudy

7. If you _____, you may go to **prison**.
   - **a.** don't follow the law
   - **b.** take a vacation
   - **c.** get an education

8. If a hotel is **unique**, there are _____ other hotels like it.
   - **a.** many
   - **b.** a few
   - **c.** no

9. This hotel is **converted**; in the past, it was _____.
   - **a.** in bad condition
   - **b.** used as a water tower
   - **c.** much smaller

10. This hotel has a **theme**. Each room has the same _____.
    - **a.** size
    - **b.** design style
    - **c.** price

11. That hotel **provides** a big breakfast. It _____ it to all guests.
    - **a.** sells
    - **b.** gives
    - **c.** shows

▶ READ AGAIN

Read "The World's Strangest Hotels" again and complete the comprehension exercises. As you work, keep the reading goal in mind.

> 📖 **READING GOAL:** To use visualization to help you remember details

Comprehension Check

A. On a separate sheet of paper, draw a simple picture of each of the hotels described in the reading. Include the most interesting features of each hotel.

B. Look at your pictures and answer the questions. Do not look back at the reading.

1. What things can you find inside each capsule room?

_____

2. What can you see on the doors and windows of Hostel Celica?

_____

3. What can you see on the walls of some rooms at Hostel Celica?

_____

4. Where do people keep their bags when they stay at the Jumbo Hostel?

_____

5. What can you watch outside your window at the Ariau Amazon Towers?

_____

6. What can you hear below you at the Ariau Amazon Towers?

_____

7. What do guests at the Hôtel de Glace sleep in to keep warm?

_____

8. How can guests reach the Jules' Undersea Lodge?

_____

C. Look back at the reading and check your answers from Exercise B.

D. Check (✓) the hotels each statement describes.

1. These hotels are very close to nature:

   _____ Hostel Celica

   _____ Jules' Undersea Lodge

   _____ Ariau Amazon Towers

   _____ Hôtel de Glace

2. These hotels were converted:

   _____ Capsule Hotel

   _____ Hostel Celica

   _____ Jumbo Hostel

   _____ Jules' Undersea Lodge

3. You can see works of art in these hotels:

   _____ Capsule Hotel

   _____ Hostel Celica

   _____ Jumbo Hostel

   _____ Hôtel de Glace

4. These hotels are located inside cities:

   _____ Capsule Hotel

   _____ Hostel Celica

   _____ Ariau Amazon Towers

   _____ Jules' Undersea Lodge

5. You can see animals outside your window in these hotels:

   _____ Capsule Hotel

   _____ Jumbo Hostel

   _____ Ariau Amazon Towers

   _____ Jules' Undersea Lodge

> DISCUSS

A. Work in small groups. Imagine you have plans to visit one of the strange hotels in the reading. Make a list of ten things you should bring with you.

1. _____   6. _____

2. _____   7. _____

3. _____   8. _____

4. _____   9. _____

5. _____   10. _____

B. Listen as other groups read their lists. Guess which hotel they plan to visit.

CHAPTER 8

Small Town, Strange Festival

> PREPARE TO READ

A. Look at the words in the list. Write the number(s) next to each word to show what you know. You may be able to write more than one number next to some of the words. You will study all of these words in this chapter.

1. I can use the word in a sentence.

2. I know <u>one meaning</u> of the word.

3. I know <u>more than one meaning</u> of the word.

4. I know how to pronounce the word.

B. Work with a partner. Look at the picture. Ask and answer the questions. If you don't know a word in English, ask your partner or look in your dictionary. Then write your new words on page 216.

1. What do you see in the picture?

2. Would you like to join the people? Why or why not?

3. What do you think is the purpose of the event you see in the picture?

_____ competition

_____ economy

_____ entertain

_____ festival

_____ host

_____ local

_____ mud

_____ occur

_____ population

_____ seek

_____ tourist

Reading Skill: Using a Graphic Organizer

You can use a graphic organizer to record the most important information in a reading. This will help you understand and remember how a reading is organized and what it's about. A graphic organizer like the one below shows the relationship between the main topic, the main ideas, the examples, and the details. Writers sometimes have one main topic and two or more main ideas about the topic. Often the writer states the topic and main ideas in one or two sentences at the end of the introductory paragraph(s). The main ideas are supported by examples and details (specific pieces of information, such as facts).

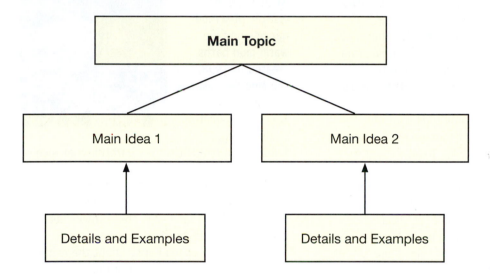

C. Read the first two paragraphs of the travel article "Small Town, Strange Festival" on the next page. Then answer the questions.

1. What is the main topic of the reading?
- **a.** Tomatoes
- **b.** Festivals
- **c.** Big Cities

2. What are the main ideas of the reading?
- **a.** Trucks deliver tomatoes. / Flying tomatoes fill the air.
- **b.** Strange festivals bring fame and fun. / They can be an expensive mess.
- **c.** Big cities have museums. / They have sports teams.

Read "Small Town, Strange Festival." Underline the sentences that tell you the topic and main ideas of the reading.

Small Town, Strange Festival

1 The town of Buñol, Spain, has a **population** of 9,000. But for one day in August, it grows to 30,000 people. This is the day of *La Tomatina*, or "the tomato **festival.**" Thousands
5 of people meet in the center of town wearing old clothes and safety glasses. Large trucks[1] deliver tomatoes. Then, suddenly, the world's biggest food fight begins. Flying tomatoes fill the air. People and buildings turn red. The
10 street becomes a river of tomato juice. Once a small **local** celebration,[2] La Tomatina has made Buñol world-famous.

Big cities have museums, sports teams, and shopping to **entertain** visitors. But for small
15 towns like Buñol, it is not so easy. Often, a strange festival is the only thing to attract **tourists**. These festivals bring fame[3] and fun. At the same time, they can be an expensive mess.[4]

One strange festival **occurs** in the town of
20 Port Lincoln, Australia. Each year the town has a **competition** to see how far people can throw a tuna fish. The festival, called Tunarama, has grown in popularity. Visitors come from all over Australia. The festival used to be a small
25 competition among locals, but the record for the longest tuna throw now belongs to an Olympic athlete. As the festival has grown, so has Port Lincoln. People are building new homes, and the local **economy** is much stronger than before.

30 Many newer festivals hope to copy the success of Tunarama and La Tomatina. One example is the Boryeong **Mud** Festival in South

Korea. During this weeklong event,
35 visitors play mud games and take warm mud baths. Created in 1998, the Mud Festival has
40 brought close to two million visitors to Boryeong.

Another unique festival—a bathtub boat race—occurs in Belgium, in the town of Dinant. Then
45 there is Kenwood, a small town in California, which **hosts** a pillow[5] fighting competition. For a short time each year, these towns become overcrowded with tourists.

But not everyone is happy about the festivals.
50 After La Tomatina, the center of Buñol requires many days of cleaning. Some people have to paint their homes again. Others say the festival is a waste of tomatoes. Tunarama causes a similar problem. Every year there are fewer tuna
55 in the ocean. In the future, people at the festival may throw plastic fish. In Kenwood, some locals say the pillow fighting festival creates too much traffic and is bad for the environment.

Although some of the festivals cause
60 problems, the fun will continue. Without them, many hotels and restaurants would lose business. As more and more small towns **seek** tourist money, expect to see stranger and stranger festivals. Who knows—your town could be next.

---

[1] **truck:** a large road vehicle that is used for carrying heavy loads

[2] **celebration:** a happy event or occasion when you do something special, for example, a party

[3] **fame:** the state of being known about by a lot of people because of your achievements

[4] **a mess:** a place or group of things that is not organized or arranged neatly

[5] **pillow:** a cloth bag filled with soft material that you put your head on when you sleep

Vocabulary Check

Write the boldfaced word from the reading next to the correct definition.
Use the correct form of the word.

1. _____ = to look for, search for

2. _____ = to happen

3. _____ = to provide space for a special event

4. _____ = travelers, visitors

5. _____ = a party, special occasion

6. _____ = to do something to interest people

7. _____ = the way money, business, and products are
organized in a particular country, area, etc.

8. _____ = all the people who live in a particular area

9. _____ = related to a particular area

10. _____ = a situation in which people try to win something by
being better or more successful than everyone else

11. _____ = earth that is soft and wet

> READ AGAIN

Read "Small Town, Strange Festival" again and complete the
comprehension exercises on the next page. As you work, keep the
reading goal in mind.

> **READING GOAL:** To understand the organization of the ideas in the
> reading

Comprehension Check

A. At which festival would you expect to see each thing? Write the initials of the festivals next to the pictures.

Bathtub boat race (BB)

La Tomatina (TO)

Mud Festival (MF)

Pillow fighting championship (PF)

Tunarama (T)

_____1.

_____2.

_____3.

_____4.

_____5.

B. Read these sentences from the reading. Write *M* if they give a main idea,
E if they give an example, and *SD* if they give a supporting detail.

    _M_   **1.** These festivals bring fame and fun.

_____ **2.** At the same time, they can be an expensive mess.

_____ **3.** People are building new homes, and the local economy is much
stronger than before.

_____ **4.** One example is the Boryeong Mud Festival in South Korea.

_____ **5.** Created in 1998, the Mud Festival has brought close to two
million visitors to Boryeong.

_____ **6.** Another unique festival—a bathtub boat race—occurs in
Belgium, in the town of Dinant.

_____ **7.** But not everyone is happy about the festivals.

_____ **8.** Although some of the festivals cause problems, the fun will
continue.

C. Complete the graphic organizer to show the main topic, ideas, examples,
and details in the reading.

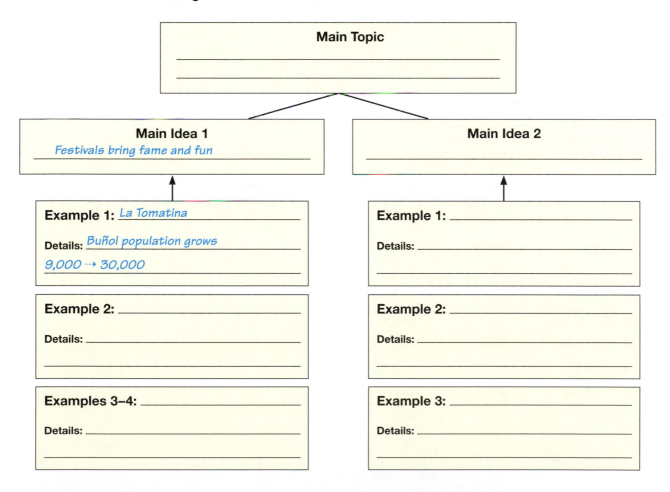

Main Topic

_____

_____

Main Idea 1

Festivals bring fame and fun

Main Idea 2

_____

Example 1: *La Tomatina*

Details: *Buñol population grows*
9,000 → 30,000

Example 2: _____

Details: _____

Examples 3–4: _____

Details: _____

Example 1: _____

Details: _____

Example 2: _____

Details: _____

Example 3: _____

Details: _____

DISCUSS

A. Work in small groups. Imagine that you and your partners live in Littleton, a small town in the mountains. Create a strange festival to attract tourists to Littleton. Discuss your answers to the questions below.

1. What is the **theme** and name of your festival?

2. What time of year will it **occur**, and how long will it last?

3. What events will it have to **entertain tourists**?

4. How will your **festival** help the **local economy**?

5. Will your **festival** create any problems? What will you do to solve the problems?

B. Listen to other groups' ideas for festivals in Littleton. Then vote for the best idea.

VOCABULARY SKILL BUILDING

Suffixes: *-ation, -ition, -sion, -ion*

In Unit 3, you learned that adding a suffix to a word can change its part of speech. Like the suffix *-ment*, the suffixes *-ation, -ition, -sion,* and *-ion* can be added to some verbs to make them nouns. Sometimes you have to remove the last letter of the verb before adding the suffix.

EXAMPLES:

inform (verb) + ***-ation*** = *information* (noun)
compete (verb) + ***-ition*** = *competition* (noun)

A. Add the suffixes to the verbs to make nouns. If necessary, remove the last letter of the verb before adding the suffix. If you are not sure about spelling, check your dictionary.

Verb	Suffix	Noun
1. populate	-ation	*population*
2. reserve	-ation	_____
3. locate	-ion	_____
4. compete	-ition	_____
5. attract	-ion	_____
6. generate	-ion	_____
7. convert	-sion	_____

B. Complete the paragraph. Use the correct form of the words from Exercise A (noun or verb). You will use only one form of each word—that is, either the noun or the verb form.

The Shetland Islands, in the northern part of the United Kingdom, are very small. In fact, they may be difficult to (1) _____ on a map. But each year, the islands become a hot spot for tourists. Every December, towns in the Shetland Islands have Fire Festivals. These festivals are a big tourist (2) _____, bringing thousands of visitors each year. At the festivals, people enjoy music, food, dancing, and nighttime celebrations. There is also a(n) (3) _____ to see who can take the best photograph. Hotel and restaurant owners love this time of year because the festivals (4) _____ a lot of business. The biggest and most successful of the Fire Festivals occurs in the town of Lerwick, which has a(n) (5) _____ of around 7,000 people. It is not uncommon for people in Lerwick to (6) _____ historical buildings into modern hotels. If you want to stay in one, however, be sure to make a(n) (7) _____ because they fill up very quickly!

Learn the Vocabulary

Using a Dictionary: Stressing the Correct Syllable

Some English words have only one syllable. For example, the target words *host* and *theme* are made up of only one syllable. Other words have two or more syllables. The target word *local* has two syllables (*lo • cal*), and *benefit* has three (*ben • e • fit*).

When a word has more than one syllable, one syllable receives the main, or primary, stress, or beat. The vowel sound in a stressed syllable is longer and louder than vowels in other syllables. In some words, another syllable receives a secondary stress, or less strong beat.

EXAMPLES:

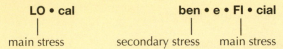

LO • cal	**ben • e • FI • cial**	
main stress	secondary stress	main stress

When you learn a new word with more than one syllable, use your dictionary to see which syllables are stressed. Dictionaries use different symbols to show which syllable receives the primary stress and which syllable, if any, receives the secondary stress. Here's how one dictionary—*The Longman Dictionary of American English*—shows stressed syllables. Notice the stress marks within the phonetic respellings of each word.

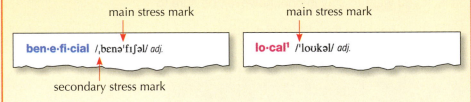

Sometimes when a word's part of speech (or form) changes, the stressed syllable also changes.

Sometimes the stressed syllable does not change when you change the word's form.

A. Use your dictionary to look up the words in the chart and their phonetic respellings. Circle the syllable in each word that receives the main stress. If another syllable receives secondary stress, underline it. Notice how the stress sometimes changes when the word's form, or part of speech, changes.

Noun	Verb	Adjective
(ben) • e • fit	(ben) • e • fit	ben • e • (fi) • cial
res • er • va • tion	re • serve	re • served
e • con • o • my	e • con • o • mize	ec • o • nom • ic
pop • u • la • tion	pop • u • late	pop • u • la • ted
con • ver • sion	con • vert	con • ver • ted

B. Complete the questions with the words from the chart.

1. Why are festivals _____ to small towns' economies?

2. What types of buildings do people _____ into hotels?

3. What is the easiest way to make a(n) _____ at a hotel?

4. Would you rather live in a big city or a town with a small _____?

5. Are you worried about _____ problems, such as finding a job and saving money?

C. Work with a partner. Check your answers to Exercise B. Then ask and answer the questions. Use the target words in your answers. Be sure that you stress the correct syllable(s) in each word.

D. Make cards for the words from Chapters 7–8 that were new to you when you started the unit. Include target words and words that you wrote on page 216. List the different forms of each word on the front of the card. Write the part of speech (for example, noun, verb, adjective, adverb) next to each word form. Circle the syllable that receives the main stress. If another syllable receives secondary stress, underline it. When you review those cards, try to remember the different forms of the word and which syllables are stressed.

E. Go back to the vocabulary list at the beginning of each chapter. What did you learn about the target words? Add your numbers to the lists.

Vocabulary Practice 4, see page 221

UNIT 5

The Food We Love

> THINK BEFORE YOU READ

A. Work with a partner. Look at the pictures. Ask and answer the questions. If you don't know a word in English, ask your partner or look in your dictionary. Then write your new words on page 216.

1. What do you see in the pictures? Point to the things you see and name them in English.

2. How is each type of food in the pictures different from the other types?

3. Do you want to try any of the food you see in the pictures? Explain.

B. Ask students in your class the questions below. Find one person who answers *yes* for each question and write his or her name below.

Questions	Name of student who answers *yes*
Did you eat a big breakfast this morning?	
Have you ordered food for delivery recently?	
Do you like to cook?	
Did you eat at a restaurant last week?	
Have you ever hosted a dinner party for many people in your home?	
Have you ever eaten a very unusual type of meat or vegetable?	
Have you ever been to a food festival?	

CHAPTER 9

What Is American Food?

> PREPARE TO READ

A. Look at the words in the list. Write the number(s) next to each word to show what you know. You may be able to write more than one number next to some of the words. You will study all of these words in this chapter.

1. I can use the word in a sentence.

2. I know <u>one meaning</u> of the word.

3. I know <u>more than one meaning</u> of the word.

4. I know how to pronounce the word.

_____	associate
_____	critic
_____	dish
_____	exotic
_____	immigration
_____	mix
_____	profit
_____	reflect
_____	sauce
_____	spicy
_____	taste

B. Work with a partner. Look at the pictures. Ask and answer the questions. If you don't know a word in English, ask your partner or look in your dictionary. Then write your new words on page 216.

1. What do you see in the pictures?

2. What is each food product made up of?

3. Which of these food products do you think Americans buy most often?

C. Preview the magazine article "What Is American Food?" on the next page. Then answer the question.

What is the main idea of the reading? Circle the letter of the correct answer.

a. Americans are eating more Asian and Mexican food.

b. Hamburgers are becoming popular in many countries.

c. People in the United States often disagree about food.

READ

Read "What Is American Food?" Underline the sentence that gives the main idea of the reading.

What Is American Food?

1   What is American food? Even for Americans, this is a difficult question. For years, many U.S. restaurants have served German-style meats and sandwiches, like the famous hamburger
5   or the hot dog. Other U.S. restaurants serve Italian-style pizza and pasta. Some of the more expensive U.S. restaurants offer French **dishes**, such as steak au poivre.[1] But now, a big change is happening. These days, Americans'
10   **tastes** are moving south and east.

Across the country, Americans are buying more and more Mexican food. In fact, Mexican salsa is now the number one **sauce** in the country. Ketchup is in second place. Americans
15   spend around $6 billion a year on tortillas, second only to white bread. Many U.S. businesses now sell nothing but Mexican food products.

One example is Mexitana Tortilla Co. in
20   Corvallis, Montana. The popularity of tortillas in Montana surprised Jonathan Whiting, the company's first owner. "We knew we'd succeed," he says. "We just never imagined it would be with tortillas." Mexitana's new owner expects
25   tortillas to become even more popular than white bread. "In a culture like this, people are taking things and throwing them into tortillas and heading to a soccer game," he says.

Business is also good for California Creative
30   Foods, the nation's largest salsa maker. This family-owned company makes over 271 different flavors of salsa, and produces over 20 million pounds of the sauce each year. "It's a very fun business to be in," says owner Meg
35   Pearson. "Everybody sort of **associates** salsa with having a good time."

Asian food is enjoying the same remarkable success. In cities around the United States, new Japanese, Thai, Korean, Vietnamese, and
40   Chinese restaurants are opening. Their **profits** are growing by 10 to 12 percent a year. Many supermarkets have added sections that sell Asian food products. Customers can now buy plum sauce from China or noodles[2] from Japan.
45   "Americans believe that Asian food is healthier than burgers, pizza, or French food," says food **critic** Susan Jimenez. "They are also excited to try **spicy** food and **exotic** things like sushi."

Experts say there is a connection
50   between the American diet and changes in **immigration**. One hundred years ago, almost 90 percent of U.S. immigrants came from Europe. As they came to the United States, they brought their traditional foods with
55   them. These foods became a regular part of the American diet. But in the last forty years, immigration has changed completely. Almost half of U.S. immigrants today are from South America. A quarter are from Asia. As
60   immigration has changed, so have Americans' eating habits. "Fifteen years ago, nobody ate sushi or Mexican food. Now everybody does," says researcher Timothy Ramey.

This makes American food even more
65   difficult to define. "It's a little bit of everything," says Jimenez. "America is a **mix** of cultures, and its food **reflects** that."

---

[1] **steak au poivre:** steak served with a pepper sauce
[2] **noodle:** a long, thin piece of soft food made from flour, water, and usually egg, which is cooked in water

Vocabulary Check

Circle the letter of the correct answer to complete each sentence. The boldfaced words are the target words.

1. When you eat something **spicy**, your mouth feels _____.
   a. cold
   b. dry
   c. hot

2. **Immigration** is when people come to another country to _____.
   a. visit
   b. live
   c. study

3. Pablo's salary at the restaurant **reflects** his good work. Pablo's salary is _____.
   a. low
   b. regular
   c. high

4. Susan Jiminez is a food **critic**. She probably writes for a _____.
   a. newspaper or magazine
   b. restaurant
   c. food market

5. Oil and water don't **mix**. They can't be _____.
   a. eaten at the same time
   b. put together to make a new thing
   c. bought at the same store

6. An example of a **dish** is _____.
   a. chicken with red sauce
   b. orange juice
   c. a crowded restaurant

7. We have the same **taste** in restaurants. We _____.
   a. eat out every night
   b. order the same dishes
   c. like the same restaurants.

8. People usually put **sauce** on _____.
   a. meat
   b. soup
   c. salads

(continued on next page)

9. That restaurant makes a good **profit**. It makes a lot of _____.

    a. dishes

    b. money

    c. salad

10. If something is **exotic**, it comes from _____.

    a. the supermarket

    b. your local area

    c. a foreign country

11. I **associate** cooking with my mother. In my mind, I _____ making food with her.

    a. connect

    b. dislike

    c. can't remember

> READ AGAIN

Read "What Is American Food?" again and complete the comprehension exercises. As you work, keep the reading goal in mind.

> **READING GOAL:** To understand the topic and main ideas

Comprehension Check

A. Find these sentences in the reading. What do the underlined words mean? Circle the letter of the correct answer. The numbers in parentheses are the paragraphs where you can find the sentences.

1. These days, Americans' tastes are moving south and east. (1)

    a. Mexican and Asian dishes are becoming more popular with Americans.

    b. Americans are moving to Mexico and Asia for the food.

    c. Many restaurants are moving to the southern and eastern parts of the United States.

2. Mexican salsa is now the number one sauce in the country. (2)

    a. newest

    b. original

    c. most popular

3. Americans spend around $6 billion a year on tortillas, second only to white bread. (2)

    a. as much as they spend on

    b. more than they spend on

    c. only a little less than they spend on

4. Many U.S. businesses now sell <u>nothing but</u> Mexican food products. (2)
   a. no
   b. only
   c. some

5. "<u>It</u>'s a very fun business to be in," says owner Meg Pearson. (3)
   a. Selling tortillas
   b. Working in a restaurant
   c. Making salsa

6. Asian food is <u>enjoying</u> the same remarkable success. (4)
   a. hoping for
   b. feeling happy about
   c. experiencing

7. As <u>they</u> came to the United States, they brought their traditional foods with them. (5)
   a. Asians
   b. Mexicans
   c. Europeans

8. <u>A quarter</u> are from Asia. (5)
   a. 25 percent of immigrants
   b. 50 percent of immigrants
   c. 75 percent of immigrants

9. <u>This</u> makes American food even more difficult to define. (6)
   a. the fact that hamburgers and hot dogs are not healthy to eat
   b. the fact that many Americans now eat sushi and Mexican food
   c. the fact that Susan Jimenez is a food critic

10. America is a mix of cultures, and its food <u>reflects that</u>. (6)
    a. is better as a result
    b. shows that America is a mix of cultures
    c. can be difficult to define

B. Complete the graphic organizer to show the main ideas, examples, and details in the reading.

Main Idea 1	Main Idea 2	Main Idea 3
Americans are eating more Mexican food.		

Example 1:
_____ *Salsa* _____

Details: *number one sauce in United States*
_____

Example 1:
_____

Details:
_____
_____

Example 1:
_____

Details:
_____
_____

Example 2:
_____ *tortillas* _____

Details:
_____
_____

Example 2:
_____

Details:
_____
_____

Example 2:
_____

Details:
_____
_____

Example 3:
_____

Details:
_____
_____

Example 3:
_____

Details:
_____
_____

Example 4:
_____

Details:
_____
_____

C. Write a short summary of the reading. Tell the three main ideas. For each main idea, give one or two examples. Use the information in your graphic organizer to help you. You do not need to use the same words and phrases as in the reading, but make sure the meaning is the same.

_____

_____

_____

_____

_____

_____

_____

_____

_____

_____

> DISCUSS

Work in small groups. Ask and answer the questions. Use the words in the lists during your discussion.

NOUNS

diet	flavor	health	mix	sauce	taste
dish	freshness	mess	salt	spice	

ADJECTIVES

exotic	fresh	messy	regular	spicy
flavorful	healthy	popular	salty	tasty

1. What do most people in your home country like to eat?

2. What do you like to eat?

3. What do you not like to eat?

4. Which foods are the best for your health?

5. Are there any dishes from your home country that you think Americans would like? Explain.

> VOCABULARY SKILL BUILDING

Suffix: -y

Like the suffix -ful, the suffix -y can be added to some nouns to make them adjectives. If the noun ends in e, you will often need to remove the e before adding the suffix. Check a dictionary if you are unsure about dropping the e.

EXAMPLES:

salt (noun) + **-y** = salty (adjective)

spice (noun) + **-y** = spicy (adjective)

A. Add or delete the suffix -y to change the form of each word. Make sure you spell the new word forms correctly.

Noun	Adjective
1. _____salt_____	salty
2. _____	spicy
3. _____	tasty
4. tourist	_____
5. noise	_____
6. mess	_____
7. scare	_____

B. Complete Susan Jimenez's restaurant review. Use the correct form of the words from Exercise A (noun or adjective). You will use only one form of each word.

Feel like Mexican food? Then try Café Mexico. The food is always fresh and

(1) _____. You'll love it! I recommend the *Pollo Rojo*, or chicken with

red sauce. This dish is really (2) _____, so you'll need something to

drink with it—try a lime soda! The only problem is that Café Mexico is near the train

station, so a lot of visitors from other cities come there. With so many visitors, and so

few locals, it can be a little (3) _____. It can also be very crowded, so it

is sometimes difficult to hear because of the (4) _____.

Another option for Mexican food is Mama's Place. The fish is excellent and has the

perfect amount of (5) _____ and pepper. The service is also fast and

friendly. Last time I ate at Mama's Place, I dropped my glass and it broke. It really gave

the other people in the restaurant a (6) _____! But my waiter quickly

came, cleaned up the (7) _____, and told a joke to make me feel better.

I'll be sure to go back.

Why Chilies Are Hot

> PREPARE TO READ

A. Look at the words (and phrases) in the list. Write the number(s) next to each word to show what you know. You may be able to write more than one number next to some of the words. You will study all of these words in this chapter.

   1. I can use the word in a sentence.

   2. I know <u>one meaning</u> of the word.

   3. I know <u>more than one meaning</u> of the word.

   4. I know how to pronounce the word.

B. Work with a partner. Look at the picture. Ask and answer the questions. If you don't know a word in English, ask your partner or look in your dictionary. Then write your new words on page 216.

   1. What is the name of the vegetable in the picture?

   2. How does it taste?

   3. How do you feel after you eat one?

   4. Which dishes are made with this vegetable?

_____ bitter

_____ chemical

_____ discover

_____ pack

_____ pain

_____ pleasure

_____ poisonous

_____ relief

_____ respond

_____ sell out

_____ variety

We often read to understand *why* something happens or is true. To understand *why*, you need to understand the relationship between *causes* and *effects*. Sometimes writers explain causes and effects directly by using signal words:

EXAMPLES:

Nathan eats too much. <u>As a result</u>, he has problems with his health.
Some people have problems with their health <u>because</u> they eat too much.

In these sentences, the phrase *as a result* introduces an effect. The word *because* introduces a cause.

Sometimes writers do not directly explain causes and effects. You have to make an *inference* about the cause-effect relationship.

EXAMPLE:

Some people eat too much. They gain weight and can have problems with their health.

Here, no word or phrase is used to introduce the cause or effect. You need to understand the cause-effect relationship by figuring out what happened (the effect: weight gain and health problems) and why it happened (the cause: eating too much).

C. Read the first paragraph of the Web site "Why Chilies Are Hot" on the next page. Then underline the sentence that gives a cause.

 READ

First, look at the picture. What do you think causes people to like hot dishes such as chili? Then read "Why Chilies Are Hot" on the next page. As you read, pay attention to the causes and their effects.

Why Chilies Are Hot

1 You eat a chili pepper. Your mouth starts to burn. Water fills your eyes. Your heart starts to beat faster. You are experiencing **pain**.

5 But after this pain comes **pleasure**. A few seconds after you eat a chili pepper, your brain **responds** and produces special **chemicals**. These chemicals give you **relief** from the pain. They make you feel relaxed and happy. And the more chilies you eat,

10 the more pain relief chemicals your brain produces.

How can a simple vegetable produce both pain and

15 pleasure? The answer is a chemical inside chilies called *capsaicin*. Capsaicin is the reason chilies

20 are spicy. Experts say this strange chemical is also the reason chilies are growing in popularity.

Around the world, people are eating more and more chilies. In the past, chilies were

25 mostly popular in countries like India, Thailand, and Mexico. Now, they are used everywhere. Americans put chilies on hamburgers, in drinks, even in chocolates. The British are **discovering** chilies as well.

30 Sales of chilies in British supermarkets increased by 29 percent in one year alone. It seems in England, the hotter the chili, the more people want to try it. One supermarket in Newcastle decided to sell the Dorset

35 Naga, an extremely spicy **variety** of chili from Bangladesh. The supermarket wasn't sure if its customers would like the strong taste of the Dorset Naga and wanted to test its popularity. They ordered 400 **packs** of this

40 super-hot chili. They thought the packs would last a month. The entire amount **sold out** in a few hours.

Experts say it is chilies' capsaicin, more than their taste, that makes them popular.

45 Scientists say dogs, monkeys, and even rats will not eat chilies. Because of the strong taste, the animals believe they are **poisonous**. Scientists compare chilies to coffee, tobacco,[1] or alcohol.[2] They taste

50 **bitter**, but they give chemical pleasure. Humans like the pleasure, and over time, they learn to like the taste.

Capsaicin has another special ability—it can make other tastes, like sweet or salty,

55 seem stronger. In one study, scientists mixed water with sugar in small bottles. Every bottle had the same amount of sugar and water. They then added capsaicin to some of the bottles. When people tasted the mixtures,

60 they believed the capsaicin bottles had more sugar than the other bottles. When scientists tried this test with salt, they had the same results. Scientists say this explains why people add chilies to food with less flavor,

65 such as rice or potatoes.

Chilies have a lot of fans around the world. They can give pleasure and change how food tastes. But scientists say that unlike coffee, tobacco, or alcohol, chilies cause no long-

70 term[3] health problems. Just don't get them in your eyes.

---

[1] **tobacco:** the dried leaves of a plant that are smoked in cigarettes

[2] **alcohol:** drinks such as beer, wine, etc., that affect your brain and make you feel drunk

[3] **long-term:** continuing for a long period of time into the future

Vocabulary Check

Write the boldfaced word from the reading next to the correct picture or definition.

1. _____ =

2. _____ =

3. _____ =

4. _____ =

5. _____ =

6. _____ =

7. _____ = finding something that was hidden or that people didn't know about before

8. _____ = reacts because of something that has occurred

9. _____ = the happy feeling you have when something scary or painful ends, or has not happened

10. _____ = a feeling of satisfaction or enjoyment

11. _____ = having a strong taste—such as black coffee

> READ AGAIN

Read "Why Chilies Are Hot" again and complete the comprehension exercises. As you work, keep the reading goal in mind.

> 📖 **READING GOAL:** To learn about why people eat chilies and the effects these hot vegetables have on our bodies

Comprehension Check

A. Explain what happens to different parts of your body when you eat chilies. Write the effects.

1. Your mouth: _____*It starts to burn*_____

2. Your eyes: _____

3. Your heart: _____

4. Your brain: _____

5. The taste of food: _____

6. Your health: _____

B. Read the pairs of sentences from the reading. Think about the relationship between the sentences in each pair. Write *C* if the underlined sentence is a cause, *E* if it is an effect. One pair of sentences does not show a cause or an effect. Write *?* next to this pair.

_____ **1.** A few seconds after you eat a chili pepper, your brain responds and produces special chemicals. <u>These chemicals give you relief from the pain</u>.

_____ **2.** How can a simple vegetable produce both pain and pleasure? <u>The answer is a chemical inside chilies called *capsaicin*</u>.

_____ **3.** <u>The British are discovering chilies as well</u>. Sales of chilies in British supermarkets increased by 29 percent in one year alone.

_____ **4.** <u>They thought the packs would last a month</u>. The entire amount sold out in a few hours.

(continued on next page)

    5. Scientists say dogs, monkeys, and even rats will not eat chilies. Because of the strong taste, the animals believe they are poisonous.

    6. They taste bitter, but they give chemical pleasure. Humans like the pleasure, and over time, they learn to like the taste.

    7. They then added capsaicin to some of the bottles. When people tasted the mixtures, they believed the capsaicin bottles had more sugar than the other bottles.

    8. Chilies have a lot of fans around the world. They can give pleasure and change how food tastes.

C. Which sentence best summarizes the reading? Check (✓) the answer.

    1. Chilies can hurt your eyes and mouth and make your heart beat faster, but scientists say they cause no long-term health problems.

    2. Chilies have a chemical called capsaicin in them that gives people pleasure and changes how food tastes; this is making chilies more popular around the world.

    3. Animals won't eat chilies because of their bitter taste, but humans have learned to enjoy the taste because chilies give pleasure.

> # DISCUSS

Work with a partner. Decide who is A and who is B.

A = You own a business that grows chilies and then sells them to supermarkets in England and the United States. Convince B to buy your chilies.

B = You own many supermarkets in Britain and the United States. You want to find new products your customers will like. Ask A as many questions as you can about chilies.

Example questions:

What makes chilies spicy?

Are chilies bad for our health?

Why do people like chilies?

What other foods go well with chili peppers?

Have chili peppers sold well in other supermarkets?

Learn the Vocabulary

A. Make cards for the words from Chapters 9–10 that were new to you when you started the unit. Include target words and words that you wrote on page 216.

B. Review your new cards one time with a partner. As your partner quizzes you, he or she will put your cards in two groups: one group for the words you remembered and one group for the words you didn't remember. Review the words you didn't remember a second time.

C. Add your cards from Units 1–4 to the new cards. Choose twenty to thirty words (Group 1) that are the most useful for you in real life. For the next three days, review these words twice a day. Review the Group 2 cards (the remaining words) once a day. Each time you review your cards, make a check (✓) in the chart.

Day one	Day two	Day three
Group 1: _____ / _____	Group 1: _____ / _____	Group 1: _____ / _____
Group 2: _____	Group 2: _____	Group 2: _____

D. After three days, put the two groups back together, change the order, and review all of the cards with your partner in class.

E. Go back to the vocabulary list at the beginning of each chapter. What did you learn about the target words? Add your numbers to the lists.

Vocabulary Practice 5, see page 222

> THINK BEFORE YOU READ

A. Work with a partner. Look at the picture. Ask and answer the questions. If you don't know a word in English, ask your partner or look in your dictionary. Then write your new words on page 216.

1. Who are the people in the picture and what are they doing? Point to the things you see and name them in English.

2. Do you have a favorite type of music? Why is it your favorite?

3. Are there any types of music you don't like? Why don't you like them?

B. On a separate piece of paper, write a question about music to ask five of your classmates. For example, you might ask, "How often do you listen to music?" or "Can you sing?" Ask five classmates your question. Write their answers.

C. Tell the class one interesting thing you learned about your classmates.

All About Music

> PREPARE TO READ

A. Look at the words (and phrases) in the list. Write the number(s) next to each word to show what you know. You may be able to write more than one number next to some of the words. You will study all of these words in this chapter.

1. I can use the word in a sentence.

2. I know <u>one meaning</u> of the word.

3. I know <u>more than one meaning</u> of the word.

4. I know how to pronounce the word.

B. Work with a partner. Look at the pictures. Ask and answer the questions. If you don't know a word in English, ask your partner or look in your dictionary. Then write your new words on page 216.

1. What do you see in the pictures?

2. What type of music are the people in each picture playing or listening to?

3. Why do humans enjoy music? On a separate sheet of paper, make a list of reasons.

4. Are humans the only living things that make music? If not, what other living things make music?

_____ appropriate

_____ beat

_____ complex

_____ content

_____ in contrast

_____ left over

_____ note

_____ pattern

_____ resemble

_____ tend to

Reading Skill: Understanding Examples

Examples help readers understand difficult ideas. A reading often starts with a short explanation of an idea, followed by an example. Don't worry if you do not understand the explanation at first. When you finish reading the examples, go back and read the explanation again. It should be easier to understand.

C. Read the first post in the blog "All About Music" on the next page. Check (✓) the examples Rachel Baines mentions in her post.

_____ **1.** It is not easy to write a popular song.

_____ **2.** Countries have national anthems.

_____ **3.** Friends usually like the same music.

_____ **4.** Humans have made music for thousands of years.

_____ **5.** Fans of different music dress differently.

D. Study the examples you checked (✓) in Exercise C. Check (✓) the main idea that the examples explain.

_____ **1.** Music makes people laugh, sing, and dance.

_____ **2.** Music helps us feel like part of a group.

_____ **3.** Music is like art for our ears to enjoy.

E. Now compare your answer in Exercise D with the first sentence of Rachel's post. Are they similar?

READ

Read "All About Music." Was your answer from Exercise B, question 4, correct? In the blog, underline the sentences that answer the question.

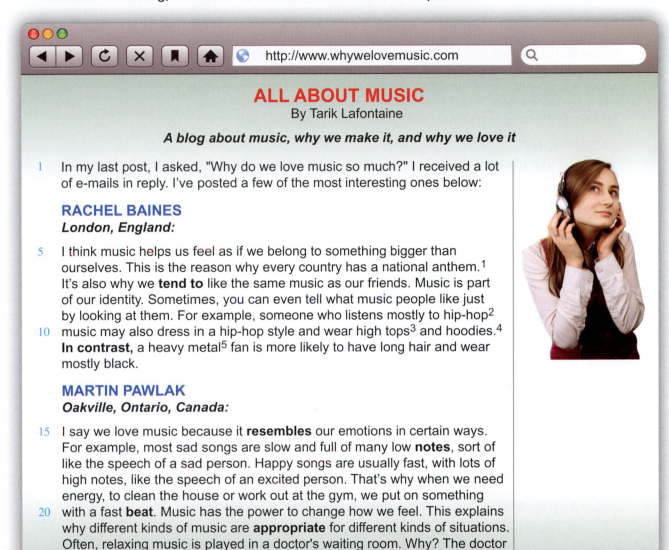

http://www.whywelovemusic.com

ALL ABOUT MUSIC
By Tarik Lafontaine

A blog about music, why we make it, and why we love it

1   In my last post, I asked, "Why do we love music so much?" I received a lot of e-mails in reply. I've posted a few of the most interesting ones below:

RACHEL BAINES
London, England:

5   I think music helps us feel as if we belong to something bigger than ourselves. This is the reason why every country has a national anthem.[1] It's also why we **tend to** like the same music as our friends. Music is part of our identity. Sometimes, you can even tell what music people like just by looking at them. For example, someone who listens mostly to hip-hop[2]
10   music may also dress in a hip-hop style and wear high tops[3] and hoodies.[4] **In contrast,** a heavy metal[5] fan is more likely to have long hair and wear mostly black.

MARTIN PAWLAK
Oakville, Ontario, Canada:

15   I say we love music because it **resembles** our emotions in certain ways. For example, most sad songs are slow and full of many low **notes**, sort of like the speech of a sad person. Happy songs are usually fast, with lots of high notes, like the speech of an excited person. That's why when we need energy, to clean the house or work out at the gym, we put on something
20   with a fast **beat**. Music has the power to change how we feel. This explains why different kinds of music are **appropriate** for different kinds of situations. Often, relaxing music is played in a doctor's waiting room. Why? The doctor wants us to relax, not feel nervous. In contrast, at a basketball game or a nightclub, music with a heavy beat such as dance music is usually played.
25   The purpose is to get the crowd excited.

(continued on next page)

---

[1] **anthem:** a formal song of praise or celebration, often for a group, such as the citizens of a country

[2] **hip-hop:** a type of dance music with a strong regular beat (rhythmical sound) and spoken words

[3] **high tops:** athletic shoes that reach above the ankles

[4] **hoodies:** hooded sweatshirts

[5] **heavy metal:** a type of rock music with a strong beat that is played very loudly on electric guitars

SUNWON CHOI
Los Angeles, California, U.S.A.

Hey, Tarik. Could it be a math thing? Our brains enjoy finding **patterns**, right?
I mean, most video games are about finding patterns—you have to find the
30 pattern to win. Well, music is also full of patterns. When we listen to a song,
our brains try to identify the pattern. We try to guess when the song will
repeat and when it will go in a new direction. Some songs have such a clear
pattern that you can sing them after the first time you hear them. A lot of pop[6]
songs are like that. I think trying to find the pattern is fun for our brains. If we
35 find it, we feel **content**. If we don't, we feel surprised. Either way, we enjoy
listening to the song. So maybe music is like a math game for our brains.

JASON HUNT
Sydney, Australia:

Tarik, I saw a report about music in the natural world on TV the other day.
40 A lot of animals use music to communicate with each other. Birds and
whales are two good examples. Birds use songs to identify their family,
friends, and enemies. Whales appear to do this as well. Each pod[7] of
whales sings its own song, and pods change their songs every year,
possibly to keep other whales from copying them. In the past, humans
45 may have used music to communicate, too. But since then our languages
have become much more **complex**. Now that we don't need our
musical ability to communicate, we use music for other things—such as
entertainment. Basically, music is **left over** from an earlier stage in human
history. Luckily, we can do something really cool with it.

---

[6] **pop:** modern music that is popular with young people

[7] **pod:** a group of sea animals, such as whales or dolphins, that swim together

Vocabulary Check

Write the letter of the correct definition next to the target word.

_____ **1.** in contrast	**a.** having many parts, difficult to understand
_____ **2.** resemble	**b.** to be likely to (do something)
_____ **3.** note	**c.** a regular series of sounds in a piece of music
_____ **4.** beat	**d.** correct or good for a particular time, situation, or purpose
_____ **5.** pattern	**e.** to look like or be similar to someone or something
_____ **6.** content	**f.** a particular musical sound or the sign in written music that represents this
_____ **7.** appropriate	**g.** remaining, kept
_____ **8.** complex	**h.** happy or satisfied
_____ **9.** left over	**i.** differently; however
_____ **10.** tend to	**j.** the regular way in which something happens, develops, or is done

Read "All About Music" again and complete the comprehension exercises. As you work, keep the reading goal in mind.

> 📖 **READING GOAL:** To use the examples in each blog post to figure out the main idea

Comprehension Check

A. Read the sentences. Check (✓) the sentence that tells the main idea of each blog post.

Post 1: Rachel Baines

_____✓_____ **a.** Music helps us feel like part of a group.

_____ **b.** Someone who listens mostly to hip-hop music may also dress in a hip-hop style.

_____ **c.** Every country has a national anthem.

Post 2: Martin Pawlak

_____ **a.** Often, relaxing music is played in a doctor's waiting room.

_____ **b.** Music has the power to change how we feel.

_____ **c.** When we need energy, we put on something with a fast beat.

Post 3: Sunwon Choi

_____ **a.** Music is like a math game for our brains.

_____ **b.** We try to guess when the song will repeat and when it will go in a new direction.

_____ **c.** Most video games are about finding patterns.

Post 4: Jason Hunt

_____ **a.** Birds use songs to identify their family, friends, and enemies.

_____ **b.** Each pod of whales sings its own song.

_____ **c.** A lot of animals use music to communicate with each other.

B. Complete the e-mail to Tarik. The main idea sentence is missing. Study the examples, then write a main idea sentence for the e-mail.

Denise Chartof
Dallas, Texas

Hi, Tarik, here's another possible explanation for why we love music:

_____.

For example, when I listen to French music, I think about the trip I took to

Paris ten years ago with my husband. Listening to U2, my favorite music

group, makes me think about college. My university friends and I listened to

U2 all the time. Classical music brings me back to my childhood—my father

loved classical music and always played it at home. For me, listening to

music is like looking at a photograph from my past.

C. These examples are not in the blog posts, but they could be added. Write the letter of the person who might write each example.

_____ **1.** Some songs mean "this is my tree, go away," or "be careful, danger coming."

_____ **2.** When we want to relax after a long day of work, we put on something soft.

_____ **3.** Music experts may prefer complex songs; it's not as easy to identify the patterns.

_____ **4.** Many sports teams have a special song they always play before games.

_____ **5.** Before humans had words, they just had simple musical sounds.

_____ **6.** Scientists say that children who listen to classical music learn math faster.

a. Rachel Baines

b. Martin Pawlak

c. Sunwon Choi

d. Jason Hunt

DISCUSS

Work in small groups. Ask and answer the questions.

1. What type of music do your friends like? Do you like the same music as they do?

   _____

   _____

2. When do you like to listen to fast music with a heavy beat?

   _____

   _____

3. When do you prefer soft, relaxing music?

   _____

   _____

4. Should people listen to music while they are studying? Why or why not?

   _____

   _____

5. In what ways do humans use music to communicate?

   _____

   _____

6. Why is the blog "All About Music" written in a more informal style than a newspaper article about the same subject?

   _____

   _____

Can't Name That Tune?

> PREPARE TO READ

A. Look at the words (and phrases) in the list. Write the number(s) next to each word to show what you know. You may be able to write more than one number next to some of the words. You will study all of these words in this chapter.

1. I can use the word in a sentence.

2. I know <u>one meaning</u> of the word.

3. I know <u>more than one meaning</u> of the word.

4. I know how to pronounce the word.

B. Work with a partner. Look at the picture. Ask and answer the questions. If you don't know a word in English, ask your partner or look in your dictionary. Then write your new words on page 216.

1. What do you see in the picture?

2. Do you like listening to someone practicing the piano or violin? Have you ever taken a music lesson?

3. Can anyone learn to play music or sing songs?

4. Does everyone in the world enjoy music? Why or why not?

_____ appreciate

_____ avoid

_____ concert

_____ condition

_____ distinguish

_____ embarrassed

_____ instrument

_____ lack

_____ turn on

_____ wish

C. Preview the article "Can't Name that Tune?" What source do you think this reading came from? Circle the letter of your answer.

a. a popular-music Web site   **b.** a science magazine   **c.** a guide to playing piano

 **READ**

Read "Can't Name that Tune?" Was your answer from Exercise B, question 4, correct?

Can't Name That Tune?

1   Music is popular around the world. We hear it everywhere. It is played at parties and sporting events. It is an important part of TV advertising and movies. We hear it in doctors' and dentists'
5 offices. And when we are in locations where no music is being played, we can always **turn on** our MP3 players.[1] For some people, however, music is no fun at all. About 4 percent of the population is what scientists call "amusic." If
10 a person is amusic, it means he or she cannot recognize or reproduce musical notes. As a result, amusic people often cannot **distinguish** one song from another. Two totally different songs, such as "Happy Birthday" and "The Star-
15 Spangled Banner," the national anthem of the United States, may sound the same.

     Many people can't sing well because they **lack** the training to do so. However, there is a difference between not being able to make
20 music and not being able to hear what music is. Most people who can't sing or play a musical **instrument** can still hear two musical notes and know which note is higher. For amusic people, the difference between the notes has to be
25 really large before they can distinguish them.

     As a result, a song will sound like noise to an amusic person. Many amusics compare the sound of music to pieces of metal hitting each other. "It sounds like you went in the kitchen
30 and threw all the pots and pans on the floor," says one amusic woman.

     Life can be hard for amusics because they can't listen to music and enjoy it. In a world filled with song, just going to a restaurant or
35 shopping mall can be uncomfortable for an amusic person. For this reason, many amusics try to **avoid** music entirely. "I used to hate parties," says Margaret, a seventy-year–old woman who only recently discovered that she
40 was amusic. By studying people like Margaret, scientists are finally starting to understand this unusual **condition**.

     Scientists say that the brains of amusics are different from the brains of people who can
45 **appreciate** music. The difference is complex, and it doesn't involving hearing. Amusics can understand other nonmusical sounds perfectly well. They also have no problems understanding ordinary speech. Scientists compare amusics to
50 people who just can't see certain colors.

     Many amusics are happy when they finally find out about and can understand their condition. For years, Margaret felt **embarrassed** about her problem with music. Now she knows
55 that there are many other people who feel the same way that she does. "When people invite me to a **concert**, I just say, 'No thanks, I'm amusic,'" says Margaret. "I just **wish** I had learned to say that when I was seventeen, and
60 not seventy."

---

[1] **MP3 player:** a small piece of electronic equipment used to play digital recordings

Vocabulary Check

Circle the letter of the correct answer to complete each sentence. The boldfaced words are the target words.

1. _____ perform at **concerts**.
   a. Musicians   **b.** Actors   **c.** Scientists

2. I can **distinguish** these two songs. I can hear the _____ between them.
   a. notes   **b.** slow parts   **c.** differences

3. I **wish** you would come to the concert. I want you to come; but I think you _____ come.
   a. will   **b.** may   **c.** won't

4. When the singer feels **embarrassed**, her _____ turn red.
   a. lips   **b.** cheeks   **c.** eyes

5. The stage is too dark. You should **turn on** the _____.
   a. window   **b.** lights   **c.** door

6. I'm trying to **avoid** my piano teacher. I don't want to _____ her.
   a. see   **b.** forget   **c.** leave

7. The violinist takes medicine because of his _____ **condition**.
   a. doctor   **b.** heart   **c.** hospital

8. An example of an **instrument** is _____.
   a. a musician   **b.** a piano   **c.** happy birthday

9. I **appreciate** classical music. I _____ this type of music.
   a. understand and enjoy   **b.** hate and avoid   **c.** don't know

10. I sing well, but I **lack** formal _____.
   a. notes   **b.** music   **c.** training

> READ AGAIN

Read "Can't Name that Tune?" again and complete the comprehension exercises on the next page. As you work, keep the reading goal in mind.

> **READING GOAL:** To understand who amusics are and why they can't appreciate music

Comprehension Check

A. Circle the letter of the correct answer to complete each sentence.

1. Amusic people are _____ .

    a. uncommon   **b.** young   **c.** unable to be happy

2. Amusics can't _____ .

    a. go to parties   **b.** enjoy music   **c.** understand their condition

3. Amusics can't tell the difference between two similar _____ .

    a. notes   **b.** words   **c.** colors

4. Amusics compare the sound of music to _____ .

    a. seeing different   **b.** pots and pans   **c.** listening to
        colors   hitting each other   ordinary speech

5. Margaret feels better because she learned _____ .

    a. about her condition   **b.** to enjoy concerts   **c.** how to dance

B. Read the statements. Write *T* (true) or *F* (false). Under each statement, write a supporting example from the reading that shows why it is true or false.

_____*T*_____ **1.** Music is popular.

      played at parties, sporting events

_____ **2.** Different songs may sound the same to amusics.

_____ **3.** Amusics like the way music sounds.

_____ **4.** Life is difficult for amusics.

_____ **5.** Amusics have problems with their ears.

_____ **6.** Margaret still feels embarrassed about her condition.

C. Complete the summary. Try not to look back at the reading. There is more than one way to complete some of the sentences. You do not need to use the same words and phrases as in the reading, but make sure the meaning is the same.

About 4 percent of people _____ . Amusic people

often cannot _____ . As a result, songs sound like

_____ . The problem is not _____ . Scientists

compare amusics to _____ . Life is _____ for

amusics because _____ and _____ . But now

that amusics finally _____ , they feel _____ .

> DISCUSS

A. Work in small groups. Imagine that you have discovered a new medicine that will help amusic people enjoy music. Make an imaginary television advertisement for your medicine. You will be the actors in the advertisement.

In your advertisement, give the following information:

- The name of your medicine
- What it means to be amusic (remember, most people do not know about this condition)
- An explanation of how your medicine works
- How amusic people will feel if they take your medicine

Suggestions:

- First, you may want to show an amusic person feeling uncomfortable. Then have a doctor explain the condition, and introduce the medicine. Finally, show the amusic person feeling better after taking the medicine.
- Use target words from this unit.

B. Perform your advertisement for the class.

> VOCABULARY SKILL BUILDING

Adjective Forms of Verbs: *-ing*, *-ed*

You can add *-ing* and *-ed* to some verbs to make them adjectives. If the verb ends in *e*, remove the *e* before adding the ending. If the verb ends in *y*, you may need to change *y* to *i* before adding *-ed*, or delete *y* when adding *-ing*. Check a dictionary if you are unsure about dropping or changing the *y*.

EXAMPLES:

confuse (verb) + **-ing** = *confusing* (adjective)

confuse (verb) + **-ed** = *confused* (adjective)

satisfy (verb) + **-ing** = *satisfying* (adjective)

satisfy (verb) + **-ed** = *satisfied* (adjective)

The endings *-ing* and *-ed* have different meanings. Study the examples below.

EXAMPLES:	**MEANING:**
*You are **confusing**.*	You are difficult to understand. You cause confusion.
*You are **confused**.*	You don't understand. You are experiencing confusion.
*John is **embarrassing**.*	John makes other people uncomfortable. He causes embarrassment.
*John is **embarrassed**.*	John is uncomfortable. He is experiencing embarrassment.

Adjectives with *-ing* tell about what something or someone causes others to feel. Adjectives with *-ed* tell about what someone or something feels, or experiences, because of others.

A. Add the endings *-ing* and *-ed* to the verbs to make adjective forms.

Verb	*-ing* Adjective	*-ed* Adjective
1. embarrass	*embarrassing*	*embarrassed*
2. interest	_____	_____
3. excite	_____	_____
4. worry	_____	_____
5. tire	_____	_____
6. relax	_____	_____

B. Complete the sentences with the adjective form of the verbs in parentheses.

1. Margaret's condition was very _____ to her. She felt
   _____ about her condition. (*confuse*)

2. I feel nervous and _____ when I sing in front of other
   people. Singing is _____ for me. (*embarrass*)

3. Playing a musical instrument is _____. After I play piano,
   I feel _____. (*satisfy*)

4. Lauren is _____ in music. Music is _____
   to Laura. (*interest*)

5. The concert was very _____. Everyone at the concert was
   _____. (*excite*)

6. I am _____ about your medical condition. Your condition
   is very _____ to me. (*worry*)

7. Dancing can be very _____. Dancing makes me
   _____. (*tire*)

8. Ji Eun does not look very _____. Maybe she should take
   a _____ vacation. (*relax*)

Learn the Vocabulary

Figuring Out Meaning from Context

When you are reading, don't use your dictionary to look up every new word. That will slow you down, and you might forget the main topic of the reading. Instead, use the context (nearby words and sentences) to figure out the meaning. Sometimes you will find a definition of the word in the context. Look at the example from "All About Music":

*Music **resembles** our emotions in certain ways. For example, most sad songs are slow and full of many low notes, <u>sort of like</u> the speech of a sad person.*

sort of like = similar to

In this example, you can guess that the verb *resemble* means "look like or be similar to something."

Other times you will get only a general idea of the meaning from the context, but that is often enough to understand the sentence.

*If we find the pattern in a song, we feel **content**. If we don't, we feel <u>surprised</u>. <u>Either way</u>, we <u>enjoy</u> listening to the song.*

surprised = positive meaning

enjoy = positive meaning

either way = whether we are surprised or content

In this example, you can guess that the adjective *content* has a positive meaning. Later you can check the exact meaning in your dictionary.

A. Read the sentences. First identify the part of speech of the boldfaced words. Then underline the words that help you understand the meaning. Don't worry if you can't figure out the exact meaning of the word. In Exercise B you will check the meaning in your dictionary.

1. Music **resembles** our emotions in certain ways. For example, most sad songs are slow and full of many low notes, <u>sort of like</u> the speech of a sad person.

   Part of speech: <u>verb</u>

   I think **resemble** means <u>to look like or be similar to something</u>.

   Dictionary definition: _____

2. Amusic people often cannot **distinguish** one song from another. Two totally different songs may sound the same.

   Part of speech: _____

   I think **distinguish** means _____.

   Dictionary definition: _____

(continued on next page)

3. These chemicals give you **relief** from the pain. They make you feel relaxed and happy.

   Part of speech: _____

   I think **relief** means _____ .

   Dictionary definition: _____

4. Hostel Celica, Slovenia: This **converted** hotel in downtown Ljubljana used to be a prison!

   Part of speech: _____

   I think **converted** means _____ .

   Dictionary definition: _____

5. The town of Buñol, Spain, has a **population** of 9,000. But for one day in August, it grows to 30,000 people.

   Part of speech: _____

   I think population means _____ .

   Dictionary definition: _____

B. Look up the words from Exercise A in your dictionary. Copy the dictionary definition that best fits the sentence. How close were your definitions to the ones in the dictionary? Even if you did not get the exact meaning, could you understand something meaningful about the word, such as whether it has a positive or negative meaning?

C. Make cards for the words from Chapters 11–12 that were new to you when you started the unit. Include target words and words that you wrote on page 216.

D. Go back to the vocabulary list at the beginning of each chapter. What did you learn about the target words? Add your numbers to the lists.

Vocabulary Practice 6, see page 223

FLUENCY PRACTICE 2

Fluency Strategy

To read more fluently, you should not read word by word. You should read in phrases (groups of words). Try these strategies to stop yourself from reading word by word:

- Read with your eyes, not with your hands. That is, do not point your finger or your pencil at the words you are reading. If it is difficult for you to do this, try sitting on your hands when you read.

- Read with your eyes, not with your mouth. That is, read silently. Do not say the words out loud. If you read out loud, you will be reading every word, rather than whole phrases. It will also slow you down.

- Do not try to translate every word you read into your native language. Instead, focus on understanding the basic meaning of sentences.

It might feel strange or difficult to read this way at first, but as you practice, you will get better at it. You will be reading more quickly and at the same time understanding more. That is, you will be on your way to becoming a fluent reader in English.

 ## READING 1

Before You Read

Preview "Dangerous Dining" on the next page. What do you think it is about? Circle the letter of the correct answer.

a. how to cook exotic seafood dishes

b. strange Japanese restaurants

c. a poisonous fish that people like to eat

Read

A. Read "Dangerous Dining." Time yourself. Write your start and end times and your total reading time. Then calculate your reading speed (words per minute) and write it in the progress chart on page 230.

Start time: _____   End time: _____   Total time: _____ (in seconds)

Reading speed:
456 words ÷ _____ (total time in seconds) x 60 = _____ words per minute

---

http://www.dangerousdining.com

Dangerous Dining

1   *Fugu* is the Japanese word for puffer fish. It is also called Japanese blowfish. Fugu are poisonous. Just a small taste of their poison can kill you. But in Japan and other countries
5   in the Far East, people pay hundreds of dollars to eat these exotic fish. It will be the last meal for some of them. Why do people eat something so dangerous? Some people say they appreciate the taste. Others like to
10   eat it *because of* the danger.

  In the wild, puffer fish use poison to protect themselves. They are very slow swimmers and have no way to avoid a hungry fish. Instead, they send a warning message to
15   any fish that come too close. First, they puff themselves up to look bigger. The puffers quickly breathe in water. They start to resemble a ball. This is enough to scare most fish away. If a fish still decides to attack
20   the puffer, it then learns about the second defense: *tetrodoxin*. This is the chemical that makes puffers poisonous. It can be found in every part of the puffers' bodies and quickly kills other fish.

25   In fact, scientists say puffers are the most poisonous fish in the world. Nobody has discovered a way to stop the bad effects of tetrodoxin. That's why, when eating puffer fish, you have to be extremely careful.

30   When chefs prepare fugu, they first need to remove the poison from the fish's body. Chefs train for years to learn how to do that. At the end of the training, they have to prepare their own fugu. To pass the test, they need to eat
35   the fish—and survive.

  Every year, about 50 people die from fugu poisoning. The deadliest year was 1958: 176 people died. In the past, if someone died after eating fugu, the chef would kill himself.
40   These days, however, fugu chefs are very well trained. You can feel safe eating fugu prepared by a chef. Most of the deaths every year are caused by untrained home cooks.

  Not everyone can prepare fugu. To be allowed
45   to serve fugu, chefs need to get a special license. All fugu restaurants must put the chef's license in the window. To get a fugu license, you must train with a licensed fugu chef. The training can take years. Then you must pass
50   two tests. First, you must take a written test. For the second test, you have 20 minutes to prepare and eat fugu. Only about 30 percent of chefs pass the second test.

  Winter is the best time to eat fugu. That is
55   when the fish are fat and not as poisonous. A fugu meal can be very expensive. Uncooked fugu, called *fugu sashi*, can cost as much as $200 per person.

B. Read "Dangerous Dining" again, a little faster this time. Write your start and end times and your total reading time. Then calculate your reading speed (words per minute) and write it in the progress chart on page 230.

Start time: _____ **End time:** _____ **Total time:** _____ (in seconds)

Reading speed:
456 words ÷ _____ (total time in seconds) x 60 = _____ words per minute

Comprehension Check

A. Circle the letter of the correct answer to complete each sentence.

1. Fugu are the _____ fish in the world.
   a. most interesting   **b.** most poisonous   **c.** fastest

2. To become a fugu chef in Japan, you need _____.
   a. a license   **b.** a restaurant   **c.** a boat

3. The test to become a fugu chef has _____ parts.
   a. two   **b.** three   **c.** four

4. These days, eating at a fugu restaurant is very _____.
   a. dangerous   **b.** expensive   **c.** uncommon

5. Today, most fugu deaths are caused by _____.
   a. restaurants that don't have fugu licenses   **b.** supermarkets that sell fugu   **c.** untrained home cooks

6. The best season to eat fugu is _____.
   a. winter   **b.** spring   **c.** summer

B. Answer the questions. Try not to look back at the reading.

1. What is fugu? _____

2. Where do people eat it? _____

3. Why do people like it? _____

4. How do people train to become fugu chefs? List two things they must do.

   _____

   _____

C. Check your answers for the comprehension questions in the Answer Key on page 231. Then calculate your score and write it in the progress chart on page 230.

_____ (my number correct) ÷ 10 x 100 = _____ %

> READING 2

Before You Read

Preview *Wild Treasures*. Answer the questions.

1. What is the topic of the reading?
   a. white truffles
   b. trained dogs
   c. the world's best restaurants

2. What is the main idea of the reading?
   a. They are expensive and hard to find.
   b. They have excellent noses for finding food.
   c. They serve exotic dishes you can't find anywhere else.

Read

A. Read "Wild Treasures." Time yourself. Write your start and end times and your total reading time. Then calculate your reading speed (words per minute) and write it in the progress chart on page 230.

Start time: _____   **End time:** _____   **Total time:** _____ (in seconds)

Reading speed:
554 words ÷ _____ (total time in seconds) x 60 = _____ words per minute

Wild Treasures

1   It has a bitter smell. Pigs love it. Great chefs do too. The best way to eat it? Cold, cut very thin, on top of a pasta dish. (The pigs don't agree about the pasta.) The taste? It's very
5   unique. Imagine the smell of dark, black, rich mud. Then mix in the taste of fine wine and very strong cheese. Where can you get it? With a lot of luck, a well-trained dog, and a plane ticket to Italy, you might find it under a tree. The price?
10   $1,200 to $2,300 a pound ($2,600 to $5,000 a kilogram).

The white truffle is a type of mushroom. It is one of the most expensive foods in the world. It comes in a variety of shapes and sizes. Some
15   look like small potatoes. Others are flat like the top of a mushroom. Truffles can weigh as little

as a third of an ounce (10 grams) or more than two pounds (1,000 grams). Large truffles are the most uncommon. They sell for the highest
20   prices. In 2007, a truffle weighing more than three pounds (1.47 kilograms) was discovered. It sold for $375,000.

In 2004, a restaurant owner in London bought a truffle that weighed almost two
25   pounds (850 grams). He put it under glass for his customers to appreciate. At night, he put it in a locked refrigerator. The chefs began to argue with him. They wanted to serve the truffle. But with his restaurant so full of excited
30   customers, the owner told them to wait. Then one night the truffle's refrigerator lost power. The truffle went bad and could not be eaten.

Like most white truffles, the 850-gram one came from Italy. When it went bad, the owner
35 sent it back to its country of origin. It was placed underground. People hoped another large truffle would grow in its place the next year. They were not so lucky because humans have not yet figured out how to grow truffles.

40 Most people do not even know how to find them. Truffles grow about 12 inches (30 centimeters) under the ground. They only grow under certain types of trees. To find these expensive food items, people need a little help.

45 Dogs and pigs, with their excellent noses, are experts at locating truffles. But pigs love the taste of truffles a little too much. That's why these days most truffle seekers use dogs.

Truffles are a big business. With so much
50 profit to be made, there is a lot of competition to find them. Most truffle hunters start at a

young age, usually when they are children. They spend years training their dogs. Giovanni Monchiero is one example. He works at a
55 school that trains truffle dogs. Monchiero knows truffle hunting is a serious, sometimes dangerous business. His dogs are sometimes stolen or poisoned.

Truffle hunters don't talk about their work
60 very much. They don't want others to know where they find their truffles. Isabelle Gianicolo is a scientist who studies the mushrooms. She says it is very difficult to get any information from truffle hunters. "They have pockets full
65 of truffles. They smell like a truffle…" says Gianicolo. But they lie and say, "No, I don't have any!"

If you want to try truffles, you might need to visit an expensive Italian restaurant. Just be
70 prepared to pay.

B. Read "Wild Treasures" again, a little faster this time. Write your start and end times and your total reading time. Then calculate your reading speed (words per minute) and write it in the progress chart on page 230.

Start time: _____ **End time:** _____ **Total time:** _____ (in seconds)

Reading speed:
554 words ÷ _____ (total time in seconds) x 60 = _____ words per minute

Comprehension Check

A. Circle the letter of the correct answer to complete each sentence.

1. _____ are very good at finding truffles.
   a. Great chefs
   b. Italians
   c. Trained dogs

2. Most truffle hunters use trained dogs, not pigs, because _____.
   a. pigs can't smell very well
   b. pigs like to eat the truffles they find
   c. dogs love to eat truffles

(continued on next page)

3. Large truffles cost the most because they _____.
   a. have the best taste
   b. are the hardest to find
   c. don't need to be cooked to be eaten

4. The restaurant owner didn't want to serve the large truffle because _____.
   a. he wanted to return it to Italy
   b. it was attracting people to his restaurant
   c. it had gone bad and couldn't be eaten

5. Giovanni Monchiero _____.
   a. trains dogs to hunt for truffles
   b. poisons truffle-hunting dogs
   c. is a scientist who studies truffles

6. Most truffle hunters _____.
   a. start their training when they are children
   b. tell others where to find the best truffles
   c. want to help scientists who study mushrooms

B. Answer the questions in your own words. Write your answers on the lines provided.

1. What are truffles?

   _____

2. Why are truffles so expensive?

   _____

3. Why are truffles hard to find?

   _____

4. Why would someone poison a dog trained to hunt truffles?

   _____

5. Why don't truffle hunters like to talk about their work?

   _____

C. Check your answers for the comprehension questions in the Answer Key on page 231. Then calculate your score and write it in the progress chart on page 230.

   _____ (my number correct) ÷ 11 x 100 = _____%

7 The Movie Business

> THINK BEFORE YOU READ

A. Work with a partner. Look at the pictures. Ask and answer the questions. If you don't know a word in English, ask your partner or look in your dictionary. Then write your new words on page 217.

1. What do you see in the pictures? Point to the things you see and name them in English.

2. What types of movies do the pictures show? What are some other types of movies?

3. What types of movies do you like to watch?

4. Do you want to see the movies in the pictures? Explain.

B. On a separate piece of paper, draw a picture of a famous movie you've seen. Don't write any words on your picture.

C. Work in small groups. Look at your partners' pictures. Talk about the movies you see.

Famous Flops

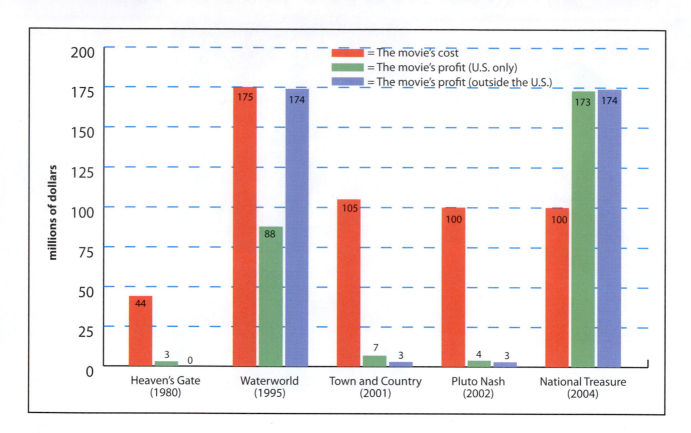

> PREPARE TO READ

A. Look at the words (and phrases) in the list. Write the number(s) next to each word to show what you know. You may be able to write more than one number next to some of the words. You will study all of these words in this chapter.

1. I can use the word in a sentence.

2. I know <u>one meaning</u> of the word.

3. I know <u>more than one meaning</u> of the word.

4. I know how to pronounce the word.

_____ audience

_____ break even

_____ career

_____ cautious

_____ comedy

_____ interact

_____ out of business

_____ review

_____ screen

_____ script

_____ set

B. Work with a partner. Look at the bar graph on page 108. Ask and answer the questions. If you don't know a word in English, ask your partner or look in your dictionary. Then write your new words on page 217.

   1. What movies do you see in the bar graph?

   2. Which movie made the most profit?

   3. Which movie lost the most money?

   4. Think about a bad movie you've seen. What didn't you like about it?

Reading Skill: Understanding Figurative Language

When a word or expression is used in a different way from its usual meaning to give you a picture or an idea in your mind, we call this *figurative* language.

EXAMPLES:

Star used with its usual (or common) meaning:
At night, you can see stars in the sky. = At night, you can see <u>bright points of light</u> in the sky.

Star used figuratively or in a special way:
This movie has a lot of stars in it. = The movie has a lot of <u>famous performers</u> in it.

Usually there is a connection between a word's usual and figurative meanings, but you may have to use your imagination to figure it out. For example, movie *stars* are in some ways like real stars in the sky: They are beautiful people who "give off light" in our minds; like the real stars at night, they are visible to people all over the world.

C. Preview the magazine article "Famous Flops" on the next page. Then read the first paragraph. Answer the questions.

   1. The title of the reading is "Famous Flops." What do you think *flops* means in this context? Check (✓) the answer.

      _____ **a.** to sit or fall down quickly, especially when you are tired (usual meaning)

      _____ **b.** a product or an idea that is not successful (figurative or special meaning)

   2. Check the meanings of *flop* in your dictionary. What is the connection between the usual and figurative meanings of this word? Write your ideas on the space provided.

      _____

      _____

      _____

Read "Famous Flops." What characteristics do flops have in common?

Famous Flops

1 When we think of flops, we usually think of bad movies, movies so bad we want to throw things at the **screen**. But for movie critics, a flop and a bad movie are not the same thing. Most
5 bad movies **break even**. Some even make a lot of money. An example is the 2004 movie *National Treasure* starring Nicholas Cage. Most critics hated it, but the action-adventure film made over $240 million in profit. Flops, in contrast, lose
10 millions of dollars. They kill the **careers** of actors and directors.[1] Movie critics say that flops have two important things in common.

First, many flops have dream-like stories that are hard to make into films. One example
15 is *Pluto Nash*. This 2002 **comedy** was about life on the moon in the future. The filmmakers used computer animation[2] to create characters to **interact** with the real actors. Although the film looked interesting, **audiences** disliked the
20 story. *Pluto Nash* cost a lot to produce, and it lost over $90 million. Another famous flop was the 1995 action movie *Waterworld*. The filmmakers tried to create a world with only water, and no land. The movie was filmed in
25 the Pacific Ocean, near Hawaii. Not only was Hawaii an expensive place to make a movie, but also the ocean cannot be controlled like a regular movie **set**. After bad weather and many accidents, *Waterworld* took twice as long to
30 make and cost twice as much as the director had planned.

If actors and directors don't pay attention to others' ideas, they can also create a flop. The director of *Waterworld* had a stormy relationship
35 with the lead actor, Kevin Costner. Costner wanted to change many parts of the movie, including the ending. Another example is the 1980 film *Heaven's Gate*. Movie company United Artists asked the director, Michael Cimino, to
40 make a two-hour western[3] love story. Cimino didn't listen and instead made a five-hour movie. *Heaven's Gate* had many excellent actors, but audiences thought it was too slow. In the end, the film nearly put United Artists **out of
45 business**. The biggest flop ever made was the 2001 comedy *Town and Country*. The movie starred well-known actors such as Warren Beatty and Diane Keaton. But the actors could not agree about the **script**. They argued with the
50 director and each other. In the end, there was nothing funny about *Town and Country*, and the film lost close to $100 million.

In truth, flops are not always bad films. Some movie critics gave *Waterworld* good
55 **reviews**. International audiences also liked the movie, and after many years, it made a profit. Since *Waterworld* and *Heaven's Gate*, however, movie companies have become much more **cautious**. Now, films are not so much
60 works of art as safe business investments. As a result, there are fewer big flops. But with nothing but "safe" films to watch, movie audiences may have lost something more important.

---

[1] **director:** someone who gives instructions to actors and other people in a movie
[2] **animation:** a movie with pictures, clay models, etc., that move and talk and are created by computers or artists
[3] **western:** a movie about life in the nineteenth century in the American West

Vocabulary Check

A. Write the letter of the correct definition next to the target word.

_____ **1.** script

a. to talk to other people and work together with them

_____ **2.** interact

b. the people watching or listening to a performance

_____ **3.** screen

c. the written form of a movie

_____ **4.** audience

d. to neither make a profit nor lose money

_____ **5.** break even

e. a large flat white surface that movies are shown on in a movie theater

B. Complete the sentences with the boldfaced words from the reading. Use the correct form of the word.

1. My uncle's film company lost too much money, and it had to close. It

went _____.

2. When the actor filmed a dangerous scene, he was very

_____; he didn't want to get hurt.

3. If a movie is a(n) _____, there are lots of funny situations

to make the audience laugh.

4. Juanita has trained to be an actor for many years, and she plans to be an

actor her entire life. Acting is her _____.

5. If you want to know whether a movie is good or not before you see it,

you should read _____ of that movie in newspapers and

magazines.

> READ AGAIN

Read "Famous Flops" again and complete the comprehension exercises on the next page. As you work, keep the reading goal in mind.

> **READING GOAL:** To identify the two characteristics of famous flops

Comprehension Check

A. Look at the sentences from the reading. Write *U* if the underlined word is used in its **usual** (or common) way. Write *F* if it is used in a **figurative**, or special, way.

_____F_____ **1.** Movie critics say that <u>flops</u> have two important things in common.

_____U_____ **2.** The action-adventure film made over $240 million in <u>profit</u>.

_____ **3.** Most <u>bad</u> movies break even.

_____ **4.** They <u>kill</u> the careers of actors and directors.

_____ **5.** This 2002 comedy was about life on the moon in the <u>future</u>.

_____ **6.** The director of *Waterworld* had a <u>stormy</u> relationship with the lead actor, Kevin Costner.

_____ **7.** The filmmakers tried to create a <u>world</u> with only water, and no land.

_____ **8.** The <u>ocean</u> cannot be controlled like a regular movie set.

_____ **9.** With nothing but "<u>safe</u>" films to watch, movie audiences may have lost something more important.

B. Complete the chart with the missing details from the reading.

Movie title	Year	Type of movie	Actors	Problem with movie	Financial result
Pluto Nash	2002				
Waterworld		action			
Heaven's Gate			many excellent actors		
National Treasure				critics hated it	
Town and Country					lost close to $100 million

C. Read the descriptions. Which movie is most likely to be a flop? Circle the name. Use the information in the chart on page 112 to help you decide.

Have a Ball: This movie is a comedy about a star athlete who falls in love with the woman who coaches his baseball team. The movie stars two actors who have had long and successful careers. The actors often disagree with each other about their performances. The director is not very famous, and some people worry that he is not in control of the set. Most of the story occurs in the athlete's apartment, on the streets of New York, and at baseball games.

Cloud City: This action movie describes life on another planet where people live in flying cities. The actors are all young and very excited to be working on the movie. Computers are used to create the flying cities. This is the director's first movie, and she is being very cautious. The movie set has been created in Los Angeles, California, and the entire movie will be filmed there.

The Search for K15: This adventure movie is about a group of scientists who must discover a special chemical in time to save the world. The scientists travel from place to place, looking everywhere for the chemical, from mountaintops to the bottom of the ocean. The movie will be filmed on five different sets. The director is very patient and friendly. The actors are interested in traveling.

Super Rockers: This action-comedy movie is about a group of musicians who also have special abilities, such as the ability to fly and to see the future. The movie stars are five very famous actors, but they don't like to interact with each other on the set. One of the characters in the movie is an animated talking dog. The director wants to make a two-hour movie, but the actors think it should be shorter. They often argue about the script.

Who's Driving? This comedy tells a story about four men who drive across the United States in a small car. Every day, something unusual and funny happens to them. The four main actors like working together and spend a lot of time studying the script. The movie set changes often, and sometimes the director gets tired of traveling.

D. Work in small groups. Compare your answers from Exercise C. Explain your answers.

> DISCUSS

A. Work with a partner. Create your own idea for a movie. Answer these questions about your movie.

1. What type of movie is it?

2. Where and when does the story occur?

3. Basically, what happens in your movie?

4. Who are the main characters in your movie? Which actors do you want to play them?

5. Where will the movie set be located? Will you need more than one set?

6. How much money will you need to make your movie?

7. What will the title of your movie be?

8. Why will audiences like your movie?

B. With your partner, work with another pair of students. Decide which pair is A and which is B. Role-play the situation. Then change roles.

A: You are filmmakers. You want a movie company to invest in your movie. Explain your idea for a movie to pair B.

B: You own a movie company. You want to invest in a movie that will make a lot of profit. Decide if pair A's movie idea is a good investment or not.

C. Tell the class whether you decided to invest in the other pair's movie idea, and explain why.

Sleeper Hits

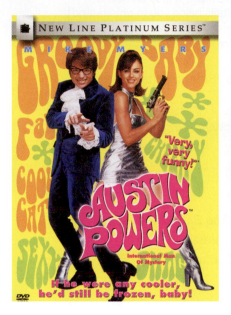
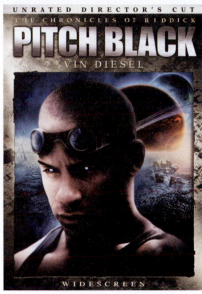

> PREPARE TO READ

A. Look at the words (and phrases) in the list. Write the number(s) next to each word to show what you know. You may be able to write more than one number next to some of the words. You will study all of these words in this chapter.

1. I can use the word in a sentence.

2. I know <u>one meaning</u> of the word.

3. I know <u>more than one meaning</u> of the word.

4. I know how to pronounce the word.

B. Work with a partner. Look at the pictures. Ask and answer the questions. If you don't know a word in English, ask your partner or look in your dictionary. Then write your new words on page 217.

1. What do you see in the pictures? Point to the things you see and name them in English.

2. Which movie looks like a comedy? How can you tell?

3. What type of movie is shown in the other picture?

4. Do all good movies cost a lot of money to make? Explain.

_____ campus

_____ factor

_____ genius

_____ hit

_____ low-budget

_____ marketing

_____ release

_____ set out

_____ state

_____ take by surprise

_____ trust

C. Read the first paragraph of the magazine article "Sleeper Hits." Then answer the questions.

1. What is the author's main idea about *The Blair Witch Project?*

   a. It was a flop.

   b. It is a good example of a sleeper.

   c. It was a horror movie.

2. What key detail supports the main idea about *The Blair Witch Project?*

   a. It told a story about three students lost in a forest.

   b. It made a huge profit, but cost only $22,000 to make.

   c. It was scary and original.

 **READ**

Read "Sleeper Hits." Underline the key details in each paragraph.

Sleeper Hits

1   The 1999 horror movie *The Blair Witch Project* **took** audiences **by surprise**. It told a story about three students lost in a forest. The film was scary and original, and it made
5   a huge profit. The film also surprised movie companies; it had cost only $22,000 to make. *The Blair Witch Project* is an example of a sleeper. Sleepers are **low-budget** films that create a surprisingly large profit. Were
10   the makers of *The Blair Witch Project* just lucky? Or are there secrets to making a sleeper?

      Marketing experts say that for a movie to become a sleeper, first it has to become
15   popular with college students. When college students see a movie they like, they tell their friends about it. Positive reviews of a film spread like fire across college **campuses**. The reason, say marketers, is that college students
20   **trust** their friends' opinions more than they trust movie critics' reviews. With enough buzz,[1] a low-budget movie becomes a big sleeper **hit**. An example is the 1997 comedy *Austin Powers*. It only made a small profit in theaters. But

---

[1] **buzz:** a lot of people speaking positively about a new product, movie, etc.

after its **release** on video, it became incredibly popular on college campuses. In the end, *Austin Powers* made more money from video sales than it did in theaters.

Another secret to sleepers is creative marketing. This often involves the Internet. Internet marketing is cheap, and it can reach a specific audience. When director David Twohy filmed the science fiction movie *Pitch Black* in the late 1990s, for example, he needed an inexpensive way to market the film. So, Twohy went on the Internet and visited science fiction chat rooms.[2] He had conversations with people about his movie. Slowly, science fiction fans became interested in the film. In the end, "Internet buzz helped make it a success," says Twohy.

College students and Internet marketing were both important **factors** in *The Blair Witch Project's* success. The filmmakers designed a Web page for the movie. It **stated** that *The Blair Witch Project* was a true story (it wasn't). It also said the three students in the film had disappeared (they hadn't). However, many people believed the Web page. Soon, college students were talking about whether the movie was real or not. Many of them wanted to see for themselves. For the film's release, theaters were completely sold out. Now, many films are marketed in the same way as *The Blair Witch Project*.

Of course, to make a tidy profit,[3] sleepers need to be good films. The makers of *The Blair Witch Project* never saw themselves as marketing **geniuses**. As Robin Cowie, who worked on *The Blair Witch Project*, says, "We never meant to change things . . . we **set out** to make a scary movie." And as anyone who has seen the film knows, they were very successful.

---

[2] **chat room:** a place on the Internet where you can have a conversation with people by writing messages to them and immediately receiving their reply

[3] **tidy profit:** a good profit; a nice amount of money

Vocabulary Check

Circle the letter of the correct answer to complete each sentence. The boldfaced words are the target words.

1. People who work in film **marketing** _____.
   a. direct movies
   b. advertise and sell films
   c. teach at film schools

2. I think the film director Ingmar Bergman was a **genius**. He was so _____.
   a. popular
   b. creative and intelligent
   c. lucky and rich

(continued on next page)

3. If a movie is a **hit**, it is very _____.

    a. successful

    b. short

    c. scary

4. My film school has a beautiful **campus** with many _____.

    a. movie sets

    b. trees and old buildings

    c. large screens

5. If you **trust** a movie review, you think that review is _____.

    a. fair and true

    b. interesting

    c. funny

6. Poor acting was a **factor** in the film's failure. Another was the _____ of the director.

    a. environment

    b. inexperience

    c. genius

7. The end of the movie **took** me **by surprise**. I was _____ what occurred.

    a. not expecting

    b. waiting for

    c. hoping for

8. The **low-budget** movie was filmed in the director's house; she had very little _____ to make the film.

    a. time

    b. ability

    c. money

9. The movie's **release** is next week. Next week, the movie will be in theaters for _____

    a. the last time

    b. the second time

    c. the first time

10. When you **state** your opinion of a book or movie, you say or write your opinion _____

    a. clearly

    b. incorrectly

    c. secretly

11. The hero of the film **set out** to save the princess. He _____ to save her.

    a. trained and prepared

    b. left home with a plan

    c. successfully found a way

❯ READ AGAIN

Read "Sleeper Hits" again and complete the comprehension exercises. As you work, keep the reading goal in mind.

> 📖 **READING GOAL:** To state the main ideas and key details about sleepers

Comprehension Check

A. Look at the sentences from the reading. Write *U* if the underlined word is used in its **usual** (or common) way. Write *F* if it is used in a **figurative**, or special, way.

_____ **1.** *The Blair Witch Project* told a story about three students lost in a <u>forest</u>.

_____ **2.** <u>Sleepers</u> are low-budget films that create a surprisingly large profit.

_____ **3.** When college students see a <u>movie</u> they like, they tell their friends about it.

_____ **4.** Positive reviews of a film spread like <u>fire</u> across college campuses.

_____ **5.** With enough buzz, a low-budget movie becomes a big sleeper <u>hit</u>.

_____ **6.** *Austin Powers* only made a small profit in <u>theaters</u>.

_____ **7.** Of course, to make a <u>tidy</u> profit, sleepers need to be good films.

B. Read the statements. Write *T* (true) or *F* (false). Then write a key detail to support your answer.

___*F*___ **1.** *The Blair Witch Project* was a flop.

    Key detail: _*It made a profit*_____

_____ **2.** *Austin Powers* became more popular after it left movie theaters.

    Key detail: _____

_____ **3.** Director David Twohy has marketed his films in creative ways.

    Key detail: _____

(continued on next page)

         4. The makers of *The Blair Witch Project* used technology to market their film.

         Key detail: _____

         5. *The Blair Witch Project* was not successful at first.

         Key detail: _____

         6. The makers of *The Blair Witch Project* hoped to change the ways movies are marketed.

         Key detail: _____

C. Your friend James is a college student who is studying to become a film director. Write a letter to James. Tell James two ways he can make his movies become successful. State the two main ideas from the reading. Use key details from the reading to support your ideas.

Dear James,

_____

_____

_____

_____

_____

_____

_____

Your friend,

_____

D. Compare letters with a partner. Did you present the same two ways to make a movie successful? Did you include the same key details?

> DISCUSS

Work in small groups. Ask and answer the questions.

1. Do you like scary movies? Tell about a scary movie you have seen. Why was it scary?

2. Do you know any other movies that were sleeper hits?

3. Are the best quality movies usually the ones that are most successful? Explain.

4. What other creative ways can people market movies?

> VOCABULARY SKILL BUILDING

Understanding Word Meaning

Many English words have more than one meaning. To figure out the meaning, look at the context in which the word is being used. Use the nearby words as clues. Also, identify the word's part of speech. This can be an important clue to meaning.

EXAMPLES:

*He **hit** me in the face.*

*The movie was a **hit** with audiences.*

In the first sentence, the context is a fight; the word *face* is a clue. *Hit* is a verb meaning "to touch suddenly and with hard force."

In the second sentence, the context is a discussion of a movie; the words *movie* and *audiences* are clues. *Hit* is a noun meaning "a movie, product, idea, etc., that is a big success."

Note that in both contexts, *hit* has the same basic, or core, meaning: "strong impact."

Study the sentences. First, check (✓) sentences that are in the context of movies. Circle the word or words that helped you figure out the context. Then write *N* if the boldfaced word is being used as a noun, or *V* if it is being used as a verb.

Movie context?	N or V?	
✓	N	1. I don't like this theater; it has a small **screen**.
_____	V	2. I don't want to talk to Mary, so I'm going to **screen** my calls.
_____	_____	3. The date of the film's **release** is September 22.
_____	_____	4. Airplanes **release** a lot of carbon dioxide.
_____	_____	5. We haven't **set** a date for our wedding yet.
_____	_____	6. The **set** of *Waterworld* was in Hawaii.
_____	_____	7. Judy went to the **market** to buy fruit.
_____	_____	8. Some filmmakers use the Internet to **market** their work.
_____	_____	9. The critic gave *The Blair Witch Project* a good **review**.
_____	_____	10. I always **review** my notes before I take a test.
_____	_____	11. The president wants to **script** his speech to the nation.
_____	_____	12. The actor forgot his **script** on the bus.

Learn the Vocabulary

A. Work in small groups. Read the definitions and example sentences, and complete the tasks in columns 1 and 2. Then complete the task in column 3.

Column 1	Column 2	Column 3
market: **definition one** a) an area outside where people buy and sell products, food, etc. b) a grocery store **Example sentence:** *We buy all our vegetables from the local market.* **Task:** Say what you can buy at a market that is close to your school.	*market:* **definition two** to tell people to buy something by advertising it in a particular way **Example sentence:** *The filmmaker marketed his movie on the Internet.* **Task:** Discuss other ways that people can market movies.	**Core meaning of *market*** **Task:** Say what the similar features/ideas are in columns 1 and 2.
release: **definition one** a) to allow someone to be free after you have kept him/her somewhere b) to stop holding something **Example sentence:** *He released her arm when she shouted.* **Task:** Explain why the police sometimes release people they are holding.	*release:* **definition two** to make a movie, product, etc., available for people to buy or see **Example sentence:** The Blair Witch Project *was released in 1999.* **Task:** Tell about some new movies and products that have been released recently.	**Core meaning of *release*** **Task:** Say what the similar features/ideas are in columns 1 and 2.
screen: **definition one** a) the flat glass part of a TV or computer on which you see words or pictures b) the large white surface that pictures are shown on in a movie theater c) a wire net that covers an open door or window **Example sentence:** *Carlos has a big-screen TV at home.* **Task:** Decide if there are screens on your classroom windows or not. Think of three electronic products that have screens.	*screen:* **definition two** to let your telephone calls be answered by a machine so that you can decide whether or not to talk to the person who calls you **Example sentence:** *When I am really busy, I screen my calls at work.* **Task:** Talk about whether or not you sometimes screen your calls and, if so, in what situations.	**Core meaning of *screen*** **Task:** Say what the similar features/ideas are in columns 1 and 2.

B. Look at the new words from Chapters 13–14 that you wrote on page 217. Then look them up in a dictionary. If a word has more than one definition, read all of the definitions and try to come up with the core meaning. Compare core meanings with a partner.

C. Make cards for the words from Exercise B. Write the core meaning under the translation, picture, or English definition of the word. When you review your cards, try to recall the core meaning as well as the definition, translation, or picture.

D. Go back to the vocabulary list at the beginning of each chapter. What did you learn about the target words? Add your numbers to the lists.

Vocabulary Practice 7, see page 224

All in the Family

> THINK BEFORE YOU READ

A. Work with a partner. Look at the picture. Ask and answer the questions. If you don't know a word in English, ask your partner or look in your dictionary. Then write your new words on page 217.

1. What do you see in the picture? How is each person related to the others?

2. In what ways do the people look similar to each other? In what ways do they look different?

B. Work with a partner. Ask and answer the questions.

1. Do you have any brothers or sisters? If so, are they older or younger than you?

2. Which family members are you most similar to? What do you have in common?

3. Do you ever argue with anyone in your family? If so, what do you argue about?

4. Why do some children behave differently from their brothers and sisters? Make a list of possible reasons.

Rebel with a Cause

> PREPARE TO READ

A. Look at the words (and phrases) in the list. Write the number(s) next to each word to show what you know. You may be able to write more than one number next to some of the words. You will study all of these words in this chapter.

1. I can use the word in a sentence.

2. I know <u>one meaning</u> of the word.

3. I know <u>more than one meaning</u> of the word.

4. I know how to pronounce the word.

B. Work with a partner. Look at the pictures. Ask and answer the questions. If you don't know a word in English, ask your partner or look in your dictionary. Then write your new words on page 217.

1. What career has the person in each picture chosen?

2. What do you think the relationship between the two women is?

3. In what ways might the two women be different? Explain.

4. What might the two women have in common?

_____ grades

_____ influence

_____ make a living

_____ obey

_____ personality

_____ raise

_____ rebel

_____ steady

_____ strict

_____ theory

_____ turn out

Reading Skill: Comparing and Contrasting

Comparing and contrasting helps you to more clearly understand what you read. When you compare, you identify how things are similar. When you contrast, you identify how things are different. To compare and contrast as you read, follow these steps:

- Look for words that show how things are similar, such as *alike, also, both, just like, the same, similarly,* and *too.*

- Look for words that show how things are different, such as *but, differently, however, in contrast, opposite, unlike, while,* and *yet.*

- Use a graphic organizer, such as the Venn diagram on page 129, to list your comparisons and contrasts.

C. Read the first paragraph of the blog post "Rebel with a Cause." Circle the comparison and contrast signal words. Then check (✓) the difference between the two sisters.

_____ **1.** hair color   _____ **3.** taste in movies

_____ **2.** eye color   _____ **4.** career

> READ

Read "Rebel with a Cause." Circle the comparison and contrast signal words.

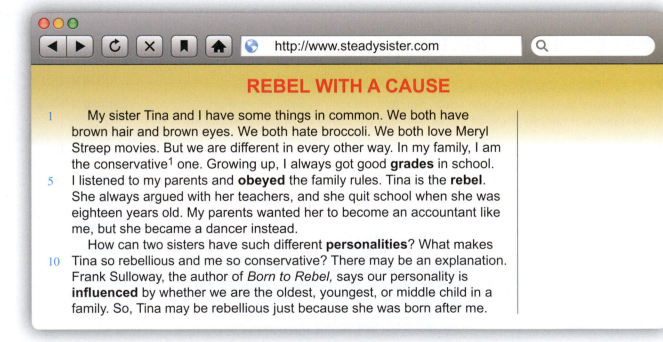

REBEL WITH A CAUSE

1   My sister Tina and I have some things in common. We both have brown hair and brown eyes. We both hate broccoli. We both love Meryl Streep movies. But we are different in every other way. In my family, I am the conservative[1] one. Growing up, I always got good **grades** in school.
5   I listened to my parents and **obeyed** the family rules. Tina is the **rebel**. She always argued with her teachers, and she quit school when she was eighteen years old. My parents wanted her to become an accountant like me, but she became a dancer instead.
     How can two sisters have such different **personalities**? What makes
10   Tina so rebellious and me so conservative? There may be an explanation. Frank Sulloway, the author of *Born to Rebel,* says our personality is **influenced** by whether we are the oldest, youngest, or middle child in a family. So, Tina may be rebellious just because she was born after me.

---
[1] **conservative:** preferring to continue doing things they way they are being done or have been done successfully in the past, instead of risking changes

Sulloway says younger siblings[2] like Tina act
15 differently to get attention from their parents. They
can't do the same things as their older brothers and
sisters, so they find other ways to stand out. They take
risks. As a child, Tina was always trying new things,
sometimes dangerous things. One time she broke her
20 arm jumping out of a tree. For Christmas one year she
asked if she could have a poisonous snake for a pet.

In contrast, older siblings like me have no reason to
rebel. We can do things sooner than our younger siblings. We can control
them. As a result, we identify with our parents. Growing up, I always
25 obeyed the rules. I did things the safe way. I wanted to be just like Mom
and Dad.

Tina believes we were **raised** differently. She thinks Mom and Dad paid
more attention to me. I don't know if that's true. I do think they were **stricter**
with me. Sulloway says this is common. He says that with first-born children,
30 parents worry about every detail. They make a lot of rules and teach their
first child to be very careful. In other words, they become really strict. With
later-born children, they are more relaxed. They think, "Oh, she'll **turn out**
fine, just like her sister." This may explain why my parents let Tina stay up
late and watch scary movies, while I had to be in bed by 10 P.M.
35 It may also explain why Tina and I took different types of jobs. I liked
accounting[3] because it was safe, **steady** work that paid well. For Tina,
dancing was a way to be different, to be free. It was also a way to rebel
against my parents. She argued with them for months after she quit
school. Some of the fights got pretty bad. Mom and Dad worried that she
40 would never be able to **make a living**. In fact, Sulloway says younger
siblings usually have lower salaries than their older brothers and sisters.

At first, making money as a dancer was difficult for Tina. These days,
however, she is very successful. She's part of an all-girl group called the
"Masters of Movement." They dance at concerts and sporting events.
45 She's been on TV a few times. Our salaries are about the same. So not
every part of Sulloway's birth order **theory** is true for us.

Sulloway says history is full of examples of his birth order theory.
He talks about Thomas Jefferson, Karl Marx, and Fidel Castro in his
book. They were all leaders of revolutions.[4] Like my sister, they were
50 all rebellious younger siblings. Bill Clinton and Jimmy Carter were older
brothers. They both became president of the United States. But Clinton's
younger brother Roger is a singer who has been in trouble with the law.
He spent time in prison. Carter's younger brother Billy got into trouble for
not paying his taxes.
55 My friends have birth order differences, too. The more I think about it,
the more I realize that Tina and I are not that unusual.

---

[2] **sibling:** your brother or sister

[3] **accounting:** the job of writing and checking financial information

[4] **revolution:** a time when people change a leader or political system, often by using force or violence

Vocabulary Check

A. Write the letter of the correct definition next to the target word.

_____ **1.** influence   **a.** an idea that explains why something happens or how something works

_____ **2.** rebel   **b.** to have an effect on the way someone behaves or thinks

_____ **3.** personality   **c.** someone's character, especially the way he or she behaves toward other people

_____ **4.** theory   **d.** someone who does not do things in the way that other people want him or her to do them

_____ **5.** strict   **e.** expecting people to obey rules and do what you say

B. Complete the sentences with the boldfaced words from the reading.

1. Because John sells so many paintings, he can _____ as an artist.

2. After his parents died, his grandparents _____ him.

3. He _____ the law, so he didn't get into any trouble.

4. She doesn't have a(n) _____ job; every month she finds new work.

5. Mary got 98 out of 100 points on the test, and I got 94 out of 100; we got good _____.

6. I'm worried; I hope everything will _____ OK in the end.

> ## READ AGAIN

Read "Rebel with a Cause" again and complete the comprehension exercises on the next page. As you work, keep the reading goal in mind.

> **READING GOAL:** To compare and contrast the author and Tina

Comprehension Check

A. Work with a partner. Use the Venn diagram to compare and contrast the author and Tina. Don't look back at the reading. Write each word or phrase under the person it describes. If it describes both people, write the word or phrase in the middle section.

always got good grades	is a sibling
broke her arm	likes taking risks
conservative	likes watching movies
does things the safe way	prefers steady work
fought with parents and teachers	raised in a strict way
has a good salary	~~rebellious~~
has brown hair	successful
identified with her parents	tried to stand out

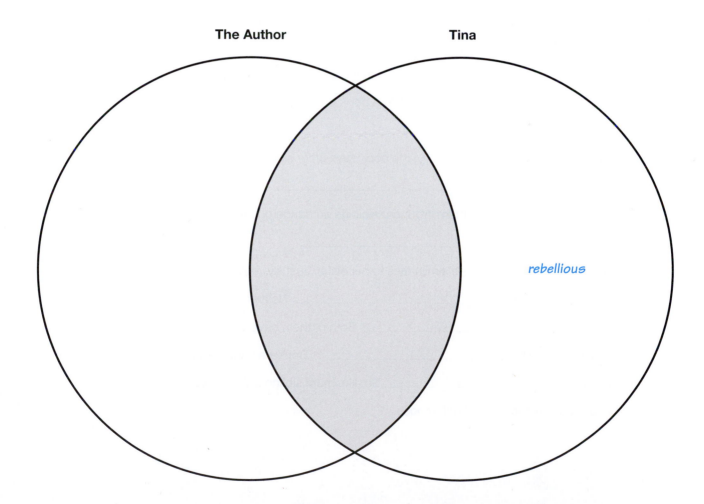

The Author   Tina

rebellious

B. Complete the summary of the reading. Use the words and phrases in the word list. Do not look back at the reading. There is one extra word.

a dancer	careers	movies	safe	steady
an accountant	identify	poisonous	siblings	take risks
broccoli	leaders of revolutions	rebellious	stand out	the rules

In her article, the author discusses the differences between younger and older (1) _____. She gives herself and her sister Tina as examples. The author says she is conservative; however, her younger sister is more (2) _____. Unlike the author, Tina isn't afraid to (3) _____, for example, jump out of a tree or ask for a(n) (4) _____ snake for a pet. The author, in contrast, does things the (5) _____ way. She works as (6) _____ and always obeys (7) _____. She says these differences are typical. She mentions a book called *Born to Rebel.* The book presents historical examples of birth order theory, such as (8) _____, who were all younger siblings. Basically, the book says older siblings are more conservative because they (9) _____ with their parents and try to act like them. Younger siblings do dangerous things because they want to (10) _____.

But the author also has some similarities to her sister. Just like her sister, she loves Meryl Streep (11) _____. Neither of them likes to eat (12) _____. Both of them have good jobs; Tina works as (13) _____. Both are successful in their (14) _____. So, like most siblings, they have some important similarities and differences.

C. Work in small groups. Ask and answer the questions. Take notes on your discussion. Then look at your notes and decide whether Sulloway's theory is true or not for the people in your group.

Questions	Example	Me	Student A	Student B	Student C
Do you have siblings? If not, imagine that you are someone who does.	Yes				
Are your siblings older or younger than you?	Of the three of us, I'm the oldest.				
In your family, which sibling: **a.** is the most rebellious?	I am.				
b. is the most conservative?	My younger sister is.				
c. takes the most risks?	My brother does.				
d. acts the most like your parents?	My sister does.				
Do your siblings work? If so, what type of job does each one have?	My sister is a piano teacher; my brother is a waiter.				

D. Tell the class one example from your group's discussion. Listen to the examples and decide whether Sulloway's theory is true for your classmates.

> ## DISCUSS

1. Have you heard other theories about why people have different personalities? Explain.

2. What do you think influences someone's personality more: environment or genetics? Explain.

3. If people want to change their personalities, what can they do?

About *The Nurture Assumption*

> PREPARE TO READ

A. Look at the words (and phrases) in the list. Write the number(s) next to each word to show what you know. You may be able to write more than one number next to some of the words. You will study all of these words in this chapter.

    1. I can use the word in a sentence.

    2. I know <u>one meaning</u> of the word.

    3. I know <u>more than one meaning</u> of the word.

    4. I know how to pronounce the word.

B. Work with a partner. Look at the picture. Ask and answer the questions. If you don't know a word in English, ask your partner or look in your dictionary. Then write your new words on page 217.

    1. What do you see in the picture? Point to the things you see and name them in English.

    2. How is the young girl feeling? Why might she be feeling that way?

    3. Do our friends influence our behavior? In what ways?

    4. Who influences our personality more—our friends or our parents? Explain.

_____ adapt

_____ credit

_____ deal with

_____ evidence

_____ fit in

_____ guilt

_____ ignore

_____ imitate

_____ mention

_____ peers

_____ psychologist

C. First, read the introduction to the online book reviews of *The Nurture Assumption*. Next, preview the two reviews. Then answer the questions.

1. Frank Sulloway says _____ influence people's personalities.

   a. parents   **b.** friends

2. Judith Rich Harris _____ with Frank Sulloway's theory.

   a. agrees   **b.** disagrees

READ

Read the online book reviews of *The Nurture Assumption*. Decide which of the two reviews is more positive.

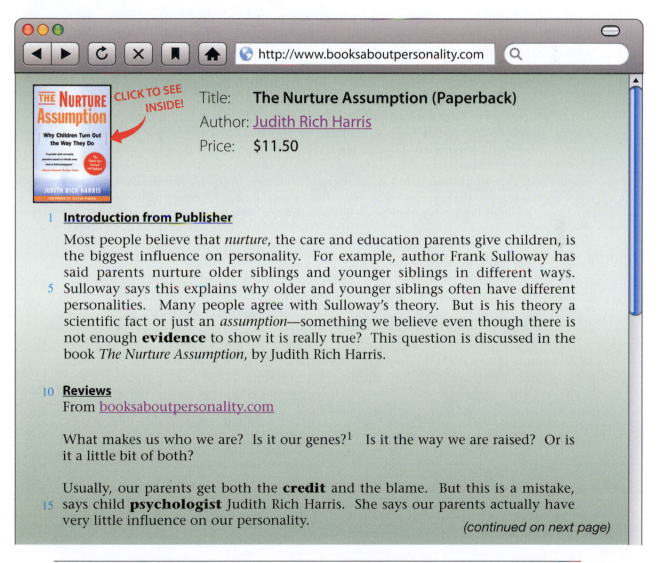

http://www.booksaboutpersonality.com

CLICK TO SEE INSIDE!

Title: **The Nurture Assumption (Paperback)**

Author: <u>Judith Rich Harris</u>

Price: $11.50

1 **Introduction from Publisher**

Most people believe that *nurture*, the care and education parents give children, is the biggest influence on personality. For example, author Frank Sulloway has said parents nurture older siblings and younger siblings in different ways.
5 Sulloway says this explains why older and younger siblings often have different personalities. Many people agree with Sulloway's theory. But is his theory a scientific fact or just an *assumption*—something we believe even though there is not enough **evidence** to show it is really true? This question is discussed in the book *The Nurture Assumption*, by Judith Rich Harris.

10 **Reviews**
From <u>booksaboutpersonality.com</u>

What makes us who we are? Is it our genes?[1] Is it the way we are raised? Or is it a little bit of both?

Usually, our parents get both the **credit** and the blame. But this is a mistake,
15 says child **psychologist** Judith Rich Harris. She says our parents actually have very little influence on our personality.

(continued on next page)

---

[1] **genes:** parts of the cells in our body that control how we develop

Her new book, *The Nurture Assumption*, provides evidence that our **peers** and not our parents make us who we are. Harris argues that we form our personality at school, not at home. At school, we **imitate** the people we like. We act like
20 the cool[2] people in school in order to **fit in**. Slowly, their behavior and style become our own. In the end, this becomes our adult personality.

Harris gives the example of immigrant families. The parents don't change much in the new country, but the children quickly **adapt**. As adults, they talk, think, and act more like their friends than their parents.

25 In *The Nurture Assumption*, Harris says children must choose their friends carefully. The book is interesting, original, and possibly life-changing. Parents with teenagers will really enjoy it.

From publishersmonthly.com

Judith Rich Harris, an author of college textbooks on child development,
30 believes that parents are not to blame for their children's behavior. Her new book, *The Nurture Assumption,* **ignores** the complex relationship between parents and children. In the book, Harris says, "Children learn separately, in each social context, how to behave in the context." This means that at home, children only learn how to **deal with** their parents and siblings. At school, with friends, at
35 soccer practice, etc., they learn other social rules. As adults, this continues; people adapt to the social rules of college or the workplace. As a result, the biggest influence on personality, says Harris, is not parents, but peer groups.

Harris argues that children don't rebel because they are angry with parents. They rebel to fit in with their peers. She gives the example of a teenager who steals a
40 car. The teenager isn't angry because he can't drive, says Harris. He just wants to appear cool to other teenagers.

Parents who have trouble controlling their children will surely appreciate this book. It allows them to feel less **guilt** about how they have raised their children. But *The Nurture Assumption* provides very little believable evidence for
45 Harris's theory. Many of the examples Harris **mentions** are from her personal life.

At one point she says, "Children who are unpopular with their peers . . . never get over that. At least I didn't." Harris's past experiences have likely influenced her opinions. Although her book is interesting, I would not recommend it to
50 people who are looking for a serious discussion of child psychology.

See All Reviews

---

[2] **cool:** popular, interesting, and attractive to other people

Vocabulary Check

Write the boldfaced word from the reading next to the correct definition. Use the correct form of the word.

1. _____ = to gradually change your behavior in order to be successful in a new situation

2. _____ = positive things that you say about someone for something he or she has done

3. _____ = to not pay attention to something or someone

4. _____ = facts or signs that show that something exists or is true

5. _____ = to copy the way someone behaves, speaks, moves, etc.

6. _____ = a person who studies the mind and how it works

7. _____ = a strong feeling of sadness when you know or believe you have done something wrong

8. _____ = people who are the same age as you

9. _____ = to do what is necessary, especially in order to solve a problem

10. _____ = to act as part of a group without standing out

11. _____ = to say or write about something, usually in a few words

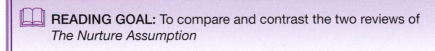 READ AGAIN

Read the book reviews of *The Nurture Assumption* again and complete the comprehension exercises on the next page. As you work, keep the reading goal in mind.

> 📖 **READING GOAL:** To compare and contrast the two reviews of *The Nurture Assumption*

Comprehension Check

A. Work with a partner. Use the Venn diagram to compare and contrast the two book reviews. Don't look back at the reading. Write each phrase under the book review it describes. If it describes both reviews, write the phrase in the middle section.

explains how Harris makes a living	says Harris's personal life influenced her
gives a negative review	says which parents will like Harris's book
gives a positive review	summarizes Harris's opinion
gives examples from Harris's book	talks about a teenager who steals a car
says Harris's book gives evidence	talks about immigrant families

Review 1: booksaboutpersonality.com   **Review 2:** publishersmonthly.com

B. Work with a partner. Check (✓) the ideas Harris agrees with.

_____ **1.** Parents are the biggest influence on personality.

___✓___ **2.** Peers are the biggest influence on personality.

_____ **3.** Children's personalities are affected by their school environment.

_____ **4.** If a child doesn't behave well, we should blame his or her friends.

_____ **5.** If children break rules, it is because they are angry with their family.

_____ **6.** Most children don't care if they are popular or not.

_____ **7.** When immigrant children grow up, they usually don't act like their parents.

_____ **8.** Parents must choose friends for their children.

_____ **9.** Adults' personalities are affected by their work environment.

_____ **10.** Children may behave differently at home than at school.

C. Complete the paragraph, which contrasts Judith Rich Harris's views with those of other psychologists. You do not have to use the same words and phrases as in the reading, but make sure the meaning is the same.

Judith Rich Harris is a psychologist. She tries to answer the question:

(1) _____?

While most psychologists think the answer is "our parents," Harris believes

(2) _____.

Harris says we form our personalities (3) _____.

We imitate (4) _____. In contrast, other

psychologists say we form our personalities at (5) _____ by

imitating our parents. When children rebel, Harris says it is because

(6) _____.

However, other psychologists say children rebel because

(7) _____.

As an example of her theory, Harris talks about immigrant families. In

these families, (8) _____

_____. In summary, Harris tries to respond to the same question as

many other psychologists, but she gives a very different answer.

> DISCUSS

1. What things do you have in common with your friends?

2. In what ways do your friends influence your behavior?

3. What things do teenagers do to appear cool?

4. What are the most important characteristics of a good friend?

> VOCABULARY SKILL BUILDING

Word Families

Most English words are part of a "family" of words. When you learn a new word, it is helpful to learn other related words because it will expand your vocabulary. Remember that words in the same word family often have the same *base word*, or main part, but may have different endings. The endings sometimes change the part of speech, but all of the words in the same family share a core meaning.

EXAMPLE:

adapt (verb)   *adaptation* (noun)   *adaptable* (adjective)

Each member of this word family shares the core meaning of *adapt* (which is "change").

A. Complete the chart with the correct word forms. Notice the endings of each word form—for example, the adjective and verb forms. Identify any that have similar patterns. Also, notice the word forms that stay the same even though the part of speech changes.

Verb	Noun	Adjective
adapt	adaptation	adaptable
	imitation	imitable
theorize		theoretical
	influence	influential
rebel		rebellious
personalize	personality	

B. Complete the sentences with the words from the chart. Be careful. You will use only one form of each word.

1. Some psychologists _____ that our genes affect our personality.

2. Harris's book changed the way I think; it had a big _____ on me.

3. Sylvia is very _____; she never does what she's told.

4. I like to _____ my favorite singer—for example, I wear the same style of clothing.

5. I have problems with my friends and family, but I don't like to talk about my _____ life with people I don't know well.

6. If our plan doesn't work, we may need to _____ it by changing some steps.

Learn the Vocabulary

A. Circle the two similar words in each group. Write *M* if their **meaning** is similar, *S* if their **sound** or **spelling** is similar, or *T* if they describe the same basic type of **thing**. Write *O* if they are **opposites**.

_____M_____ **1.** (locate)   athlete   regular   (discover)   spicy

_____ **2.** release   advertising   shape   marketing   fan

_____ **3.** passenger   turn out   converted   remarkable   turn on

_____ **4.** improve   chair   rebel   table   script

_____ **5.** psychologist   cautious   resemble   appropriate   appreciate

_____ **6.** instrument   sweet   theory   bitter   extra

_____ **7.** blame   credit   towers   originally   reach

_____ **8.** peers   set out   sell out   investment   exotic

B. Make cards for the new words from Chapters 15–16 that you wrote on page 217. Review them with a partner.

C. Add your new cards to your old cards. Now put your cards into groups of thirty to forty cards each. Look through each group of cards carefully to make sure it doesn't have similar words. If you find two similar words in the same group, put one of those words into a different group of cards. Review each group of cards separately for the next week.

D. Go back to the vocabulary list at the beginning of each chapter. What did you learn about the target words? Add your numbers to the lists.

Vocabulary Practice 8, see page 225

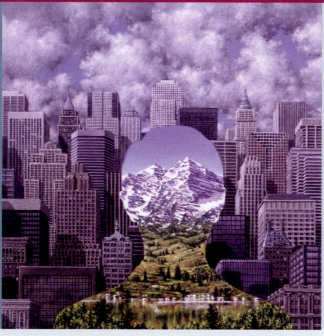

> THINK BEFORE YOU READ

A. Work with a partner. Look at the picture. Ask and answer the questions. If you don't know a word in English, ask your partner or look in your dictionary. Then write your new words on page 217.

1. What do you see in the picture? Point to the things you see and name them in English.

2. Which part of the picture most resembles where you live? What does it have in common with your hometown?

3. Is it better to live in the city or in the country? Explain.

B. Work in small groups. Complete the chart with your ideas.

Benefits of living in a city	Benefits of living in nature

C. Compare charts with another group. Add any new ideas to your chart.

The Haiku Master

Matsuo Basho   Some of Basho's Travels

 PREPARE TO READ

A. Look at the words in the list. Write the number(s) next to each word to show what you know. You may be able to write more than one number next to some of the words. You will study all of these words in this chapter.

  1. I can use the word in a sentence.

  2. I know <u>one meaning</u> of the word.

  3. I know <u>more than one meaning</u> of the word.

  4. I know how to pronounce the word.

B. Work with a partner. Look at the picture and map. Ask and answer the questions. If you don't know a word in English, ask your partner or look in your dictionary. Then write your new words on page 217.

  1. What do you see in the picture and map?

  2. Who do you think Matsuo Basho was, and when do you think he lived?

  3. Why might someone like to travel as much as Basho did?

_____ admirable

_____ countryside

_____ empty

_____ encourage

_____ inspiration

_____ journey

_____ master

_____ overrated

_____ poet

_____ robber

_____ season

_____ sign

C. Scan the textbook article "The Haiku Master." Find the answers for questions 2 and 3 in Exercise B.

 READ

Read "The Haiku Master." Check your answer to question 4 in Exercise B.

❧ The Haiku Master ☙

1   In 1694, at the age of forty-nine, a remarkable Japanese **poet** died. Before his death, Matsuo Kinsaku, better known as "Basho," wrote this final poem:

> *Fallen sick on a **journey***
> *my dream goes wandering*[1]
5   > *over a field of dried grass*

Basho's last poem, like much of his work, was a *haiku*—a traditional Japanese poetic form. Most haiku share certain characteristics. First, they are short: only three lines long. Second, they describe a remarkable moment in a few simple words. Third, they mention nature in some way—usually the **seasons**.

10   Matsuo Basho was one of the greatest **masters** of haiku; he wrote over 1,000 of these small, surprising poems. His haiku reflect his life experiences.

Matsuo's life began in 1644 in Ueno, a small town in Iga Province. After the death of his father in 1656, Matsuo left home and became a servant. His master was Todo Yoshitada, a wealthy young man. Todo and Matsuo quickly discovered
15   they had something in common: They both loved writing poetry. One of their favorite poetic subjects was an old cherry blossom[2] tree in Todo's garden. Matsuo wrote many haiku about it, such as this one from 1664:

> *The old-lady cherry*
> *is blossoming—in her old age*
20   > *an event to remember*

Until 1666, Matsuo enjoyed a simple life of working and writing poetry. Then Todo suddenly died. Matsuo lost his job and best friend. Filled with sadness, he

---

[1] **wandering:** walking slowly, without having a clear direction or purpose
[2] **cherry blossom:** a tree that produces cherry fruit and pink flowers in springtime

traveled to the capital of Edo (modern-day Tokyo) to start a new life. There, he
studied and wrote poetry. His poetry began to attract fans. Soon, Matsuo had his
own school and many students. His life was comfortable again.

Inside, however, Matsuo felt **empty**. Although his friends liked the many
shops and crowded streets of Edo, Basho felt city life was **overrated**. He wanted a
change. Looking for **inspiration**, he moved to a small hut[3] outside of Edo in the
winter of 1680. In front of this simple house, he planted a banana tree, called a
basho in Japanese. It became the subject of many haiku:

> *Having planted a banana tree,*
> *I'm a little contemptuous[4]*
> *of the bush clover[5]*

Because he loved his banana tree so much, Matsuo's friends began calling him Basho.
The poet enjoyed this and began **signing** his poems *Basho*. Then one cold winter day,
a fire burned down his hut. For the third time in his life, Basho was without a home.

Feeling lost and without purpose, Basho set out to travel the **countryside** of Japan.
He planned to visit the twelve provinces between Edo and Kyoto, Japan's second largest
city. Now forty years old, Basho knew the trip would be difficult and dangerous. He
expected to die from illness or be killed by **robbers**. But he traveled safely. Basho began
to enjoy his long journey. He met many people and made new friends. As he traveled,
the topics of his haiku began to change. He focused less on his feelings and more on
nature. While on the road, Basho wrote some of his best haiku:

> *How **admirable**!*
> *to see lightning and not think*
> *life is fleeting[6]*

For the rest of his life, Basho traveled the Japanese countryside. His travels
took him east to the Pacific coast. He climbed the mountains of Honshu in the
north. He traveled west to the inland sea. His final journey was south to the city
of Osaka, where he wrote his final poem. During his travels, he wrote many great
books of poetry. Today, his haiku inspire writers and readers from countries all
over the world. His poems **encourage** people to see their lives and the things
around them in a new way.

---

[3] **hut:** a small wooden building with only one or two rooms

[4] **contemptuous:** showing that you believe something or someone does not deserve any respect

[5] **bush clover:** a flowering bush that blooms in late summer and fall

[6] **fleeting:** happening only for a moment

Vocabulary Check

Complete the sentences with the boldfaced words from the reading.

1. My parents and teachers always _____ me to do my best.

2. The _____ from here to my hometown takes four hours.

3. People who love nature should spend time in the _____.

4. Hiking in the mountains gives me the _____ to paint.

5. When I finish a poem, I enjoy _____ my name below it.

6. There are four _____, and summer is my favorite.

7. This book got great reviews, but in my opinion it's _____.

8. The police caught the two _____ who took my money.

9. There is nothing inside this hut; it is completely _____.

10. Juan has many good qualities; he is very _____.

11. No one is better than Julie at tennis; she's one of the _____.

12. The American _____ Robert Frost wrote a lot about the people and countryside of New England.

> READ AGAIN

Read "The Haiku Master" again and complete the comprehension exercises. As you work, keep the reading goal in mind.

> 📖 **READING GOAL:** To identify key events and details in the life of Basho

Comprehension Check

A. Scan to find the answer to each question.

1. Where was Basho born?

2. What was the name of his first master?

3. What was the city of Tokyo called during Basho's lifetime?

4. During which season did Basho's hut burn down?

5. How many provinces are there between Edo and Kyoto?

6. In which city did Basho write his final poem?

B. Put the events from the **first part of Basho's life story** into the correct sequence. Write *1* next to the first event, *2* next to the second, and so on.

_____ **1.** Todo dies.

_____ **2.** Basho starts his own school.

_____ **3.** Basho goes to the capital city of Edo.

_____ **4.** Todo and Basho write haiku together.

_____ **5.** Basho's father dies.

_____ **6.** Basho becomes a servant.

C. Put the events from the **second part of Basho's life story** into the correct sequence. Write *1* next to the first event, *2* next to the second, and so on.

_____ **1.** Basho travels to Osaka.

_____ **2.** Basho travels from Edo to Kyoto.

_____ **3.** Basho plants a banana tree.

_____ **4.** Basho writes his final poem.

_____ **5.** Basho's poems inspire people around the world.

_____ **6.** Basho's hut burns down.

_____ **7.** Basho moves to a small hut.

D. Work in small groups. Use your answers to Exercises B and C to create a time line of key events in Basho's life. Scan the reading and add as many dates as you can.

1644
Basho born
in Ueno

1694
Basho dies
in Osaka

E. With your group, use the time line to take turns talking about Basho's life. Include as many details as you can, such as the names of people and places and the dates when things occurred. Don't look back at the reading. If someone makes a mistake, correct it before continuing the story.

> DISCUSS

Work in small groups. Which of the words and phrases in the list describe Matsuo Basho? Explain your answers with details from the reading.

admirable	a happy person	cautious	creative	popular
a genius	athletic	close to nature	lucky	successful

> VOCABULARY SKILL BUILDING

Prefix: over-

A *prefix* is a word part that is added to the beginning of some words. Unlike suffixes, prefixes don't change the word's part of speech. They change its meaning. For example, the prefix *over-* can mean "too much" or "more than is necessary." The following examples show what happens when *over-* is added to certain verbs, nouns, and adjectives.

EXAMPLES:

Words with *over-*	Meaning
overwork (verb)	to work too much
overeater (noun)	someone who eats too much
overcrowded (adjective)	too crowded

A. Write *A* if the word is an adjective, *N* if it is a noun, and *V* if it is a verb.

___V___ **1.** overworks   _____ **5.** overrated

___N___ **2.** overeater   _____ **6.** overcooked

___A___ **3.** overcrowded   _____ **7.** overpopulation

_____ **4.** overslept   _____ **8.** overpriced

B. Complete the sentences with the words from Exercise A. Keep the same part of speech and the same form for each word.

1. I wanted to wake up at 8:00 A.M., but I _____ and woke up at 8:45 A.M.

2. John goes to the office seven days a week; I think he _____.

3. In the summer, the beach can become so _____ with tourists that there is nowhere to sit.

4. I can't believe how much money that watch costs—it's _____, in my opinion.

5. Almost 20 million people live in the capital city; _____ is a big problem there.

6. Everyone says he is the best poet of all time, but I think his work is _____.

7. The meat is not very soft. I think we _____ it.

8. He can't stop putting food on his plate; I think he's a(n) _____.

CHAPTER 18

So You Want to Write Haiku?

> PREPARE TO READ

A. Look at the words (and phrases) in the list. Write the number(s) next to each word to show what you know. You may be able to write more than one number next to some of the words. You will study all of these words in this chapter.

1. I can use the word in a sentence.

2. I know <u>one meaning</u> of the word.

3. I know <u>more than one meaning</u> of the word.

4. I know how to pronounce the word.

B. Work with a partner. Look at the pictures. Ask and answer the questions. If you don't know a word in English, ask your partner or look in your dictionary. Then write your new words on page 217.

1. What animal do you see in the pictures? What is it doing?

2. Where does this animal live?

3. Do you think this animal is beautiful? Explain.

_____ approach

_____ challenging

_____ go on and on

_____ have trouble

_____ mood

_____ nap

_____ on your mind

_____ skip

_____ syllable

_____ system

_____ unit

C. Read the first three paragraphs (through Step 1) of the textbook article "So You Want to Write Haiku?" Then answer the questions.

1. What process does the reading tell about?
   a. how to understand Basho's most famous haiku
   b. how to figure out the topic of a haiku
   c. how to write your own haiku

2. What is the first step of the process?
   a. Look at an example haiku.
   b. Create a picture in your mind.
   c. Decide which topic to write about.

A Basho Poem

 **READ**

Read "So You Want to Write Haiku?" Notice the steps in the process.

So You Want to Write Haiku?

1 If you are interested in writing haiku, take a look at this famous example by Basho:

The old pond
a frog jumps in
sound of water
5   —Basho (translated by Robert Hass)

Notice how simple and direct the poem is. Other poets might **go on and on** about frogs singing, but Basho just describes the sound of a frog hitting the water. The poem clearly mentions nature. It also contrasts something—the quiet of the pond with the noise of the frog. Finally, it has a feeling of *sabi*, a Japanese word
10 meaning something like "peaceful sadness." Basho's haiku creates a picture in your mind. You can easily imagine sitting alone by the pond, listening to the sounds of nature.

Haiku can be a lot of fun to write. In this simple, short poetic form, you can describe your environment, explain how you feel about something, or present a
15 funny situation. To write your own haiku, just follow the steps below.

STEP 1: First, figure out what you want to write about. Traditional haiku focus on nature, but they can be about anything. A lot of modern haiku discuss city life, work, or school. Take a look at these examples:

20
> *Still in a meeting*
> *boss talks, nightfall* **approaches**—
> *dreams of the weekend*
>> —Sandra Duque

> *English class is here*
> *my favorite time of day;*
25
> *chance for a nice* **nap**
>> —David Clayton

You might want to write about something you love, something you hate, the things around you, or anything else that is **on your mind**.

STEP 2: Decide on the form of your haiku. Japanese haiku use a **system** of
30
sound counting. A Japanese haiku must have exactly seventeen *on*, or "**units of sound**." To write haiku in English, some writers use a system of **syllable** counting. The first line has five syllables. The second line has seven syllables, and the third line has five. Count the syllables in the next example.

> *Summer has arrived*
35
> *see children running outside—*
> *fresh smell of cut grass*
>> —Jessica Andrea

Some haiku writers prefer not to follow the seventeen-syllable form. It can be hard to do in English, as this example shows:

40
> *To con-vey[1] one's* **mood**
> *in sev-en-teen syl-la-bles*
> *is ve-ry dif-fic*
>> —John Cooper Clarke

STEP 3: The next step is the most **challenging**: Include a change or contrast
45
in your haiku. Look at the examples above. The haiku that begins *Still in a meeting* contrasts work with dreams of the weekend. *English class* contrasts something serious, a class, with a funny idea—taking a nap in school. *Summer has arrived* contrasts something that you see (children running) with something that you smell (fresh cut grass) The contrast doesn't have to be big; it could just be a description of
50
something and a related statement. Some writers use special punctuation, such as a dash (—) or semicolon (;) to show the contrast in their poem.

STEP 4: Include a season word, if possible. This word tells the reader what time of year it is in your poem. For example, if the haiku mentions "cherry blossoms," the reader knows it's spring. If the haiku mentions snow, the reader pictures
55
winter. Depending on the topic you choose, you may need to **skip** this step.

STEP 5: Practice, practice, practice! The more haiku you write, the better you will get at it. It also helps to read a lot of haiku. Be sure to read a variety of types—traditional, modern, serious, sad, funny, and so on.

STEP 6: Have fun with it! Don't worry if you **have trouble** at first. With
60
enough time, you'll soon be able to write your own great haiku.

---

[1] **convey:** to communicate a message or information, with or without using words

Vocabulary Check

Circle the letter of the correct answer to complete each sentence. The boldfaced words are the target words.

1. A **unit** is one whole part of something _____.
   - **a.** important
   - **b.** bigger
   - **c.** smaller

2. If your friend **goes on and on** about something, you may want him to _____.
   - **a.** stop talking
   - **b.** come closer to you
   - **c.** answer your questions

3. If an activity is _____, you may **have trouble**.
   - **a.** overrated
   - **b.** difficult
   - **c.** enjoyable

4. _____ is **challenging**.
   - **a.** Watching a movie
   - **b.** Climbing a mountain
   - **c.** Eating a meal

5. The word *understand* has _____ **syllables**.
   - **a.** one
   - **b.** two
   - **c.** three

6. If you are in a good **mood**, you _____.
   - **a.** are a genius
   - **b.** have a big salary
   - **c.** feel happy

7. If a person is **on your mind**, you are _____ about that person.
   - **a.** thinking
   - **b.** learning
   - **c.** forgetting

8. When something **approaches** you, it gets _____.
   - **a.** darker
   - **b.** closer
   - **c.** smaller

9. If you **skip** lunch, you will feel _____.
   - **a.** full
   - **b.** healthy
   - **c.** hungry

10. When you take a **nap**, you sleep for _____.
    - **a.** the entire night
    - **b.** a short time
    - **c.** one week

11. I organize my papers using a **system**. I follow _____.
    - **a.** my own ideas
    - **b.** my feelings
    - **c.** rules and steps

> READ AGAIN

Read "So You Want to Write Haiku?" again and complete the comprehension exercises. As you work, keep the reading goal in mind.

> 📖 **READING GOAL:** To understand the steps involved in the process of writing haiku

Comprehension Check

A. Work with a partner. Answer the questions in your own words. Don't look back at the reading.

1. Why is Basho's frog poem a good example of a haiku?

_____

2. How are modern haiku different from traditional haiku?

_____

3. After choosing a topic, what is the next step in writing a haiku?

_____

4. Which step is the most challenging, according to the reading?

_____

5. How do writers show contrast in their haiku?

_____

6. Which step do haiku writers sometimes skip, according to the reading?

_____

7. What can people do to get better at writing haiku?

_____

B. Now look back at the reading. Check your answers.

C. Study each example haiku in the reading. Then write the letter of the haiku next to the person who wrote it. Except for number 1, the answers are not in the text—you have to infer them.

_____*a*_____ **1.** the Japanese poet Basho   **a.** *The old pond*

_____ **2.** a teacher   **b.** *Still in a meeting*

_____ **3.** a student   **c.** *English class is here*

_____ **4.** a joker   **d.** *Summer has arrived*

_____ **5.** a worker   **e.** *To con-vey one's mood*

D. Prepare to write your own haiku. Write your ideas in the section "My haiku." You will complete the other sections later.

	My haiku	Student A's	Student B's	Student C's
Topic:				
Form / number of syllables:				
Contrast:				
Season:				
Season word:				

E. On a separate sheet of paper, write one or more drafts of your haiku. Use your ideas from the chart to help you. Then write your final haiku below.

_____

_____

_____

F. Work in small groups. Listen to your classmates read their haiku. As you listen, complete the spaces in the chart above.

> DISCUSS

Work in small groups. Ask and answer the questions.

1. How did you feel while you were writing your haiku?

2. Is a haiku easy to write? Explain.

3. Have you ever written a poem in your native language? If so, what was it about?

4. Is it better to write poetry when you are in a good mood or in a bad mood? Explain.

Learn the Vocabulary

A. Make cards for the words from Chapters 17–18 that were new to you when you started the unit. Include target words and words that you wrote on page 217. Then add example sentences to the back of the cards.

B. Choose a word with one example sentence and draw a picture of the sentence on the back of the card.

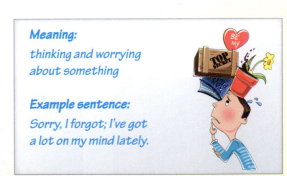

on my mind

Meaning:
thinking and worrying about something

Example sentence:
Sorry, I forgot; I've got a lot on my mind lately.

C. Work in small groups. Fold your word card in half so that only the picture is showing. Look at one another's pictures. Say which word you think is on the other side of the card.

D. Go back to the vocabulary list at the beginning of each chapter. What did you learn about the target words? Add your numbers to the lists.

Vocabulary Practice 9, see page 226

FLUENCY PRACTICE 3

Fluency Strategy

To increase your reading speed, don't focus on the meaning of every word. Divide sentences into groups of words, or "chunks." For example, the following sentence can be broken into three chunks.

The quick green frog • jumped over • the old gray cat.

The first chunk (*the quick green frog*) is the subject, the thing that does the action. The next chunk (*jumped over*) is the verb phrase, the description of the action. The third chunk (*the old gray cat*) is the object, the thing that receives the action.

If you think of the sentence as three chunks instead of 10 words, it is easier to understand.

 READING 1

Before You Read

A. Work with a partner. Look at the pictures. Ask and answer the questions.

1. What creatures do you see?

2. What special abilities does each one have?

3. Do you know any stories in which insects and animals behave like people? Explain.

B. Preview "Folktales" on the next page. Answer the questions.

1. What example of a folktale is given in the beginning of the reading?

2. How many different kinds of folktales does the reading discuss?

Read

A. Read "Folktales." Time yourself. Write your start and end times and your total reading time. Then calculate your reading speed (words per minute) and write it in the progress chart on page 230.

Start time: _____   **End time:** _____   **Total time:** _____ (in seconds)

Reading speed:
527 words ÷ _____ (total time in seconds) x 60 = _____ words per minute

---

๑ **Folktales** ๛

The Ant and the Grasshopper

1   One sunny winter day, an ant was eating in the sun. A hungry grasshopper walked by. He asked the ant if he could share his meal.
"Why do you ask me for food? What were you doing in the summer?" asked the ant.
"Oh," answered the grasshopper, "I was singing all summer."
5   "Well then," said the ant, "you sang all summer, you can dance all winter."

"The Ant and the Grasshopper" is a *folktale*. Folktales are very old stories. They explain something about human behavior or the natural world. This example folktale shows the importance of hard work. The ant worked hard during the summer. He is not hungry in the winter. The grasshopper spent the summer
10   having fun. Now he has to suffer as a result.
The types of animals in folktales are usually chosen for a reason. Take "The Ant and the Grasshopper," for example. The ant reminds us of hard work. When we see ants, they are usually busy. Grasshoppers, in contrast, are known for their singing. Most people associate singing with having a good time. By
15   comparing human and animal behavior, the message of folktales becomes easier to remember.
Folktales usually have long histories. In most cases, the original tale was not written down. It was passed on from one generation to the next. Parents told it to their children and they told it to their children, and so on.
20   Interestingly, every culture on earth has folktales. The stories are different, but the ideas are often the same. There are many different kinds of folktales. Each kind serves a different purpose. Here are four kinds of folktales.

Fables

In a fable, the characters are animals, but they behave like humans. A fable
25   always teaches something. This is called the *moral*. Sometimes the moral is told at the end of the story. Other times the listener has to think about it. "The Ant and the Grasshopper" is a fable.

Pourquoi Stories

Pourquoi means *why* in French. Pourquoi stories explain something about the
30   natural world. Many cultures have them. One pourquoi story from Africa explains why the sun and moon live in the sky. (The reason? The ocean was too crowded with fish.) In the Philippines, there are stories about the origin of each kind of

(continued on next page)

fruit. Other common pourquoi stories answer the questions "Why is the grass green?" or "Why is the ocean blue?"

Trickster Tales

35   Children must learn about good behavior. They must also learn what *not* to do. *Trickster* tales show examples of bad behavior. Tricksters are characters who don't obey the rules. They tell lies and rob others. Tricksters are often animals. Usually, they don't get into trouble for their bad behavior, but the other animals don't
40   trust them. Children learn to behave better. They also learn not to trust everyone they meet.

Fairy Tales

A fairy tale has one or more characters with magical powers. There are good characters and bad characters. The bad characters are punished, and the story
45   most often ends happily. Usually, the purpose is to entertain. That's why fairy tales are the inspiration for so many animated movies. For all of human history, audiences have just loved happy endings!

B. Read "Folktales" again, a little faster this time. Write your start and end times and your total reading time. Then calculate your reading speed (words per minute) and write it in the progress chart on page 230.

Start time: _____   **End time:** _____   **Total time:** _____ (in seconds)

Reading speed:
527 words ÷ _____ (total time in seconds) x 60 = _____ words per minute

Comprehension Check

A. Complete the chart. Check (✓) the characteristics of the different types of folktales.

Characteristics	Fable	Pourquoi story	Trickster tale	Fairy tale
A main character who can't be trusted				
A happy ending				
A moral at the end				
An explanation of something in the natural world				

B. Answer the questions.

1. What is the moral of "The Ant and the Grasshopper"?

2. What can trickster tales teach children?

3. Why are most animated movies adapted from fairy tales?

C. Check your answers for the comprehension questions in the Answer Key on page 231. Then calculate your score and write it in the progress chart on page 230.

_____ (my number correct) ÷ 7 x 100 = _____ %

> READING 2

Before You Read

Look at the pictures. Ask and answer the questions.

1. What creatures do you see?

2. What characteristics do you associate with each creature?

3. Do you know any folktales about these creatures? If so, name them.

Read

A. Read "Anansi Tales" on the next page. Time yourself. Write your start and end times and your total reading time. Then calculate your reading speed (words per minute) and write it in the progress chart on page 230.

Start time: _____   **End time:** _____   **Total time:** _____ (in seconds)

Reading speed:
521 words ÷ _____ (total time in seconds) x 60 = _____ words per minute

❧ Anansi Tales ❧

1 The following folktale is an example of an *Anansi* tale. Anansi is a spider. Anansi stories originated in West Africa. Anansi has since become a common character in many cultures' folktales. In the Caribbean, he is called *Ananse*, or *Nanzi*. He is known as *Anancy* in much of Central America. In the United States,
5 he appears as a woman and is known as *Aunt Nancy*.

Anansi is an example of a trickster. He has only one thing on his mind: food. Often, he is able to influence others into giving him their food. Other times, he lies to avoid giving away his own. His character never changes. The secret to living with Anansi is to adapt to his methods, as the following story shows.

10 ## Anansi and Turtle

One day, Anansi the spider was eating his evening meal when his friend Turtle walked by. "Hello, Anansi," said Turtle. "That smells great!"

Anansi loved to eat, and he didn't like to share. But in spider culture, you always share your food with a friend. So Anansi said, "Come in, Turtle, and eat
15 with me."

Turtle sat down with a smile, but before he could start eating, Anansi said, "Turtle, your hands are dirty! In my culture, we wash our hands before we eat."

Turtle looked at his dirty hands and felt embarrassed. "Sorry, excuse me," he said to Anansi. He got up and went to the river to wash his hands. When he got
20 back, Anansi was already eating.

"I didn't want the food to get cold," Anansi explained.

Turtle sat down at the table. Now he was really hungry, but Anansi said, "Turtle, your hands are still dirty!"

Turtle looked down. Anansi was right! "I'm so sorry! I don't know what
25 happened. I'll wash them again," Turtle said.

This time, Turtle walked back from the river on the grass. His hands were clean when he got to the table. But to his surprise, all of the food was gone! "I'm sorry, Turtle, but you took so long! I couldn't wait," Anansi explained.

The next day Turtle was swimming in the river when he saw Anansi. "Hello,
30 Anansi, would you like to have lunch with me?"

"Oh yes!" said Anansi.

"Then follow me!" said Turtle.

Turtle and Anansi swam to the bottom of the river. There, Anansi saw a table and a lot of food. He was very hungry, but there was a problem. Every time he
35 tried to sit down, he floated back up to the surface of the river.

Then Anansi had a clever idea. He put some rocks in his jacket and swam back down to the bottom of the river. He sat down at the table and smiled. But before he could eat anything, Turtle said, "In my culture, we don't wear our jackets at the table."

Anansi saw that Turtle wasn't wearing a jacket. He realized that if he wanted to
40 eat, he would have to take off his jacket as well. But as soon as he took his jacket off, he rose up to the surface again. On the river bottom below, Turtle smiled and started eating.

B. Read "Anansi Tales" again, a little faster this time. Write your start and end times and your total reading time. Then calculate your reading speed (words per minute) and write it in the progress chart on page 230.

Start time: _____   **End time:** _____   **Total time:** _____ (in seconds)

Reading speed:
521 words ÷ _____ (total time in seconds) x 60 = _____ words per minute

Comprehension Check

A. Put the events from the *first part of the story* into the correct sequence. Write *1* next to the first event, *2* next to the second, and so on.

_____ **1.** There was no more food because Anansi had eaten it all.

_____ **2.** Turtle sat down to eat, but Anansi told him that his hands were dirty.

_____ **3.** Turtle washed his hands two times.

_____ **4.** Anansi invited Turtle to share his meal.

B. Put the events from the *second part of the story* into the correct sequence. Write *1* next to the first event, *2* next to the second, and so on.

_____ **1.** As soon as Anansi took off his jacket, he floated back up to the surface.

_____ **2.** Anansi put rocks in his jacket pockets.

_____ **3.** Anansi sat down to eat with his jacket on, but Turtle asked him to take it off.

_____ **4.** Turtle invited Anansi to lunch at the bottom of the river.

C. How does Turtle adapt to Anansi's methods?

_____

_____

_____

D. Check your answers for the comprehension questions in the Answer Key on page 232. Then calculate your score and write it in the progress chart on page 230.

_____ (my number correct) ÷ 9 x 100 = _____%

Big Buildings

The World's Five Tallest Buildings, 2010

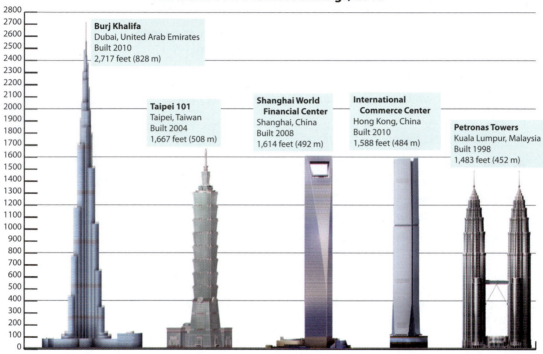

Burj Khalifa
Dubai, United Arab Emirates
Built 2010
2,717 feet (828 m)

Taipei 101
Taipei, Taiwan
Built 2004
1,667 feet (508 m)

**Shanghai World
Financial Center**
Shanghai, China
Built 2008
1,614 feet (492 m)

**International
Commerce Center**
Hong Kong, China
Built 2010
1,588 feet (484 m)

Petronas Towers
Kuala Lumpur, Malaysia
Built 1998
1,483 feet (452 m)

❯ THINK BEFORE YOU READ

A. Work with a partner. Look at the diagram. Ask and answer the questions.
If you don't know a word in English, ask your partner or look in your
dictionary. Then write your new words on page 217.

1. What do you see in the diagram?

2. How is each building's design different from the others?

3. Which building design do you like best? Explain.

B. Work with a partner. Ask and answer the questions.

1. In which part of the world are most of the tallest skyscrapers located?

2. Why do you think this part of the world has so many skyscrapers?

Race for the Sky

Chrysler Building   Empire State Building   40 Wall Street

> PREPARE TO READ

A. Look at the words in the list. Write the number(s) next to each word to show what you know. You may be able to write more than one number next to some of the words. You will study all of these words in this chapter.

   1. I can use the word in a sentence.

   2. I know <u>one meaning</u> of the word.

   3. I know <u>more than one meaning</u> of the word.

   4. I know how to pronounce the word.

B. Work with a partner. Look at the pictures. Ask and answer the questions. If you don't know a word in English, ask your partner or look in your dictionary. Then write your new words on page 217.

   1. Do you know the buildings in the pictures?

   2. In which city are the buildings located?

   3. Which of the buildings do you think is the tallest?

C. Scan the textbook article "Race for the Sky" on the next page. Check your answers for questions 2 and 3 from Exercise B.

_____ architect

_____ construction

_____ crush

_____ enemy

_____ floor

_____ former

_____ height

_____ honor

_____ intense

_____ limited

_____ race

_____ symbol

READ

Read "Race for the Sky." Circle the paragraph that tells the main idea of the reading.

ᖇ Race for the Sky ᖇ

1　In 1924, in the heart of New York, a competition began between two **architects**. Each planned to build the tallest building in the world. **Former** friends and business partners, they had started to fight over their differences. They were now bitter **enemies**. The first

5　architect, William Van Alen, was very creative. He imagined a unique, modern design. With money from a car company, he built the famous Chrysler Building. The second architect, Craig Severance, was a smart businessperson. He had rich and powerful friends. They helped him build a skyscraper at 40 Wall Street.

10　From the first day of **construction**, Van Alen and Severance competed to make their building the tallest. They watched as each other's buildings quickly grew. They frequently changed their plans to increase the **height** of their buildings. In order to win, Severance planned to make his building 927 feet (283 meters) tall, slightly taller

Taipei 101

15　than what he thought the height of the Chrysler Building would be. Van Alen had a surprise for him, however. During the last week of construction, Van Alen added a 185-foot (56-meter) spire[1] to his building, giving it a total height of 1,046 feet (319 meters). Van Alen won the competition, but he only had a year to enjoy the **honor**—in 1930, work started on an even taller skyscraper. This building—paid

20　for by General Motors, a car company that was in competition with Chrysler—became the now-famous Empire State Building. At 1,454 feet (443 meters), including its lightning rod, it was the tallest building in the world for over forty years, until the construction of the World Trade Center was completed in 1973.

These tall buildings became **symbols** of the power and wealth of the

25　businesspeople who created them. But today competitions are no longer between businesspeople, and they are not **limited** to one city or country. **Races** to build the tallest buildings are occurring around the world. Countries compete in order to show their economic power. And with so many countries in the game, the competition is becoming more **intense**.

30　As the economic power of Asia has grown, so has the size of its buildings. Of the fifteen tallest buildings in the world, eleven are now in Asian countries. Ten of those eleven are in China and Taiwan. The tallest of them, as of 2010, is the Taipei 101, in Taiwan. It stands at 1,667 feet (508 meters). It is more than 200 feet (61 meters) taller than the Empire State Building. For the 2004 opening in

35　Taipei, the Taiwanese people held a big celebration,[2] with concerts, speeches, and a fireworks[3] show. But no celebration could last forever. Competition was already brewing[4] in another part of the world.

---

[1] **spire:** a thin metal tower on the top of a building

[2] **celebration:** a party because of a particular event or special occasion

[3] **fireworks:** burning objects that produce colored lights and noise in the sky

[4] **brewing:** happening soon

The builders of the Burj Khalifa, in the United Arab Emirates, didn't simply want to create the world's tallest building. They wanted to **crush** the international record. At over 2,717 feet (828 meters), the Burj Khalifa is about 60 percent taller than the Taipei 101. It is almost twice as tall as the Empire State Building. Designers say that the Burj Khalifa is "a symbol of the new Middle East." The building certainly is a symbol of economic power—it cost more than $4 billion to complete.

40

Although the Burj Khalifa opened in January 2010, the builders have said that they might add more **floors** to the building in the future. This isn't a bad idea. Architects in Delhi, India, have blueprints[5] for an even taller building. Once again, competition is brewing.

45

---

[5] **blueprints:** a print of the plan for a building or machine

Vocabulary Check

Write the boldfaced words from the reading next to the correct picture or definition. Use the correct form of the word.

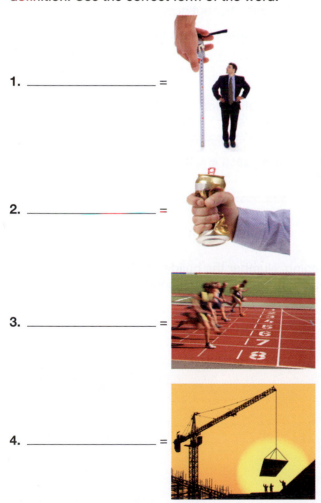

1. _____ =

2. _____ =

3. _____ =

4. _____ =

(continued on next page)

5. _____ =

6. _____ =

7. _____ = the levels in a building, especially in tall buildings

8. _____ = very extreme, strong

9. _____ = an object that has a special meaning or makes you think of a particular quality or idea

10. _____ = existing or happening only in a particular place

11. _____ = existing or happening in the past, but not now

12. _____ = the respect that someone gets from other people

> READ AGAIN

Read "Race for the Sky" again and complete the comprehension exercises. As you work, keep the reading goal in mind.

 READING GOAL: To identify and summarize the main ideas and key details

Comprehension Check

A. Work with a partner. Don't look back at the reading. Number the buildings in order of height. Write *1* next to the tallest building, *2* next to the second tallest, and so on.

_____ **a.** 40 Wall Street

_____ **b.** Taipei 101

_____ **c.** Empire State Building

_____ **d.** Burj Khalifa

_____ **e.** Chrysler Building

B. Answer the questions in your own words. Many of the answers are not in the reading. You will need to infer them.

1. Why did Van Alen and Severance want to win the competition so badly?

   _____

2. Why did Van Alen wait until the final day of construction to add a spire to the Chrysler building?

   _____

3. Why did General Motors want to build the Empire State Building?

   _____

4. Which building in the reading was not the tallest in the world when it was built?

   _____

5. Why is China building so many skyscrapers?

   _____

6. Why do you think the skyscraper in Taipei is called the "101"?

   _____

7. Why did the Taiwanese hold a celebration when the Taipei 101 opened?

   _____

8. In what ways is the Burj Khalifa "a symbol of the new Middle East"?

   _____

9. Why would the builders of the Burj Khalifa add more floors to the building in the future?

   _____

10. Are the countries in the reading similar to Van Alen and Severance? Explain.

   _____

Burj Khalifa on the right

C. Write a short paragraph comparing and contrasting the skyscraper competitions of the past with those occurring today. Use the words (and phrases) in the list. Give examples of buildings from the reading.

| businesspeople | intense competition | skyscrapers |
| countries | show economic power | the tallest building in the world |

_____

_____

_____

_____

_____

_____

> DISCUSS

A. Work with a partner. You are architects. Design your own skyscraper. Ask and answer the questions.

1. Where will the skyscraper be located?

2. Will the skyscraper be a symbol of something (e.g., a particular country or a particular idea such as economic power)?

3. What will the height of the skyscraper be?

4. How many floors will the skyscraper have?

5. What will you have inside the skyscraper (e.g., offices, apartments, or restaurants)?

6. How long will the construction of the skyscraper take?

7. What will make the skyscraper unique?

8. What will you name the skyscraper?

B. On a separate sheet of paper, draw a picture or diagram of your skyscraper. Add a label that tells the building's name, location, date when it will be built, and height in feet (and meters).

C. Share your drawing with the class. Listen to your classmates talk about their skyscrapers. Look at their drawings. Then choose your favorite skyscraper (don't choose your own). Explain why it is your favorite.

Anybody Want to Buy a Stadium?

> PREPARE TO READ

A. Look at the words (and phrases) in the list. Write the number(s) next to each word to show what you know. You may be able to write more than one number next to some of the words. You will study all of these words in this chapter.

1. I can use the word in a sentence.

2. I know <u>one meaning</u> of the word.

3. I know <u>more than one meaning</u> of the word.

4. I know how to pronounce the word.

B. Work with a partner. Look at the picture. Ask and answer the questions. If you don't know a word in English, ask your partner or look in your dictionary. Then write your new words on page 217.

1. What do you see in the picture? Point to the things you see and name them in English.

2. Where is the building located? Why was it built?

3. Is there a stadium in your hometown? What is it used for?

_____ add up

_____ circular

_____ controversial

_____ fade

_____ maintenance

_____ manager

_____ named after

_____ operation

_____ rent

_____ roof

_____ status

_____ worth it

Reading Skill: Recognizing Text References

Writers often *refer to* an idea from a previous sentence or paragraph in a reading. It is important to understand which idea the writer is referring to. Look at the examples from "Race to the Sky."

EXAMPLES:

*Van Alen and Severance each wanted to **build the tallest building in the world** . . .*
Van Alen won the <u>competition</u>.

↓

= to build the tallest building in the world

*The builders of the Burj Khalifa have said that they might **add more floors to the building** in the future. <u>This</u> isn't a bad idea.*

↓

= adding more floors to the building

C. Read the first paragraph of the magazine article "Anybody Want to Buy a Stadium?" Then answer the question.

What "really big thing" do host cities have to worry about?
a. tourists going home   **b.** excitement slowly fading   **c.** operation of stadiums

 READ

Read "Anybody Want to Buy a Stadium?" Notice the text references.

Anybody Want to Buy a Stadium?

1   The Olympic Games bring fame, **status**, and excitement to their host city. They also bring economic benefits. At the 2008 Summer Games in Beijing, China, for example, tourists spent
5   more than $2 billion. But then the tourists go home. The excitement slowly **fades**. The host city now has something to worry about—something really big. "The **operation** of stadiums after the Olympics," says one
10   stadium **manager** in Beijing, "is a worldwide problem."

Most stadiums cost $7–10 million per year to operate. A lot of the money goes into **maintenance**. In addition, there are
15   other costs, from paying stadium workers' salaries to fire insurance.[1] As the costs **add up**, the stadiums can become a big economic headache.
      When Nagano, Japan, hosted the 1998
20   Winter Games, the city built five stadiums. The plan was for people to enjoy the stadiums after the Olympics were over. But today, only two are used. One, the bobsled[2]

---

[1] **insurance:** an agreement in which you regularly pay money to a company, and it pays the costs if anything bad happens to you

[2] **bobsled:** a sport in which people race a small vehicle down a special ice road

168   UNIT 10 ■ Big Buildings

stadium, is closed all but two months of the
25 year. It costs $13,000 a day to keep the ice
frozen.³

Athens, Greece, host of the 2004 Summer
Games, has the same problem. All but one
of its twenty-two stadiums are now empty.
30 There is no water in the Olympic swimming
pool. Even so, the city has spent almost
$1 billion on maintenance. The situation has
many people in Athens feeling upset. "I used
to think the Olympics were **worth it**," says
35 Stelious Thanelas, who lives near one of the
empty stadiums. "Now I don't. The stadiums
aren't being used and nothing has been done."
The Greek government hopes to **rent** or sell
many of the stadiums to private⁴ companies.
40 So far, it has had little luck.

It seems that the bigger a stadium is,
the bigger the economic problem it creates.
Perhaps the most famous example is the
Olympic Stadium of Montreal, Canada. This
45 stadium, built for the 1976 Summer Games,
was originally called "The Big One" because of
its **circular** shape. But today it is more often
called "The Big Owe." The stadium's architect
wanted "The Big One" to be one of the greatest

50 buildings in the world. He created a complex
design, with a large tower on one side of
the stadium and swimming pools at the base
of the tower. He also created a special **roof**
that could open and close. The design was so
55 complex that workers were unable to complete
it in time for the opening of the Games. In
fact, construction on the stadium was not
completed until 1990, fourteen years later.
Originally expected to be around $115 million,
60 the stadium's final cost was over ten times
that amount. Canadian taxpayers⁵ only finished
paying for the stadium in 2006, after thirty
years. Today the stadium is in poor condition
and rarely used.

65 To solve its stadium problem, the city
of Montreal will need fresh ideas. Sydney,
Australia, may have the answer. This city, the
host of the 2000 Summer Games, found a way
to deal with its Olympic stadium problem.
70 In 2002, the Australian government sold the
rights⁶ to name the stadium. For six years,
the stadium was **named after** a telephone
company. Now the naming rights belong to a
bank, at a cost of $20 million over seven years.
75 The city also rents the stadium to local sports
teams. "For the first time, we expect to break
even," says a manager.

Beijing hopes to break even on its stadiums
as well. But the idea of naming rights is very
80 **controversial** in China. As one writer said,
"These are buildings of historical importance.
We cannot change their names just to make
money." Beijing, however, may not have any
other choice. As the people of Montreal know,
85 a big stadium, if not carefully managed, can
become a big mistake.

---

³ **frozen:** made very hard or turned to ice because of cold temperatures

⁴ **private:** not relating to or owned by the government

⁵ **taxpayers:** people who must pay money to the government, based on how much they earn, what they buy, etc.

⁶ **the rights:** things you can do according to the law

Vocabulary Check

Complete the sentences with the boldfaced words from the reading.

1. When I take a vacation, I usually _____ a car.

2. My name is Jack, and my father's name is Jack. I'm _____ my father.

3. Everyone argues about the plan; it is very _____.

4. When it rains, the _____ of your house gets wet.

5. A ring has a(n) _____ shape.

6. If you wash a shirt many times, the color _____.

7. The stadium cost a lot to build, but it has so many benefits. I think the stadium was _____.

8. Doctors are well respected in society; they have a lot of _____.

9. The _____ told the workers to go home.

10. The building needs _____: The floors are dirty, the paint is old, and one light doesn't work.

11. A pilot is responsible for the _____ of an airplane.

12. Ice cream isn't expensive, but if you buy it every day, it can _____ to a lot of money.

> READ AGAIN

Read "Anybody Want to Buy a Stadium?" again and complete the comprehension exercises on the next page. As you work, keep the reading goal in mind.

> **READING GOAL:** To identify the main reasons why stadiums cause problems

Comprehension Check

A. Complete the chart with information from the reading.

Host city	Olympics	Stadium problem
Montreal, Canada		
	1998 Winter Games	
		had to sell naming rights to a phone company, bank
	2004 Summer Games	
Beijing, China		

B. Find the sentences in the reading. What do the underlined words refer to? Circle the letter of the correct answer. The numbers in parentheses are the paragraphs where you can find the sentences.

1. They also bring economic benefits. (1)
   a. host cities
   b. status and excitement
   c. the Olympic Games

2. A lot of the money goes into maintenance. (2)
   a. $7–10 million per year
   b. workers' salaries and fire insurance
   c. $13,000 a day

3. When Nagano, Japan, hosted the 1998 Winter Games, the city built five stadiums. (3)
   a. the 1998 Winter Games
   b. Nagano
   c. Japan

(continued on next page)

4. But today, only <u>two</u> are used. (3)

    a. bobsleds

    b. stadiums

    c. games

5. Athens, Greece, host of the 2004 Summer Games, has the same <u>problem</u>. (4)

    a. hosting the Winter Olympics

    b. renting or selling stadiums to private companies

    c. paying for maintenance of empty stadiums

6. "I used to think the Olympics were worth <u>it</u>," says Stelious Thanelas, who lives near one of the empty stadiums. (4)

    a. the high cost of hosting the Olympics

    b. the excitement of being the host city

    c. putting water in the Olympic swimming pool

7. So far, <u>it</u> has had little luck. (4)

    a. maintenance

    b. the Greek government

    c. the stadium

8. Originally expected to be around $115 million, the stadium's final cost was over ten times <u>that amount</u>. (5)

    a. $115 million

    b. $20 million over seven years

    c. $1 billion

9. Sydney, Australia, may have the <u>answer</u>. (6)

    a. how to design a roof that opens and closes

    b. how to become the host city of the Olympic Games

    c. how to solve the stadium problem

10. Beijing, however, may not have any other <u>choice</u>.

    a. about selling naming rights

    b. about building a stadium

    c. about breaking even

C. Your home city wants to host the Olympics. Write a letter to the editor of your local newspaper telling your opinion. Say if hosting the Olympics is a good idea or not. Use details from the reading to support your opinion.

Dear Editor:

_____

_____

_____

_____

_____

_____

_____

_____

_____

_____

_____

_____

Sincerely,

_____

D. Compare letters with a classmate. Do you have the same opinion?

> DISCUSS

Work in small groups. Ask and answer the questions.

1. Has your home country ever hosted the Olympics? If so, when was it?

2. Would you like your home country to host the Olympics in the future? Explain.

3. Do you enjoy watching the Olympics? Which Olympic sports do you enjoy watching the most?

4. In what other ways could host cities solve their stadium problems?

> VOCABULARY SKILL BUILDING

Collocation Patterns

When you are learning new words, pay attention to patterns in the way they are used. Notice how certain words often pair up with specific words—this is called *collocation*. Learning common collocations will help you use words the way native English speakers do. For example, English speakers say *tall building*, not *high building*. Study these examples of collocation patterns.

EXAMPLES:

noun + verb	*architect designs*
verb + noun	*deliver news*
adjective + noun	*tallest skyscraper*
noun + noun	*status symbol*

A. Use each target word in the list to form two collocations. Sometimes the target word comes first and sometimes it comes second.

construction	~~intense~~	race
enemies	limited	rent

1. _____*intense*_____
   a. _____*intense*_____ competition
   b. _____*intense*_____ discussion

2. _____
   a. _____ time
   b. _____ budget

3. _____
   a. former _____
   b. bitter _____

4. _____
   a. _____ site
   b. _____ worker

5. _____
   a. foot _____
   b. _____ car

6. _____
   a. _____ increase
   b. _____ an apartment

B. Use two collocations above to write two sentences of your own.

1. _____

   _____

2. _____

   _____

Learn the Vocabulary

A. Write a definition for each boldfaced word. Your understanding of the word parts will help you. Pay attention to the context.

1. The Olympics is an **international** competition.

   definition of **international**: _____ *between countries* _____

2. I have an **unlimited** train pass, so I hope to do a lot of traveling.

   definition of **unlimited**: _____

3. My ticket cost less than Mary's; I think they **undercharged** me.

   definition of **undercharge**: _____

4. The team did not play fairly; the players' actions were **dishonorable**.

   definition of **dishonor**: _____

5. The new stadium is **unnamed**; I wonder what they will call it.

   definition of **unnamed**: _____

6. This skyscraper Web site allows you to **interact** with other people who are interested in tall buildings.

   definition of **interact**: _____

7. I think your behavior at the game last night was **inappropriate**.

   definition of **inappropriate**: _____

(continued on next page)

8. This sport is **underappreciated**; I feel as if I'm the only fan!

definition of **underappreciated**: _____

9. Sydney **renamed** its Olympic stadium; now it is called ANZ Stadium.

definition of **rename**: _____

10. The workers hope they can **reconstruct** the building damaged by the storm.

definition of **reconstruct**: _____

B. Now find the words from Exercise A in your dictionary and check your answers.

C. Make cards for the words from Chapters 19–20 that were new to you when you started the unit. Include target words and words that you wrote on page 217.

D. Go back to the vocabulary list at the beginning of each chapter. What did you learn about the target words? Add your numbers to the lists.

Vocabulary Practice 10, see page 227

UNIT 11

Body Language: The Science of Pheromones

"I wonder what pheromones she's wearing."

> THINK BEFORE YOU READ

A. Work with a partner. Look at the cartoon. Ask and answer the questions. If you don't know a word in English, ask your partner or look in your dictionary. Then write your new words on page 217.

    1. What do you see in the cartoon? Point to the things you see and name them in English.

    2. Why is the cartoon humorous? Explain.

    3. What do you think "pheromones" are?

B. Work with a partner. Ask and answer the questions.

    1. What do people do to be attractive to others? On a separate sheet of paper, make a list of ideas.

    2. Of the ideas on your list, which things do animals also do? Explain.

Pheromone Perfume

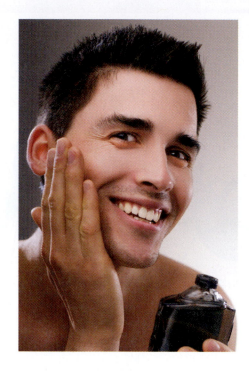

▶ PREPARE TO READ

A. Look at the words in the list. Write the number(s) next to each word to show what you know. You may be able to write more than one number next to some of the words. You will study all of these words in this chapter.

  1. I can use the word in a sentence.

  2. I know <u>one meaning</u> of the word.

  3. I know <u>more than one meaning</u> of the word.

  4. I know how to pronounce the word.

B. Work with a partner. Look at the pictures. Ask and answer the questions. If you don't know a word in English, ask your partner or look in your dictionary. Then write your new words on page 217.

  1. What are the people in the pictures doing to be attractive?

  2. What else do you see in the pictures? Point to the things you see and name them in English.

_____ biologist

_____ claim

_____ debate

_____ detect

_____ industry

_____ insect

_____ likely

_____ nevertheless

_____ process

_____ proof

_____ surgery

_____ sweat

C. Read the first two paragraphs of the magazine article "Pheromone Perfume." Check (✓) the statement about pheromones that is an opinion.

_____ **1.** Pheromones are chemicals produced by animals' bodies.

_____ **2.** Pheromone perfume makes the people who wear it more attractive to others.

 **READ**

Read "Pheromone Perfume." Underline three facts about pheromones.

Pheromone Perfume

1   People do many things to be attractive. They spend money on clothes, haircuts, and makeup. Some even undergo[1] plastic **surgery**. But there may be an easier way. The secret could
5 be pheromones. Pheromones are chemicals produced by animals' bodies. Some scientists believe that these chemicals can influence human behavior. These scientists think that if they add pheromones to perfume, the people
10 who wear it will become more attractive to others. They **claim** to have evidence that these pheromone perfumes really work. Other scientists have some doubts.
    "Nobody's really identified a [human]
15 pheromone," says **biologist** Richard Doty. In Doty's opinion, pheromones are just a way for the perfume **industry** to make more profits. So what is the truth? Do human pheromones exist? And can they really make people more
20 attractive?
    Although the topic of human pheromones is controversial, scientists know that animal pheromones exist. Over the last fifty years, scientific experiments have discovered
25 evidence of pheromones in dogs, cats, pigs, rats, rabbits, many types of **insects**, and even plants. These living things use pheromones to find each other and communicate. Insects, for example, use pheromones to find mates.
30 Studies show that flowers use pheromones to

(continued on next page)

---

[1] **undergo:** if you undergo something, it happens to you or is done to you

attract bees.[2] Some scientists believe humans may use pheromones in the same way—as chemical attractors.

There are, however, many questions about
35 how this chemical **process** would actually work in humans. Scientists are unsure, for example, how humans could **detect** pheromones. The theory is that people release pheromones when they **sweat**, and the pheromones then stay in
40 the air and are detected by other people. But pheromones cannot be seen, heard, tasted, touched, or smelled. Some scientists have suggested that humans detect pheromones through an undiscovered sixth sense.[3] Then
45 there is the question of how pheromones influence human behavior. "Even if pheromones do work," says Dr. Stuart Firestein, a biologist, "they're not **likely** to create an attraction all by themselves." In other words, being
50 attractive to other people probably requires more than pheromones.

Nevertheless, many companies are selling pheromone perfume. One example is the

Athena Institute, started in 1986 by biologist
55 Dr. Winnifred Cutler. In its advertisements, the Pennsylvania-based company claims its perfume works for 75 percent of people. But are pheromones the only possible explanation? "Maybe just knowing that you're wearing the
60 stuff will help," said Firestein. It could be that pheromones only exist in the minds of customers.

A recent study by ABC News makes the pheromone **debate** more interesting. In the
65 study, ABC tested pheromone perfume from the Athena Institute on twins.[4] Scientists gave one twin, Sarah, pheromone perfume, and her sister, Bridgette, regular perfume. The twins didn't know which perfume they were wearing.
70 They then talked to ten men, for five minutes each. Afterwards, nine of the ten men said they wanted to meet Sarah again. But only five said the same about Bridgette. ABC then tested pheromone perfume on male twins with
75 similar results.

Dr. Cutler often mentions the ABC study in her advertisements. "I think our product is the only product that has any **proof** behind its claims," she says. But most scientists are not
80 so sure. They say more studies will be necessary to prove the existence of human pheromones. Then there is the question of how much, if at all, pheromones influence human behavior. This research may take years to complete. For now,
85 pheromone perfume is selling for about $100 a bottle on Dr. Cutler's Web site.

---

[2] **bees:** black and yellow flying insects that make honey

[3] **sixth sense:** a special ability to know things without using any of your five ordinary senses such as hearing or sight

[4] **twins:** two children born at the same time to the same mother

Vocabulary Check

A. Write the letter of the correct definition next to the target word.

_____ **1.** surgery   **a.** facts, information, etc., that show something is true

_____ **2.** claim   **b.** medical treatment in which a doctor cuts open your body to fix something

_____ **3.** process   **c.** to notice something, especially something that is not easy to see, hear, etc.

_____ **4.** detect   **d.** a discussion on a subject in which people express different opinions

_____ **5.** debate   **e.** to say that something is true even though it might not be

_____ **6.** proof   **f.** a series of actions or changes that happen naturally

B. Complete the sentences with the boldfaced words from the reading.

1. It was raining; _____ I went for a walk outside.

2. Look at those dark clouds; I think it is _____ to rain later.

3. Those companies all make computers; they are part of the same _____.

4. He studies living things; he is a(n) _____.

5. I have screens on my window so that _____ won't come in the house.

6. If you _____ a lot when you exercise, your clothes will get wet.

Read "Pheromone Perfume" again and complete the comprehension exercises. As you work, keep the reading goal in mind.

> 📖 **READING GOAL:** To identify the facts and opinions about pheromones

Comprehension Check

A. Find the sentences in the reading. What do the underlined words refer to? Circle the letter of the correct answer. The numbers in parentheses are the paragraphs where you can find the sentences.

1. The secret could be pheromones. (1)
  a. how to undergo surgery
  b. how to be attractive
  c. how become a scientist

2. And can they really make people more attractive? (2)
  a. scientists
  b. perfume
  c. pheromones

3. There are, however, many questions about how this chemical process would actually work in humans. (4)
  a. how flowers use pheromones to attract bees
  b. how pheromones are produced and detected
  c. how scientific experiments have discovered pheromones

4. One example is the Athena Institute, started in 1986 by biologist Dr. Winnifred Cutler. (5)
  a. a business that advertises its products
  b. a company that sells pheromone perfume
  c. a university that teaches biology

5. But are pheromones the only possible explanation? (5)
  a. why the Athena Institute advertises its products
  b. why the Athena Institute's perfume works for some people
  c. why Dr. Winnifred Cutler started the Athena Institute

6. "Maybe just knowing that you're wearing <u>the stuff</u> will help," said Firestein. (5)

  a. attractive clothing

  b. pheromone perfume

  c. makeup

7. "I think our product is the only product that has <u>any proof</u> behind its claims," she says. (7)

  a. Dr. Firestein's research

  b. the ABC study

  c. the Athena Institute's advertising

8. <u>This research</u> may take years to complete. (7)

  a. finding out what percentage of scientists believe in human pheromones

  b. studying how much customers will pay for a bottle of pheromone perfume

  c. learning whether human pheromones exist, and how they work

B. There are eight mistakes (including the example) in the summary of "Pheromone Perfume." Find the mistakes and correct them. When you finish, look at the reading again to check your answers.

(1) bodies

Pheromones are chemicals produced by animals' ~~minds~~. Scientists think

that pheromones might also influence human behavior. They may help us

to ignore others. Some scientists have created pheromone drinks. But do

these products really work?

In nature, pheromones are chemical attractors. For example, some plants

use pheromones to attract sunlight. One theory is that we release pheromones

when we swim, and other people detect the pheromones using all five senses.

There is some evidence that pheromone perfume really works. One

study tested pheromone perfume on rats. The study suggested that

pheromone perfume makes a person twice as attractive as regular perfume.

Most scientists agree that no more research is needed on pheromones. For

now, pheromone perfume is selling for about $100 a bottle.

C. Read the conversation between two students. Are the underlined statements facts or opinions? Write *F* or *O*.

_____ **Chen:** I can't believe this topic. <u>You can't attract people just with pheromones</u>.

_____ **Lucy:** Well, I'm not so sure. <u>Animals use pheromones as chemical attractors</u>; maybe we do too.

_____ **Chen:** There's no proof human pheromones exist. <u>Pheromones are just a way for the perfume industry to make profits.</u>

_____ **Lucy:** Well, I guess <u>the pheromone perfume *is* overpriced.</u>

_____ **Chen:** I'll say! <u>It sells for $100 a bottle!</u> Why would people waste their money?

_____ **Lucy:** I don't know, Chen, there is some evidence the perfume works. Remember, <u>ABC tested pheromone perfume on twins named Bridgette and Sarah.</u> Nine out of ten men wanted to meet Sarah again, the one wearing the perfume.

_____ **Chen:** The men didn't want to meet Sarah again because she was wearing pheromone perfume. <u>It was because of something else, like her personality.</u>

_____ **Lucy:** You should be more open-minded. You'll see, Chen. <u>One day, scientists will prove pheromone perfume really works.</u>

> DISCUSS

A. Work in small groups. Imagine that you are on a television show about pheromones. One student is the host of the show. The other students should each choose a different character from the list. The host welcomes the guests. The host then asks the guests questions. Guests should only answer one question at a time.

Characters:

Richard Doty	Sarah (the twin from the ABC study)
Dr. Winnifred Cutler	a flower that uses pheromones to attract bees
Dr. Stuart Firestein	

EXAMPLE QUESTIONS:

What are pheromones?

How do pheromones work?

How important are pheromones in your life?

What is your opinion about pheromone perfume?

B. Work in small groups. What is your opinion about pheromone perfume? Ask and answer the questions.

1. Do you think pheromone perfume really works?

2. Do you want to try pheromone perfume? Why or why not?

3. How much would you pay for pheromone perfume?

4. What other studies could scientists do to find out if pheromone perfume really works?

The Language of Pheromones

> PREPARE TO READ

A. Look at the words (and phrases) in the list. Write the number(s) next to each word to show what you know. You may be able to write more than one number next to some of the words. You will study all of these words in this chapter.

    1. I can use the word in a sentence.

    2. I know <u>one meaning</u> of the word.

    3. I know <u>more than one meaning</u> of the word.

    4. I know how to pronounce the word.

B. Work with a partner. Look at the pictures. Ask and answer the questions. If you don't know a word in English, ask your partner or look in your dictionary. Then write your new words on page 217.

    1. Which insects and other living things do you see in the pictures?

    2. What special abilities does each creature have?

    3. What does each creature eat?

_____ alarm

_____ attack

_____ blocked

_____ care for

_____ depend on

_____ head toward

_____ species

_____ stage

_____ trail

_____ trap

_____ vision

_____ weapon

C. Read the introduction of "The Language of Pheromones." Then answer the questions.

1. Which sentence in the introduction tells the main idea of the reading?

_____

2. What is the main idea of the reading? Rephrase it.

_____

> READ

Read "The Language of Pheromones" on the next page. Underline the sentence that gives the main idea of the whole reading.

A Mountain Alcon Blue Butterfly

The Language of Pheromones

1   Florida farmer Henry Lohfner doesn't like moths. "They eat my vegetables," he complains. But Lohfner has a secret **weapon** in his fight against moths: pheromones.

5   Lohfner uses **traps** that release a female moth pheromone that is very attractive to male moths. Lohfner says that his traps catch almost 100 moths a week. For these moths, following pheromones causes their death.

10 Nevertheless, for other moths and many insects, life would not be possible without pheromones.

For moths, pheromones are a matter of life and death. Moths have poor **vision**, and

15 most cannot use sound to communicate. As a result, most moths **depend on** pheromones to send messages. Female moths release pheromones from their legs and wings. These pheromones can stay in the air for

20 hours. A male moth can identify female moth pheromones from as many as five miles away.

Like moths, ants use pheromones to find each other; they also use pheromones to find their homes and food. When an ant finds food,

25 it takes a piece and **heads toward** home. Along the way, it releases a **trail** of pheromones. Other ants follow the trail to find the food. If the trail becomes **blocked**, the ants look for a new way to reach the food. When they find

30 the shortest way, they create a new trail of pheromones. In this way, pheromones help ants adapt to changes in their environment.

Ants even have different pheromones for different purposes. When an ant is

35 hurt, it produces an "**alarm**" pheromone. Other ants identify the alarm pheromone and immediately come to help the hurt ant. The more serious the alarm, the more pheromones the ant produces. In this way,

40 ants can quickly organize when they are in danger. Large groups of ants will form to fight insects hundreds of times their size. Some **species** of ants even use "trick" pheromones. Fire ants,[1] for example, use trick pheromones

45 to **attack** the homes of other ants. The trick pheromones confuse other ants and cause them to attack each other.

Some insects, remarkably, can use trick pheromones to imitate other species. This

50 can help them to find a meal, or in the case of the Mountain Alcon Blue butterfly,[2] to avoid becoming the meal. During its caterpillar **stage**, this unusual insect releases a pheromone similar to that of an ant. If ants

55 find a Mountain Alcon Blue butterfly caterpillar in the forest, they carry it home. There, instead of eating it, they **care for** it—as if it were a family member. The caterpillar is given a private room and lots of food. If attacked, the

60 mistaken ants will give their lives to protect the caterpillar, just as they would for their offspring.[3]

Another creature has even learned how to use pheromones in the same way as farmer

65 Henry Lohfner—to catch moths. The bolas spider, a species common in South America and Africa, produces a pheromone similar to that of a female moth. It waits in trees for a male moth to arrive. Hoping to find a

70 female, the moth becomes a meal for the spider instead.

To sum up, pheromones are involved in every part of insect life, from communication to finding food and protecting the home.

75 Many biologists say pheromones are the true language of insects. And now, it is a language biologists are starting to understand.

---

[1] **fire ant:** a species of ant that builds large piles of earth to live in and has a painful bite

[2] **butterfly:** an insect with large and usually very colorful wings

[3] **offspring:** an animal's baby or babies

Vocabulary Check

Circle the letter of the correct answer to complete each sentence. The boldfaced words are the target words.

1. When children _____, mothers **care for** them.
   a. don't behave well
   b. are sick
   c. get good grades

2. You hear an **alarm** when there is a _____.
   a. fire
   b. party
   c. delivery

3. An example of a **weapon** is a _____.
   a. television
   b. gun
   c. moth

4. The road was **blocked** by a _____.
   a. rain cloud
   b. dark night
   c. fallen tree

5. People **attack** _____.
   a. enemies during a war
   b. a building after a bad storm
   c. an idea they agree with

6. In the morning, students **head toward** _____.
   a. books
   b. school
   c. tests

7. You can find a **trail** _____.
   a. inside a building
   b. into the ocean
   c. up a mountain

8. The **stages** of life are _____.
   a. food, sleep, and a home
   b. childhood, adulthood, and old age
   c. friends, family, and teachers

(continued on next page)

9. Children **depend on** _____.

   a. playing games

   b. television

   c. their parents

10. If you have poor **vision**, you probably _____.

    a. wear glasses

    b. need training

    c. speak loudly

11. One **species** of butterfly is _____.

    a. a caterpillar

    b. the Mountain Alcon Blue butterfly

    c. a biologist

12. One use of a **trap** is to _____.

    a. catch a mouse

    b. take a picture

    c. hold a liquid

> READ AGAIN

Read "The Language of Pheromones" again and complete the comprehension exercises. As you work, keep the reading goal in mind.

📖 **READING GOAL:** To summarize the main ideas about how insects and spiders use pheromones

Comprehension Check

A. Check (✓) the ways each insect or spider uses pheromones.

	To find mates	To find food	To trick others	To send an alarm message
Moths				
Fire ants				
Mountain Alcon Blue butterflies				
Bolas spiders				

B. Check (✓) the statement that best summarizes each paragraph.

1. Paragraph 2:

   _____ **a.** Only female moths release pheromones.

   _____ **b.** Moths need pheromones to communicate.

   _____ **c.** Male moths can identify pheromones from far away.

2. Paragraph 3:

   _____ **a.** Ants use pheromones to change their environments.

   _____ **b.** Ants follow pheromone trails so they don't get lost.

   _____ **c.** Ants use pheromones to find food and bring it home.

3. Paragraph 4:

   _____ **a.** Ants also have trick and alarm pheromones.

   _____ **b.** Ants are not afraid to fight other species because of pheromones.

   _____ **c.** Ants are able to confuse other ants with pheromones.

4. Paragraph 5:

   _____ **a.** Some ants use pheromones to find caterpillars.

   _____ **b.** The Mountain Alcon Blue butterfly uses trick pheromones to imitate an ant.

   _____ **c.** Ants will give their own lives if they detect caterpillar pheromones.

5. Paragraph 6:

   _____ **a.** Moths often die because they follow pheromones.

   _____ **b.** Insects in South America and Africa use pheromones in unusual ways.

   _____ **c.** The bolas spider uses pheromones to catch moths.

C. Write a summary of the main ideas of the reading. Use the main idea sentences you identified in the reading and your answers to Exercise B to help you. Be sure to use your own words to summarize the reading.

_____

_____

_____

_____

_____

_____

_____

> VOCABULARY SKILL BUILDING

Knowing the Meanings of Roots

Some words in English contain a *root*—usually a Greek or Latin word part. Like a prefix, a root has a special meaning, but it is not a word in English by itself. Instead, it appears as a part of other words with related meanings that contain the same root. For example, *bio* is a Greek root. It means *life*. It is part of the target word *biologist*. It appears in other words with related meanings, such as *biofuel* (fuel made from living things).

Knowing the meanings of common word roots in English will help you figure out the meanings of other words that contain the same roots.

A. Study the chart of common roots and example words. Complete the chart with the correct meanings from the list. Your understanding of the example words will help you.

against	good	people	step
believe	~~life~~	place	

Roots	Example words	Meanings of roots
bio	*bio*logy, *bio*logist	life
pop	*pop*ular, *pop*ulation	
loc	*loc*al, *loc*ation	
bene	*bene*fit, *bene*ficial	
cred	*cred*it, in*cred*ible	
grad	*grad*es, *grad*uate	
contro / contra	*contro*versial, in *contra*st	

B. Study the boldfaced words. Circle the letter of the correct definition. Your understanding of the meanings of roots will help you.

1. Scientists are **gradually** learning more about pheromones.
   a. suddenly, quickly
   b. slowly, over time

2. I think the idea of human pheromones is **credible**.
   a. interesting
   b. believable

3. His wife always **contradicts** what he says.
   a. disagrees, says the opposite of
   b. agrees, has the same opinion as

4. The book's **locale** changes many times.
   a. story, main idea
   b. place where something happens

5. The science center was built with the help of a **benefactor**.
   a. someone who gives money for a good purpose
   b. someone who owns a construction company

6. Hong Kong is a **populous** city.
   a. expensive
   b. full of people

7. I'm reading a **biography** of a famous scientist.
   a. a book that tells someone's life story
   b. a magazine that contains articles about science

Learn the Vocabulary

The Keyword Technique

There are many ways to remember the meaning of a new word. Research on language learners shows that the keyword technique works well for many learners. Here's how it works:

1. Look at the new word and choose a *keyword*. A keyword is a word in your native language that sounds similar to the beginning or all of the new word in English. Look at the example from a native speaker of Spanish.

   EXAMPLE:

   New word = *trail*
   Keyword (Spanish word for "three" that sounds similar to *trail*) = *tres*

2. Imagine a picture that connects the meaning of the new word and the meaning of the keyword in some way. The connection can be strange. In fact, strange pictures are often easier to remember!

3. To remember the word *trail* in English, think of the image of the *tres* trails, or the *tres* in the sky, as shown on the word card.

4. Draw the picture on the back of your word card, with the English word and its pronunciation (phonetic respelling) on the front.

A. Think of five target words from the unit and write them. Then write keywords next to the target words.

Target word

Keyword (a word in your native language that sounds similar to the beginning or all of the new word)

1. _____   _____

2. _____   _____

3. _____   _____

4. _____   _____

5. _____   _____

B. Now imagine a picture to connect the target word and the keyword for each of the new words in Exercise A. Draw the picture on the back of a word card. Write the new word on the other side of the card.

C. Show your cards to a classmate. Explain your pictures by pronouncing the keywords and telling your partner the meanings in your native language.

D. Look at the new words you wrote on page 217. Make word cards for any additional words from Chapters 21–22 that you want to study.

E. Add the new cards to your other cards. Review all of your cards with a partner.

F. Go back to the vocabulary list at the beginning of each chapter. What did you learn about the target words? Add your numbers to the lists.

Vocabulary Practice 11, see page 228

UNIT 12 High Seas, High Tech

> THINK BEFORE YOU READ

A. Work with a partner. Look at the picture. Ask and answer the questions. If you don't know a word in English, ask your classmate or look in a dictionary. Then write your new words on page 217.

    1. What do you see in the picture? Point to the things you see and name them in English.

    2. Have you ever been sailing? If so, what was it like?

B. Imagine you are setting out on a one-year sailing trip. What will you bring? On a separate sheet of paper, make a list of ten things.

C. Work with a partner. Compare your lists. Together choose five of the most important things to take with you. Explain your ideas to another pair of students.

The Chronometer

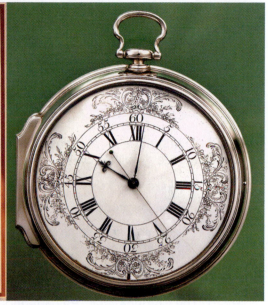

 PREPARE TO READ

_____	accurate
_____	century
_____	constant
_____	deserve
_____	endure
_____	invent
_____	model
_____	observe
_____	on board
_____	repair
_____	sailor
_____	tough

A. Look at the words (and phrases) in the list. Write the number(s) next to each word to show what you know. You may be able to write more than one number next to some of the words. You will study all of these words in this chapter.

    1. I can use the word in a sentence.

    2. I know <u>one meaning</u> of the word.

    3. I know <u>more than one meaning</u> of the word.

    4. I know how to pronounce the word.

B. Work with a partner. Look at the picture and map. Ask and answer the questions. If you don't know a word in English, ask your partner or look in your dictionary. Then write your new words on page 217.

    1. What do you see in the picture and map?

    2. Why is a map useful to have on a sailing ship?

    3. Are maps easy to make? Explain.

Reading Skill: Identifying Problems and Solutions

Identifying problems and solutions helps you better understand what you read. Many readings include a problem that a person, group, or imaginary character has to solve. To identify problems and solutions as you read, ask yourself questions such as these:

- What problem does the person or group of people have?
- What does the person or group do to try to solve the problem?
- How is the problem eventually solved?

The person, group, or character may have more than one problem to solve, but the problems are usually related in some way. If you understand the basic problem in a reading, and the solution to that problem, it will help you understand how the reading is organized. It will also make the text easier for you to summarize.

C. Read the first three paragraphs of the textbook article "The Chronometer." Check (✓) the problem John Harrison set out to solve.

_____ **1.** the sextant problem

_____ **2.** the longitude problem

_____ **3.** the ship captain problem

 **READ**

Read "The Chronometer." Pay attention to the problems John Harrison has to solve.

ೞ **The Chronometer** ಞ

1   It was the greatest scientific problem of the time. As **sailors** traveled the world's oceans, they did not know the exact location of their ships. Some ships entered dangerous waters. Powerful storms sent them to the bottom of the ocean. Other ships sailed into rocks. Those who survived often could
5   not find their way home. It was a dangerous time to be a sailor.

    This was the eighteenth **century**. To make a safe journey, a ship's captain needed to know his ship's longitude and latitude. Longitude and latitude are lines on a map of the Earth. They are used to pinpoint[1] an exact location. Latitude lines go from left to right and tell north-
10 south position. Longitude lines go up and down and tell east-west position. By **observing** the sun, moon, and stars with a sextant,[2] eighteenth century ships were able to find their latitude but not their longitude. As a result, maps were not **accurate**. Ship captains had to guess their longitude, often with disastrous results.

---

[1] **pinpoint:** to say exactly what something is, or exactly where someone or something is

[2] **sextant:** an instrument that measures the angle between two objects in the sky to figure out location or direction

15   In 1714, the British government decided to offer an award of 20,000 pounds (several million dollars today) to anyone who could solve the longitude problem. Clockmaker John Harrison (1693–1776) decided to make solving the problem his life's work.

20   Although Harrison had little formal education, he had always been interested in clocks. No one knows for sure when Harrison's interest in clocks began. Some say his parents gave him a clock when he was six and Harrison entertained himself by studying every moving part. As a teenager, Harrison started **repairing** broken clocks. By age twenty, he had built his own clock. Then one day he wondered, "What if a clock could tell a ship's longitude?"

25   In theory, the idea was simple. Time changes depending on one's position in the world. The time moves forward as one travels east and backward as one travels west. Therefore, if a ship captain knows the local time in two places, he knows how far apart they are. For example, if the time difference is twelve hours, the captain knows that the places are on opposite sides of the world. The time

30   difference is the same as the difference in longitude between the two places. Harrison understood this and decided to **invent** a new type of clock called a chronometer. The chronometer would tell London time. A traveling captain could compare his local time (using the sun's position) to the time in London. The farther the ship was from London, the greater the difference in time would

35   be between the two locations. In order for the chronometer to work, however, Harrison needed to solve two more problems.

The big, wooden clocks that were common in the eighteenth century would not work **on board** a ship. Most of them lost time after a few days. Harrison's clock would have to keep time[3] for months, even years. To keep ticking[4] day

40   after day on a ship, the clock would also need to be very **tough**. It would have to survive **constant** movement. It would have to **endure** storms. Even worse, it would have to work under any weather conditions, extreme heat, cold, or rain. It would need to be the strongest and most accurate clock ever built.

For the next thirty years, Harrison built many different chronometers and

45   tested them on land and at sea. He made each **model** smaller, stronger, and more accurate. Finally, he felt he had the perfect design. His model looked like a pocket watch and was made of metal, glass, and stone.

In 1761, the sixty-eight-year-old Harrison tested his model. He sent his chronometer with his son William to the Caribbean island of Jamaica. When the

50   ship arrived months later, the clock was only five seconds slow. It had predicted the longitude within 1 mile.

It would take another twelve years for Harrison to be given the longitude award. Many people couldn't believe that Harrison's clock was really that accurate. Some thought he had just been lucky. Harrison finally received the

55   award in 1773, but only after the king had personally tested the clock. At eighty years of age, just three years before his death, Harrison received the fame and money he **deserved**.

Harrison's life work was a big success. Because of his chronometer, sea captains could finally make accurate maps. Even today, every ship has a chronometer.

60   Sailors know the exact location of their ships. Thanks to Harrison, life at sea is much less dangerous.

---

[3] **keep time:** to stay accurate and always tells the correct time

[4] **ticking:** making a short sound every second

Vocabulary Check

Complete the text with the boldfaced words from the reading.

Today in the twenty-first (1) _____, John Harrison is a
hero to (2) _____, the people who live and work on ships. But
Harrison was not the only person who hoped to (3) _____,
or create, a method for measuring longitude. Other clockmakers tried and
failed. Their clocks could not (4) _____ life on a ship; after a
few weeks, the clocks stopped working. The clocks were not very
(5) _____: They were made of wood and broke easily.
Once they broke, (6) _____ them was impossible.
Only a clockmaker knew how to fix them. Other clocks were not
(7) _____: They started telling the wrong time after a couple
days. None were as perfect or tough as Harrison's chronometers, such as
the H4—the (8) _____ that won the longitude award.

Nevil Maskelyne, an astronomer,[1] thought he could figure out longitude
by watching, or (9) _____, the moon's position.
In 1764, Harrison's chronometer was tested against Maskeylne's system.
Maskelyne traveled (10) _____ a ship with the H4 for
three months. The test showed that Maskelyne's system was less
accurate than Harrison's. His system also required (11) _____
effort—many times each day, Maskelyne had to carefully observe the
sun and moon.

Nevertheless, Maskelyne said that he (12) _____ to win
the longitude award. He said that the H4 did not work. Most people believed
Maskelyne because he was a famous astronomer. Fortunately for Harrison,
the king did not.

---

[1] **astronomer:** a scientist who studies the stars and planets

Read "The Chronometer" again and complete the comprehension exercises. As you work, keep the reading goal in mind.

> 📖 **READING GOAL:** To understand the problems that John Harrison faced and how he solved them

Comprehension Check

A. Check (✓) the best explanation of the longitude problem.

_____ **1.** During bad weather, ship captains could not observe the sun or find their ship's north-south or east-west position.

_____ **2.** By observing the sun, ship captains could tell their north-south position, but not their east-west position.

_____ **3.** Using a sextant, ship captains could tell their east-west position, but not their north-south position.

_____ **4.** By reading a map, ship captains could not be sure if their ship was heading north, south, east, or west.

B. Put the events from the story into the correct sequence. Write *1* next to the first event, *2* next to the second, and so on.

_____ **1.** Harrison is given the longitude award.

_____ **2.** The British government offers an award.

_____ **3.** Harrison feels he has finally gotten the perfect design.

_____ **4.** Harrison decides to invent the chronometer.

_____ **5.** The chronometer is sent to Jamaica.

_____ **6.** The king tests the chronometer himself.

_____ **7.** Many people do not believe the chronometer really works.

_____ **8.** Harrison tests the early models of the chronometer.

C. Answer the questions in your own words. Some of the answers are not in the reading. You will need to infer them.

1. How has sailing changed since the eighteenth century?

_____

2. Why was it more difficult for ship captains to figure out longitude than latitude?

_____

3. Why did Harrison's chronometer tell London time, not a ship's local time?

_____

4. Why was Harrison not satisfied with the early models of the chronometer?

_____

5. Why did Harrison use metal, glass, and stone instead of wood to build his chronometer?

_____

6. Which paragraph in the reading describes how Harrison solved the basic problem?

_____

7. Why do you think some people felt Harrison had just been lucky?

_____

8. Why do you think the king tested Harrison's clock himself?

_____

9. How do you think Harrison felt when he finally won the award?

_____

D. Compare answers from Exercise C with a partner's. If your answers are different, explain your ideas. Decide who is correct.

> DISCUSS

Work in small groups. Ask and answer the questions.

1. Have you used a map recently? Explain.

2. Do you know any other famous inventors?

3. What new thing would you like to invent? What problem would your invention solve?

CHAPTER 24

The Treasure of the SS *Central America*

The Wreck of the SS *Central America* by J. Childs

> PREPARE TO READ

A. Look at the words (and phrases) in the list. Write the number(s) next to each word to show what you know. You may be able to write more than one number next to some of the words. You will study all of these words in this chapter.

    1. I can use the word in a sentence.

    2. I know <u>one meaning</u> of the word.

    3. I know <u>more than one meaning</u> of the word.

    4. I know how to pronounce the word.

B. Work with a partner. Look at the picture. Ask and answer the questions. If you don't know a word in English, ask your partner or look in your dictionary. Then write your new words on page 217.

    1. What do you see in the picture? Point to the things you see and name them in English.

    2. What might the reading be about? Invent a story using the picture.

_____ coast

_____ convince

_____ desperate

_____ determined

_____ equipment

_____ insure

_____ investigate

_____ mystery

_____ sink

_____ task

_____ the rest

_____ ton

C. Read the first three paragraphs of the magazine article "The Treasure of the SS *Central America*." Then answer the questions.

1. Who is the most important person in the reading?

2. What problem is this person trying to solve?

 **READ**

Read "The Treasure of the SS *Central America*." Underline the problems the main character has to solve.

The Treasure of the SS *Central America*

1　　As a child, Tommy Thompson (1952–) loved science. At age eight, he built his own telephone. He also loved secrets. Perhaps that was why he became interested in the ocean
5　as he grew older. It was full of secrets. And shipwrecks fascinated him, particularly one: the wreck of the SS *Central America*.

　　In 1857 the SS *Central America* was sailing from Panama to New York with twenty-one
10　**tons** of gold on board. The ship was also carrying hundreds of gold miners[1] and their families. One hundred sixty miles off the **coast**, a hurricane hit the ship. For three days, the sailors fought to save the ship. Each day the
15　storm grew stronger. As the ship slowly took on water, the **desperate** passengers realized that the fruits of their labor[2] were about to be lost. They threw their gold into the ocean, but it was too late to save themselves. The
20　SS *Central America* **sank**, taking 425 of the 578 passengers down with it.

　　For years, treasure seekers had searched for the sunken ship, with no success. However, Thompson was **determined** to find

25　the SS *Central America*. He read hundreds of historical news reports
30　about the disaster and tried to figure out the ship's location. He also **convinced** investors to pay for his research. With their money, he bought
35　advanced sonar[3] **equipment**. Using airplanes and a research ship, Thompson set out to find the SS *Central America*.

　　The **task** would not be easy. The ship had sunk in a part of the ocean that was over
40　8,500 feet (2,590 meters) deep. As soon as Thompson began his search, other ships started to follow him. At times, they came dangerously close to his ship.

　　To locate the shipwreck, Thompson used
45　sonar to create images of the ocean floor. On a clear day in 1987, he got lucky. The sonar found an object in the shape of a ship. Thompson sent down a robotic[4] submarine with

---

[1] **gold miners:** people who work in gold mines (deep holes in the ground, from which gold is dug)

[2] **labor:** work

[3] **sonar:** equipment on a ship or submarine that uses sound waves to find out the position of objects under the water

[4] **robotic:** run by a machine that can do the work of a person

a camera to **investigate**. As the submarine got closer to the bottom, Thompson noticed something yellowish. Everywhere he looked, he saw gold bars and coins. He described it as "a garden of gold."

Thompson had found the treasure, but the real work was just beginning. Somehow, he had to get the gold to the surface. Thompson returned to his investors for more money. He needed a special submarine that could lift the gold up 8,500 feet (2,590 meters). Excited by the idea of gold, the investors quickly agreed. News of Thompson's discovery was everywhere. Soon, thirty-seven companies filed suit[5] for the money. They had **insured** the gold on the SS *Central America*. When the ship sank, they lost a lot of money. Now, they wanted their money back. Some said the gold was worth $100 million. Others said it was worth much more, perhaps even $1 billion.

For weeks, Thompson slowly brought the gold to the surface and hid it in a secret location. After years of legal fighting, a court awarded the insurance companies a small share of the gold, worth $5.5 million. Before long, Thompson's former workers were also asking for money. They said Thompson had promised them a share of the treasure. Then Tommy's investors began to complain. They wanted Tommy to pay them back.

In 2006, after secretly selling a large amount of gold to a California businessman, Thompson disappeared. Some believed he was hiding **the rest** of the gold. His fans said he was looking for other shipwrecks. Others believed he was hiding from his investors. The last time Tommy Thompson's name appeared in the news, his whereabouts[6] were unknown. Is the person who always loved secrets searching for another shipwreck? Will he solve another deep-sea mystery? Only time will tell.

---

[5] **file suit:** to bring to a court of law a problem or complaint to be settled, especially for money

[6] **whereabouts:** the place where someone or something is

Vocabulary Check

A. Write the letter of the correct definition next to the target word.

_____ **1.** coast

_____ **2.** insure

_____ **3.** task

_____ **4.** desperate

_____ **5.** ton

_____ **6.** equipment

_____ **7.** convince

a. the land next to the ocean

b. a unit of weight equal to 2,000 pounds

c. the tools, machines, etc., that you need for a particular activity

d. to make someone feel certain that something is true

e. a job or particular thing that you have to do

f. to pay a company regularly so the company will pay the costs if anything bad happens

g. willing to do anything to change a bad situation

B. Complete the sentences with the boldfaced words from the reading.

1. If I found a lot of money, I'd keep a little and give _____ to my family.

2. No one can explain what happened; it is a(n) _____.

3. The ship _____; now it is on the bottom of the ocean.

4. The task is difficult, but I will not quit until I succeed; I'm

   _____.

5. The scientist wanted to find out the truth, so he decided to

   _____.

> READ AGAIN

Read "The Treasure of the SS *Central America*" again and complete the comprehension exercises. As you work, keep the reading goal in mind.

> 📖 **READING GOAL:** To understand the problems Tommy Thompson faced and how he solved them

Comprehension Check

A. Rephrase the problems Tommy Thompson has to solve. Find as many examples as you can in the reading.

He has to figure out the ship's location.

_____

_____

_____

_____

_____

_____

B. Work with a partner. Write *T* (true) or *F* (false). If it is not possible to tell, write *?*.

_____ **1.** When the SS *Central America* sank, everyone on board died.

_____ **2.** Before Thompson found the SS *Central America*, other people knew it existed.

_____ **3.** Thompson could not have found the SS *Central America* without the help of his investors.

_____ **4.** One of Thompson's airplanes first located the SS *Central America*.

_____ **5.** Thompson worked alone while he was searching for the SS *Central America*.

_____ **6.** The SS *Central America* sank near the coast.

_____ **7.** Thompson used different submarines for different purposes.

_____ **8.** The gold Thompson found was worth almost $1 billion.

_____ **9.** Thompson sold some of the gold he found.

_____ **10.** Now, Thompson is looking for other shipwrecks.

C. Work in small groups. Your teacher will give each group a number. Each group will act out a different part of a play called *Tommy Thompson and the Missing Gold*. Find your group's part of the play below:

1. The SS *Central America* sinks in a hurricane.

2. Young Tommy Thompson becomes interested in science and the ocean.

3. Thompson convinces investors to give him money and prepares to set out.

4. Thompson finds the wreck of the SS *Central America*.

5. Thompson brings the gold to the surface.

6. Everyone wants their money, but where is Tommy Thompson?

D. With your partners, follow these steps to prepare for your acting:

- Decide basically what happens in your part of the play.
- Decide which characters each student in your group will play (for example, one student is Tommy Thompson, another student is a sailor on his ship, etc.).
- Write what you will say on pieces of paper.
- Practice reading your lines together. Try to remember what you will say.

E. Watch the other groups act out their parts of the story. Do they get the details right?

> DISCUSS

Work in small groups. Which of the words and phrases in the list describe Tommy Thompson? Explain your answers with details from the reading.

admirable	a robber	intelligent	rebellious
a hard worker	controversial	likely to reappear	remarkable
a risk-taker	inspiring	lucky	trustworthy

VOCABULARY SKILL BUILDING

Suffix: -able

Like the suffix -ful, the suffix -able can be added to some verbs to make them adjectives. The suffix -able means "able to." For example, if a ship is *sinkable*, the ship is *able to sink*. If the verb ends in *e*, you will usually have to remove the *e* before adding the suffix.

EXAMPLES:

sink (verb) + **-able** = *sinkable* (adjective)

insure (verb) + **-able** = *insurable* (adjective)

A. Add the suffix -able to the verbs and write the adjective form.

Verb	Adjective
1. sink	*sinkable*
2. insure	*insurable*
3. endure	_____
4. detect	_____
5. repair	_____
6. debate	_____
7. depend	_____
8. honor	_____

B. Complete the sentences with the words from Exercise A. The boldfaced words will help you choose the correct word.

1. **People do not agree** about how much gold Thompson found. The amount of gold is _____.

2. You **can locate** shipwrecks. They are _____ with sonar.

3. On a good ship, people **can survive** three months at sea. Three months at sea is _____.

4. Thompson's behavior **doesn't deserve credit or awards**. His behavior is not _____.

5. The ship **can be fixed**. It is _____.

6. This equipment **always works when I need it**. It is very _____.

7. If you have a ship, you **can buy insurance**. Ships are _____.

8. The *Titanic* **is on the bottom of the ocean**. It was _____.

Learn the Vocabulary

Choosing Words to Learn

There are many words in English. You should learn the most frequent words first. That is why it is important to know how frequent a word is before you learn it. Words that can be used in many different contexts or that have more than one meaning or usage are more likely to be frequent. If a word is less frequent, it probably has a specific meaning that is only used in one context.

There are two places where you can find information about word frequency: a good English-English dictionary for English language learners and the Internet. Each dictionary shows frequency differently, so you will need to read the guide at the beginning of your dictionary. Here's how one dictionary, *The Longman Advanced American Dictionary*, shows the most frequent 3,000 words in spoken and written English.

ar·gu·ment /ˈɑrgyəmənt/ S2 W2 *n.* **1** [C] a situation in which two or more people disagree, often angrily.

The 3,000 most frequent words in spoken and written English are highlighted in red. This shows you the important words you need to know. S1 S2 S3 show which are the most frequent 1,000/2,000/3,000 words in spoken English. W1 W2 W3 show which are the most frequent 1,000/2,000/3,000 words in written English.

To find information about word frequency on the Internet, type the keywords "word frequency" and "English" in a search box, or ask your teacher for help.

Some of the Web sites have lists of the most frequent words in English. Some of them have a place where you can enter a word, a paragraph, or a whole text into a program. Then the program will "read" your text and give you information about the frequency level of the word(s).

If the word you checked has a high frequency level, make a word card for it right away. If its frequency level is not very high, don't make a card for it until you have seen it two more times.

A. Work with a partner. From the target words in this unit, choose five that you think are the most frequent. Choose five that you think are less frequent.

B. Check the frequency of the words you chose in Exercise A on a word frequency Web site or in a dictionary. Were your guesses correct?

C. Look at the new words you wrote on page 217. Make word cards for any additional words from Chapters 23–24 that you want to study.

D. Go back to the vocabulary list at the beginning of each chapter. What did you learn about the target words? Add your numbers to the lists.

Vocabulary Practice 12, see page 229

FLUENCY PRACTICE 4

 READING 1

Before You Read

First, scan "BIOMIMICRY: Frequently Asked Questions" on the next page. Then answer the questions.

1. What does *biomimicry* mean?

_____

2. What is one thing that has been designed using biomimicry?

_____

Read

A. Read "BIOMIMICRY: Frequently Asked Questions" on the next page. Time yourself. Write your start and end times and your total reading time. Then calculate your reading speed (words per minute) and write it in the progress chart on page 230.

Start time: _____   **End time:** _____   **Total time:** _____ (in seconds)

Reading speed:
534 words ÷ _____ (total time in seconds) x 60 = _____ words per minute

BIOMIMICRY: Frequently Asked Questions

1 ***What is biomimicry?***
Bio- means "life," and *mimic* means "imitate or copy." Biomimicry is the science of imitating things in the natural world.

5 ***Why should we copy the natural world?***
Living things have evolved over thousands of years. Nature has found the simplest, easiest ways to do many things. Nature is also efficient. It is not wasteful. And it does 10 most things in a way that is safe for the environment. Designers who use biomimicry investigate nature. They seek and find answers to today's problems in the natural world.

15 ***Can you give some examples?***
There are many examples. Here are two. In the first, designers copied a fish. In the second, they copied a termite.

In 2005, DaimlerChrysler designed a new car. 20 It is similar to a type of fish called the boxfish. They have the same basic shape. Both the boxfish and the car are powerful and fast. They operate without wasting any energy. They can move well in small places. They 25 don't weigh very much, but they are tough. They can endure the constant force of wind and water.

An architect in Zimbabwe, Africa, was designing an office building. He was inspired 30 by a small hill, or mound, of African termites. The African termite survives by eating the mold, or decaying material, that grows inside its mound. The mold only grows if the temperature inside the mound stays the 35 same. But it is very hot in Zimbabwe. Why doesn't the mound get hotter and hotter during the day? The termites control the temperature.

How do they do it? Termites build their 40 mounds so that air enters under the ground. Why? It is colder underground than on the land's surface. As the cool air rises, it cools the inside of the mound. If the air temperature inside the mound gets too cool, 45 the termites make holes in the walls. Then hot air from the outside enters the mound. If the air inside gets too hot, the termites close the holes.

To make the office building energy efficient, 50 the architect designed it to be similar to a termite mound. Air enters the building under the ground. Then vents (holes) in the building open and close all day to control the temperature. The building costs 90 percent 55 less to heat and cool than similar buildings in the same city.

What are some possible future uses of biomimicry?
One day biomimicry may solve our energy 60 problems. Scientists are studying how plants use energy. Plants are able to convert sunlight and water into fuel. If people can figure out how to copy this technology, the benefits will be endless.

65 Imagine a house that gets all its energy naturally. There would be special equipment on the roof of every home. This equipment would trap sunlight and water. It would then convert it into energy. There would be 70 enough energy to operate your TV, computer, refrigerator, and everything else in your house. This technology would also reduce pollution. Today our energy use releases a lot of carbon dioxide. Plants, in contrast, take 75 carbon dioxide from the air. Imagine a home that worked like a plant and actually took carbon dioxide from the air!

B. Read "Biomimicry: Frequently Asked Questions" again, a little faster this time. Write your start and end times and your total reading time. Then calculate your reading speed (words per minute) and write it in the progress chart on page 230.

Start time: _____   **End time:** _____   **Total time:** _____ (in seconds)

Reading speed:
534 words ÷ _____ (total time in seconds) x 60 = _____ words per minute

Comprehension Check

A. Circle the letter of the correct answer to complete each sentence.

1. DaimlerChrysler based its new car on the design of _____.
   a. termite mounds   **b.** boxfish   **c.** plants

2. An architect in Zimbabwe was inspired by _____ when designing an energy-efficient office building.
   a. termite mounds   **b.** boxfish   **c.** plants

3. Termites are able to _____ inside their mounds.
   a. endure the force   **b.** turn sunlight and   **c.** control the
       of wind and water   water into fuel   temperature

B. Answer the questions. Use your own words.

1. When a designer uses biomimicry, what does he or she do?

2. What are the benefits of imitating or copying nature?

3. Which of the examples of biomimicry did you find most interesting? Why?

C. Check your answers for the comprehension questions in the Answer Key on page 232. Then calculate your score and write it in the progress chart on page 230.

_____ (my number correct) ÷ 6 x 100 = _____%

❯ READING 2

Before You Read

Preview *"Swarm Intelligence"* on the next page. Answer the questions.

1. What creature does the reading discuss?

2. Does the reading say positive or negative things about this creature?

Read

A. Read "Swarm Intelligence." Time yourself. Write your start and end times and your total reading time. Then calculate your reading speed (words per minute) and write it in the progress chart on page 230.

Start time: _____   **End time:** _____   **Total time:** _____ (in seconds)

Reading speed:

505 words ÷ _____ (total time in seconds) x 60 = _____ words per minute

Swarm Intelligence

The next time you see an ant in your kitchen, think twice before you kill it. Why? Scientists believe that ants can help us solve some serious problems.

Ants are very successful animals. They can be found in every part of the Earth except for Antarctica and a few small islands. Over 12,500 species of ants exist. Their populations number in the millions. In fact, biologists say that if you weighed every living thing on the planet, 15–25 percent of the total weight would be made up by ants.

What explains ants' success? They have very small brains and no leader. But as a group, they are organized, efficient, and excellent at solving problems. For example, they are always able to find the fastest way to get to food. Thousands of them can travel to the same place at the same time without getting into a traffic jam (something humans have not been able to figure out how to do). How can they do these things with such small brains?

The answer is simple. Any one ant doesn't need to know much; it just needs a few simple rules. When it follows those rules, it becomes one small part of a large group brain. This is called *swarm intelligence*.

We're going to look at an example of swarm intelligence, but first, here are the rules:

1. When an ant finds food, it doesn't eat it. It takes it back to its home.
2. Ants release pheromones when they find food. Pheromones are special chemicals released by animals and insects. They influence the behavior of other members of the same species. Pheromones send simple messages such as "help" or "I found food."
3. Ants always follow one another's pheromones.

Now, let's see what happens when a swarm of ants follows these three simple rules.

Several ants find some bread. They each take a little of the bread back to their home. By chance, one of the ants takes the shortest, fastest trail and gets home first. The other ants in the ant home don't know that's the best trail to the food, but they don't need to. They just need to follow the rules. They follow the pheromones of that ant back to the bread. When they find the bread, they add their pheromones to the trail. This trail, the shortest, fastest path to a meal, now has the most pheromones on it. It becomes the main trail for all of the ants. Simple, efficient—and very intelligent.

Scientists now hope to imitate ants' organizational power. Computer scientists think it can help in communication. They are using swarm intelligence to find the fastest way to send messages over the Internet.

Other scientists are making simple robots that work in swarms, like ants. One day, they hope to use these robots to investigate dangerous places. They also think that the cells in our bodies might use swarm intelligence. If so, the lessons learned from ants might one day help us treat a variety of medical conditions.

B. Read "Swarm Intelligence" again, a little faster this time. Write your start and end times and your total reading time. Then calculate your reading speed (words per minute) and write it in the progress chart on page 230.

Start time: _____ End time: _____ Total time: _____ (in seconds)

Reading speed:
505 words ÷ _____ (total time in seconds) x 60 = _____ words per minute

Comprehension Check

A. Read the statements about ants. Write *T* (true) or *F* (false).

_____ **1.** They live in large groups.

_____ **2.** They think before they act.

_____ **3.** They follow rules.

_____ **4.** They follow one leader.

_____ **5.** They are very efficient at collecting food.

_____ **6.** They take a long time to find the best path to food.

B. Circle the correct answer to complete each sentence.

1. Because ants use swarm intelligence, they are very <u>stupid / successful / small</u>.

2. Ants use swarm intelligence to <u>treat diseases / survive in Antarctica / find food</u>.

3. A swarm intelligence activity is always <u>difficult / good / fun</u> for the group's survival.

4. The rules for swarm intelligence are <u>difficult / easy / strange</u>.

5. The members of the group <u>always / sometimes / never</u> follow the rules.

6. There is <u>a group of leaders / one leader / no leader</u> of a swarm intelligence activity.

7. The group members do not <u>like / remember / think about</u> what they are doing.

8. The group is more intelligent than the <u>leaders / members / other groups</u>.

C. Check your answers for the comprehension questions in the Answer Key on page 232. Then calculate your score and write it in the progress chart on page 230.

_____ (my number correct) ÷ 14 x 100 = _____ %

Unit 3 Quiz: How Green Are You? (page 30)

A. First, read the questions. Then circle your answers in the chart.

Questions	1 point	2 points	3 points
Where do you live?	in a village	in a town	in a city
How do you go to work / school?	by walking / bicycle	by train / bus / subway	by driving a small car
How many times a year do you fly on airplanes?	0–1	1–2	2–3
How many hours of electricity do you use each day (e.g., watching TV, turning on lights)?	0–6 hours	6–12 hours	12–18 hours
How often do you recycle?[1]	almost always	often	sometimes

Total Points	Result
7	Less than the average person
8–10	As much pollution as the average person
11–13	A little more pollution than the average person
14–15	A lot more pollution than the average person

B. Count your total points and check your result on the table. Compare scores with a partner.

[1] **recycle:** to put used objects or materials through a special process so that they can be used again

New Words

UNIT 1

UNIT 2

UNIT 3

UNIT 4

UNIT 5

UNIT 6

New Words

UNIT 7

UNIT 8

UNIT 9

UNIT 10

UNIT 11

UNIT 12

VOCABULARY PRACTICE 1

THINK ABOUT MEANING

Read each set of words or phrases. Are the meanings of the two words or phrases similar or different? Write *S* or *D*.

_____ 1. frequently / often

_____ 2. genetic / passed down from parents

_____ 3. imaginary / real

_____ 4. in control / anxious

_____ 5. things in common / differences

_____ 6. break out of / escape

_____ 7. perform / watch

_____ 8. acquire / get

_____ 9. get over / overcome

_____ 10. crowded / full

PRACTICE A SKILL: Parts of Speech

Read the sentences. Underline all the adjectives. Circle all the adverbs.

1. Mary is a shy person.
2. Shyness is remarkably common.
3. Some superstars feel scared when they perform.
4. When I feel sad, I pretend I'm in an imaginary world.
5. The prisoner anxiously prepared to break out of the crowded prison.
6. Bill frequently blames others for his failures.
7. Scientists think shyness can be acquired genetically.
8. Because the actor was nervous, he took frequent breaks.
9. The movie became increasingly scary, so I stopped watching.
10. My coach helped me be successful.

PRACTICE A STRATEGY: Making Word Cards

Make word cards for 10 more words that you learn this week. Add them to the cards that you made for this unit. Review your cards every day. Always change the order of your cards before you review them.

VOCABULARY PRACTICE 2

THINK ABOUT MEANING

Look at the words in the list. Circle the words that have a positive meaning (something good), and underline the words that have a negative meaning (something bad).

argue	award	fan	improve	quit
attract	doubt	hero	mind	stand out

PRACTICE A SKILL: Compound Nouns

A. Complete the sentences with the compound nouns from the list.

advertising contract	football	hometown	investment plan	star player
ballgame	home team	Internet post	sports fan	team player

1. Junko's _____ is Tokyo, but she's living in London.

2. Most of the fans wanted the _____ to win the game.

3. Chen doesn't work well with others; he's not a(n) _____.

4. I'm not a(n) _____; I'd rather read a book than watch a game.

5. The athlete has a(n) _____ with a car company.

6. I went online and read your _____.

7. I want to be rich in the future, so I created a(n) _____.

8. Why don't we bring a(n) _____ to the park to throw around.

9. The players couldn't focus, so the team lost the _____ 5-2.

10. The _____ has a contract that pays him a high salary.

PRACTICE A STRATEGY: Using Word Cards with Parts of Speech

Review your word cards for this unit. Write the part of speech of each word on the front of the card, under the word. If you are not sure about a word's part of speech, check the word in your dictionary. Be careful—sometimes two different forms of a word have the same spelling.

THINK ABOUT MEANING

Complete the sentences with the words from the list. The boldfaced words and the words in the list are the target words.

afford	attract	genetic	quit	satisfied	wasteful
athletes	crowded	posts	salary	stands out	worry

1. The **customer complained** because she wasn't _____ with her order.

2. The train was very _____; there were hundreds of **passengers**.

3. Some businesses offer free **delivery** to _____ new **customers**.

4. Some people _____ humans are hurting the **environment**.

5. The red hair in my family passes from one **generation** to the next; it is _____.

6. John takes **extra materials**, but he doesn't use them; that is so _____.

7. I can't _____ to go; they are **charging** too much for tickets.

8. The all-star team is **made up of** famous _____.

9. Sofia wanted to _____ school, but her parents didn't **allow** it.

10. My **luggage** is red, so it _____ and is easy to find at the airport.

PRACTICE A SKILL: Suffixes: *-ful, -ment*

Add the suffixes to the words below. Make one new form of each word.

Adjective suffix: *-ful*		Noun suffix: *-ment*	
1. waste	*wasteful*	6. enjoy	_____
2. require	_____	7. thank	_____
3. agree	_____	8. use	_____
4. hope	_____	9. excite	_____
5. ship	_____	10. mind	_____

PRACTICE A STRATEGY: Using Word Cards with Example Sentences

Review your word cards for this unit. If a word is difficult for you to remember, add an example sentence to the back of the card. You can copy the sentence from the reading, or you can copy an example sentence from your dictionary.

VOCABULARY PRACTICE 4

THINK ABOUT MEANING

Circle the letters of all the possible words or phrases that can complete each sentence. The boldfaced words are the target words.

1. You can **host** a _____.
   - **a.** dinner
   - **b.** hotel
   - **c.** festival

2. People **compete** for _____.
   - **a.** mud
   - **b.** jobs
   - **c.** awards

3. You can **check out** _____.
   - **a.** from a prison
   - **b.** a book from the library
   - **c.** of a hotel

4. _____ have **populations**.
   - **a.** Cities
   - **b.** Countries
   - **c.** Themes

5. You can **reserve** a _____.
   - **a.** table in a restaurant
   - **b.** room in a hotel
   - **c.** seat in a prison

6. You can find **mud** _____.
   - **a.** on your shoes
   - **b.** on the ground
   - **c.** in a tree

7. It is not healthy to eat an **entire** _____.
   - **a.** sandwich
   - **b.** cake
   - **c.** banana

8. Restaurants always **provide** _____.
   - **a.** plates
   - **b.** entertainment
   - **c.** something to drink

9. _____ attract **tourists**.
   - **a.** Festivals
   - **b.** Ancient towers
   - **c.** Local economies

10. **Extreme** sports include _____.
    - **a.** riding your bike in the park
    - **b.** jumping out of an airplane
    - **c.** SCUBA diving with sharks

PRACTICE A SKILL: Suffixes

Look at the words in the list. If a word has a suffix, circle the suffix. Not all the words have suffixes.

attraction	entertainment	positively	reservation	seek
doubtful	local	regularly	salary	unique

PRACTICE A STRATEGY: Using Word Cards with Compound Names

Review your word cards for this unit. Look up the new words in your dictionary to see if they can form compound nouns (for example: a **tourist attraction**). Add the compound to the front of the card, under the word.

THINK ABOUT MEANING

Circle the letters of all the possible words and phrases that can complete each sentence. The boldfaced words are the target words.

1. Some people work as _____ **critics**.
   a. movie   **b.** taste   **c.** music

2. Some _____ can be **poisonous**.
   a. chemicals   **b.** roads   **c.** animals

3. Some medicines give you **relief** from _____.
   a. pleasure   **b.** anxiety   **c.** pain

4. You can buy a **pack** of _____.
   a. cards   **b.** cars   **c.** gum

5. If this tastes too **bitter**, add _____.
   a. sugar   **b.** honey   **c.** salt

6. You can **respond** to a(n) _____.
   a. question   **b.** e-mail   **c.** profit

7. You can see your **reflection** in _____.
   a. the sky   **b.** a mirror   **c.** the water

8. _____ sometimes **sell out**.
   a. Customers   **b.** Tickets   **c.** Products

PRACTICE A SKILL: Suffixes

Look at the words in the list. If the word has a suffix, circle the suffix. Not all words have suffixes.

associat**ion**	improvement	painful	saucy	tasteful
bitter	muddy	poison	spicy	tasty

PRACTICE A STRATEGY: Using a Dictionary

Use an English-English dictionary to answer the questions about the words.

1. immigration—How many syllables are there in the word and which one receives the main stress?

2. relief—What is the verb form of the word? The adjective form?

3. pain—What does the expression **a pain in the neck** mean?

THINK ABOUT MEANING

Complete the sentences with the words from the list. The boldfaced words are the target words. There are two extra words in the list.

complex	frequently	look	poisonous	refrigerator	treat
entertainment	local	mud	profit	scary	variety

1. How can I **distinguish** _____ mushrooms from the ones that are safe to eat?

2. I didn't finish my dinner, so I put the food that was **left over** in the _____.

3. This radio station always plays the same music; I **wish** there was more _____.

4. It is not **appropriate** for young children to watch extremely _____ movies.

5. Gustav is amusic, and there is no way to _____ his **condition**.

6. If you like simple music, then you won't **appreciate** _____ jazz songs.

7. Please **avoid** bringing _____ into the house. I like to keep the floor clean.

8. I _____ a lot like my mother; we **resemble** each other.

9. Let's **turn on** the TV; I think we need some _____.

10. Miguel **tends to** play loud music at night. His neighbors _____ complain.

PRACTICE A SKILL: Parts of Speech

Read the paragraph. Are the boldfaced words adjectives or verbs? Circle the adjectives, and underline the verbs.

The strangest thing happened yesterday. I was **bored**, so I went for a walk in the park. A really **entertaining** jazz band was playing there. A lot of people were **relaxing** and having fun. The band even played my favorite song, "A Time to Remember." That really **excited** me, so I got up and started dancing. Then I fell over—how **embarrassing**! But the singer of the band came over, and asked if I was OK. He was **worried**. He **helped** me up, and we talked for a while. He is a really **interesting** person! Now I have a new friend—can you believe it?

PRACTICE A STRATEGY: Changing the Order and Grouping of Word Cards

Review your cards every day. If you remember a word correctly three times, remove that card and put it away in a safe place. (Don't throw it away!) Then after a few days, put that card back with the other cards, change the order, and review all of your cards again.

VOCABULARY PRACTICE 7

THINK ABOUT MEANING

Look at the target words in the list. Think about their meanings, and decide where to put them in the chart. Some of the words can go in more than one place in the chart. Be ready to explain your decisions.

| audience | campus | low-budget | ~~out of business~~ | screen |
| break even | career | marketing | review | script |

Business	Theater	Student
out of business		

PRACTICE A SKILL: Understanding Word Meaning

Read each set of sentences. Is the meaning of the boldfaced words the same or different in the two sentences? Write *S* or *D*.

_____ 1. My friend is always able to **beat** me at chess. / Put on something with a fast **beat** and let's dance!

_____ 2. First-year college students usually live on **campus**. / He lived near the **campus**, so he didn't need to drive.

_____ 3. Thanks for cooking; I'll wash the **dishes**. / This restaurant serves a lot of spicy **dishes**.

_____ 4. I like singing, but I have difficulty with the high **notes**. / To do well in class, it helps to take **notes**.

_____ 5. Mia is professional athlete who has had a long **career**. / To change **careers**, you can to go back to school.

_____ 6. The critic usually **states** her opinion of a film. / Judy has traveled all over the U.S.; she's been to all fifty **states**.

PRACTICE A STRATEGY: Figuring Out Meaning from Context

Read the sentences. The boldfaced words are related to target words from the unit. Can you figure out their meanings? Underline the words that help you understand the meaning. Then check your answers in a dictionary.

1. Mark wrote a **screenplay**. A director wants to use it for his next movie.

   Screenplay means _____

2. I like this movie; it stars my favorite **comedian**. She always makes me laugh!

   Comedian means _____

3. Kirk isn't **trustworthy**. I wouldn't believe what he says.

   Trustworthy means _____

THINK ABOUT MEANING

The sentences below do not make sense. Replace the underlined words with words from the list so that the sentences make sense.

credit	evidence	movies	quit
environment	fit in	obey	requirements

1. I **imitate** my **peers**. I want to <u>stand out</u>.

2. My parents are **strict**; they expect me to <u>ignore</u> their rules.

3. My parents **raised** me well; I <u>blame</u> them for my success.

4. No one believes the psychologist's **theory**; he doesn't have enough <u>mistakes</u>.

5. When children change schools, they have to **adapt** to their new <u>personality</u>.

6. Students have to **deal with** a lot of <u>good grades</u>.

7. Joe doesn't need **steady** work; so he likes to <u>keep</u> his job every few months.

8. Some parents worry that their children are **influenced** by <u>vegetables</u>.

PRACTICE A SKILL: Word Families

First, circle the part of speech (**adjective, noun, verb**) that is missing in the sentences. Then complete the sentences with the correct form of the words in the list.

adapt	influence	obey	personal	theory

1. Over thousands of years, animals have _____ to their environments. (adj/n/v)

2. At this point, his idea about birth order is only _____ ; he has no proof. (adj/n/v)

3. I think this video game will have a negative _____ on young people. (adj/n/v)

4. I want to add a _____ touch to my room, so I'll paint it my favorite color. (adj/n/v)

5. My dog Spot always does what I say; he is very _____. (adj/n/v)

6. She is a rich and _____ businesswoman; everyone pays attention to her. (adj/n/v)

PRACTICE A STRATEGY: Using a Dictionary

Use your dictionary to check your answers to Practice a Skill. Correct any spelling mistakes.

THINK ABOUT MEANING

Complete the sentences with the words from the list. The boldfaced words are the target words.

contract	deal with	ignore	set out	successful
critics	falling	script	steady	traveling

1. If a problem is always **on your mind**, then you should _____ the problem.

2. His parents always **encouraged** him; they told him he would be _____.

3. The man who wrote the _____ said his own life was the **inspiration** for the movie.

4. I disagree with the _____; this movie about Basho is **overrated**.

5. After the company increased his salary, Juan **signed** a four-year _____.

6. We _____ weeks ago, and finally we are **approaching** the end of our **journey**.

7. The teacher was **going on and on** about small details, so we began to _____ him.

8. I wanted to take a **nap**, but I **had trouble** _____ asleep.

PRACTICE A SKILL: The Prefix over-

A. Make new words by adding the prefix *over-* to some of the words below. If you cannot add the prefix *over-* to a word, write *X*. If you are not sure, look in your dictionary.

	over- + word			*over-* + word
1. admirable	*X*	**4.** inspirational		_____
2. crowded	*overcrowded*	**5.** act		_____
3. payment	_____	**6.** fishing		_____

B. Write the words from Exercise A next to the definitions.

Word	Definition
1. _____	to perform with too much emotion or movement
2. _____	filled with too many people or things
3. _____	the act of paying too much money for something
4. _____	the process of taking too many fish from the sea, a river, etc.

PRACTICE A STRATEGY: Choosing Which Words to Study

Study the new words from Practice a Skill. Decide which words are most useful to you in real life. Make word cards for those words.

THINK ABOUT MEANING

Look at the target words in the list. Think about their meanings, and decide where to put them in the chart. Some of the words can go in more than one place in the chart. Be ready to explain your decisions.

architect	enemy	honor	manager	~~rent~~
construction	floor	intense	named after	roof
crush	height	maintenance	race	status

Building	Leader	Competition
rent		

PRACTICE A SKILL: Collocations

Complete each collocation with the correct target word. The boldfaced words in the sentences form collocations with the words in the list.

construction	express	race	robber	symbol	trouble

1. The new hotel is currently **under** _____; it will be completed next year.

2. John Dillinger was a famous **bank** _____; eventually the police caught him.

3. If something is on your mind, poetry is a great way to _____ **yourself**.

4. Mr. Brown drives a really expensive Rolls Royce; it's a **status** _____.

5. I think you can do this by yourself, but if you **have** _____, let me know. I can help you.

6. Some _____ **cars** can travel over 250 miles per hour (350 kph).

PRACTICE A STRATEGY: Finding the Core Meaning of Words

Work with a partner. Look up target words from this unit in your dictionary. Find words that have more than one definition. Talk about the similar features/ideas in each definition for the word.

THINK ABOUT MEANING

Circle the letters of all the possible words or phrases that can complete each sentence. The boldfaced words are the target words.

1. You can **prove** _____.
   a. a theory
   b. a book of poetry
   c. that a person is guilty

2. Biologists study _____.
   a. plants
   b. the environment
   c. technology

3. You **sweat** when _____.
   a. the air is cold
   b. you exercise
   c. you eat spicy food

4. I want to work in the _____ **industry**.
   a. fashion
   b. vision
   c. travel

5. _____ **care for** other people.
   a. Parents
   b. Doctors
   c. Robbers

6. If you are **trapped** in a room, try to _____.
   a. break out
   b. set out
   c. turn out

7. You can **debate** a _____.
   a. living room
   b. theory
   c. controversial topic

PRACTICE A SKILL: Knowing the Meanings of Roots

Complete the words in the sentences with a root from the list.

bene	bio	contra	cred	loc

1. A(n) _____graphical movie tells a story about someone's life.

2. The act of moving from place to place is called _____omotion.

3. If something is _____ible, people are likely to believe it.

4. If you _____dict someone, you disagree with what he or she says.

5. If you are a _____volent person, you behave in a kind and generous way.

PRACTICE A STRATEGY: Adding a Picture for Example Sentences

Review your word cards for this unit. If a word is difficult for you to remember, add an example sentence to the back of the card. Use your imagination to picture the meaning of the example sentence in your head. Then draw a picture on the back of the card.

VOCABULARY PRACTICE 12

THINK ABOUT MEANING

Complete the sentences with the words from the list. The boldfaced words and the words in the list are the target words.

biologists	leftover	passengers	surgery
journey	map	poet	worth it

1. Meredith's **insurance** paid for her stomach _____.

2. The _____ is not **accurate**; many streets have the wrong names.

3. If you want to be a _____, the only **equipment** you need is pen and paper.

4. Don't throw away the _____ food; I'll eat **the rest** later.

5. To **investigate** the natural world, _____ use a variety of **equipment**.

6. The **desperate** _____ jumped off the **sinking** ship.

7. To successfully cross the ocean, birds have to **endure** a **tough** _____.

8. Learning a new language is not an easy **task**, but I'm **convinced** it is _____.

PRACTICE A SKILL: The Suffix -able

A. Add the suffix -able to create new forms of the words.

Verb	Adjective	Verb	Adjective
1. afford	*affordable*	4. profit	_____
2. allow	_____	5. reach	_____
3. avoid	_____	6. treat	_____

B. Complete the sentences with the words from Exercise A.

1. This condition is _____; there is medicine you can take for it.

2. Ella's business is very _____; it makes thousands of dollars every day.

3. Two things in life are not _____: death and taxes.

4. I think that apple is too high in the tree; it isn't _____.

5. Missing one day of work is _____; but missing a whole week is against the rules.

PRACTICE A STRATEGY: The Keyword Technique

Review the words that were new to you from this unit. If a word is difficult for you to remember, think of a keyword from your first language that sounds similar to that word. Imagine a picture where the meaning of the new word and the meaning of the keyword are connected in some way.

Fluency Progress Charts

FLUENCY PRACTICE 1

	Words per Minute	
	First Try	Second Try
Reading 1		
Reading 2		
Comprehension Check Score _____ %		

FLUENCY PRACTICE 2

	Words per Minute	
	First Try	Second Try
Reading 1		
Reading 2		
Comprehension Check Score _____ %		

FLUENCY PRACTICE 3

	Words per Minute	
	First Try	Second Try
Reading 1		
Reading 2		
Comprehension Check Score _____ %		

FLUENCY PRACTICE 4

	Words per Minute	
	First Try	Second Try
Reading 1		
Reading 2		
Comprehension Check Score _____ %		

Fluency Practice Answer Key

Count only the Comprehension Check answers (not the Read answers) toward your Comprehension Check Score.

Fluency Practice 1
Reading 1
Comprehension Check, p. 47

A.

1. a **2.** c **3.** a **4.** a **5.** c **6.** a

B.

1. a. people in the United States and other countries
   b. in a swimming pool
   c. run, walk, or mind-body practice in the water
2. It's easier than exercising on land, better for your knees than walking or running, and you burn more calories in the pool than in the gym.

Reading 2
Read, p. 50

C. Answers will vary but may include strength, calmness under pressure, persistence, and a positive outlook.

Comprehension Check, p. 50

A.

1. T **2.** T **3.** T **4.** F **5.** F **6.** F

B.

1. swimmer **4.** feet **7.** failures
2. success **5.** kick **8.** anxious
3. body **6.** positively

Fluency Practice 2
Reading 1
Comprehension Check, p. 103

A.

1. b **2.** a **3.** a **4.** b **5.** c **6.** a

B.

1. puffer fish—a poisonous Japanese blowfish
2. in Japan and other countries in the Far East
3. Some appreciate the taste; some like the danger.
4. They must train with a licensed fugu chef and pass two tests—a written test and a test in which they must prepare and eat fugu in only 20 minutes.

Reading 2
Comprehension Check, p. 105

A.

1. c **2.** b **3.** b **4.** b **5.** a **6.** a

B.

1. a type of mushroom
2. They're hard to find.
3. They grow under the ground and only under certain kinds of trees.
4. Truffle hunters compete for these expensive mushrooms and want to prevent a competitor's dogs from finding truffles.
5. They want to keep the location of the truffles a secret.

Fluency Practice 3
Reading 1
Comprehension Check, p. 156

A.

Characteristics	Fable	Pourquoi story	Trickster tale	Fairytale
A main character who can't be trusted			✓	
A happy ending				✓
A moral at the end	✓			
An explanation of something in the natural world		✓		

B.

1. Hard work is important. If you don't work hard, you'll suffer.
2. how to behave better and not trust everyone they meet
3. They are entertaining, and they usually have happy endings.

(continued on next page)

Reading 2

Comprehension Check, p. 159

A.

4, 2, 3, 1

B.

4, 2, 3, 1

C.

Turtle learns from Anansi how to trick the trickster. He uses a similar method to keep Anansi from eating. Just as Anansi gets to eat all the food by shaming Turtle into washing his hands, Turtle is able to keep all the food for himself by making Anansi take off his jacket under the water.

Fluency Practice 4

Reading 1

Comprehension Check, p. 212

A.

1. b   **2.** a   **3.** c

B.

1. He or she investigates and copies nature in order to find answers to today's problems.
2. Nature has the simplest, easiest ways of doing many things; it is efficient, not wasteful. It does things in a way that is safe for the environment.
3. Answers will vary.

Reading 2

Comprehension Check, p. 214

A.

1. T   **2.** F   **3.** T   **4.** F   **5.** T   **6.** F

B.

1. successful   **4.** easy   **7.** think about
2. find food   **5.** always   **8.** members
3. good   **6.** no leader

Pronunciation Table

Vowels

Symbol	Key Word
i	b**ea**t, f**ee**d
ɪ	b**i**t, d**i**d
eɪ	d**a**te, p**ai**d
ɛ	b**e**t, b**e**d
æ	b**a**t, b**a**d
ɑ	b**o**x, **o**dd, f**a**ther
ɔ	b**ough**t, d**o**g
oʊ	b**oa**t, r**oa**d
ʊ	b**oo**k, g**oo**d
u	b**oo**t, f**oo**d, st**u**dent
ʌ	b**u**t, m**u**d, m**o**ther
ə	b**a**n**a**n**a**, **a**mong
ɚ	sh**ir**t, m**ur**d**er**
aɪ	b**i**te, c**r**y, b**u**y, **eye**
aʊ	ab**ou**t, h**ow**
ɔɪ	v**oi**ce, b**oy**
ɪr	b**eer**
ɛr	b**are**
ɑr	b**ar**
ɔr	d**oor**
ʊr	t**our**

/t/ means that /t/ may be dropped.
/d/ means that /d/ may be dropped.
/'/ shows main stress.
/ˌ/ shows secondary stress.

Consonants

Symbol	Key Word
p	**p**ack, ha**pp**y
b	**b**ack, ru**bb**er
t	**t**ie
d	**d**ie
k	**c**ame, **k**ey, **qu**i**ck**
g	**g**ame, **g**uest
tʃ	**ch**urch, na**t**ure, wa**tch**
dʒ	**j**u**dg**e, **g**eneral, ma**j**or
f	**f**an, **ph**otogra**ph**
v	**v**an
θ	**th**ing, brea**th**
ð	**th**en, brea**th**e
s	**s**ip, **c**ity, p**s**ychology
z	**z**ip, plea**s**e, goe**s**
ʃ	**sh**ip, ma**ch**ine, sta**t**ion, spe**c**ial, discu**ss**ion
ʒ	mea**s**ure, vi**s**ion
h	**h**ot, **wh**o
m	**m**en, so**m**e
n	su**n**, **kn**ow, **pn**eumonia
ŋ	su**ng**, ri**ng**ing
w	**w**et, **wh**ite
l	**l**ight, **l**ong
r	**r**ight, **wr**ong
y	**y**es, **u**se, m**u**sic
t̬	bu**tt**er, bo**tt**le
t̚	bu**tt**on

Vocabulary Index

The numbers following each entry are the pages where the word appears. All words followed by asterisks* are on the Academic Word List.

A

accurate* /ˈækyərɪt/ 197, 198, 199
acquire* /əˈkwaɪɚ/ 2, 4
adapt* /əˈdæpt/ 132, 134, 158, 188
add up / æd ʌp/ 167, 168
admirable /ˈædmərəbəl/ 141, 143
advertising /ˈædvɚˌtaɪzɪŋ/ 23, 24, 25, 93
afford /əˈfɔrd/ 16, 18
alarm /əˈlɑrm/ 186, 188
allow /əˈlaʊ/ 31, 33, 134
anxious /ˈæŋkʃəs, ˈæŋʃəs/ 2, 4, 46, 49
appreciate* /əˈpriʃiˌeɪt/ 92, 93, 102, 104, 134
approach* /əˈproʊtʃ/ 147, 149
appropriate* /əˈproʊpriɪt/ 85, 87
architect /ˈɑrkəˌtɛkt/ 161, 162, 211
argue /ˈɑrgyu/ 16, 18, 104, 110, 113, 126, 127, 134
associate /əˈsoʊʃiˌeɪt, -siˌeɪt/ 69, 70, 155
athlete /ˈæθlit/ 16, 18, 49, 60, 113
attack /əˈtæk/ 186, 188, 102
attract /əˈtrækt/ 23, 24, 25, 60, 143
audience /ˈɔdiəns/ 108, 110, 116, 117, 156
avoid /əˈvɔɪd/ 92, 93, 102, 158, 188
award /əˈwɔrd/ 16, 18, 49, 199

B

beat /bit/ 85, 87
benefit* /ˈbɛnəfɪt/ 37, 38, 46, 49, 54, 168, 211
biologist /baɪˈɑlədʒɪst/ 178, 179, 180, 188, 213
bitter /ˈbɪtɚ/ 77, 79, 104, 162
blame /bleɪm/ 2, 4, 49, 133, 134
blocked /blɑkt/ 186, 188
break even /breɪk ˈivən/ 108, 110, 169
break out of /breɪk aʊt əv/ 8, 9

C

campus /ˈkæmpəs/ 115, 116, 117
care for /kɛr fɚ/ 186, 188
career /kəˈrɪr/ 108, 110, 113
cautious /ˈkɔʃəs/ 108, 110, 113
century /ˈsɛntʃəri/ 197, 198, 199
challenging* /ˈtʃæləndʒɪŋ/ 147, 149
charge /tʃɑrdʒ/ 31, 33
check out /tʃɛk aʊt/ 52, 54
chemical* /ˈkɛmɪkəl/ 77, 79, 102, 113, 179, 180, 213
circular /ˈsɚkyələ/ 167, 169
claim /kleɪm/ 178, 179, 180
coach /koʊtʃ/ 8, 9, 18, 113
coast /koʊst/ 203, 204
comedy /ˈkɑmədi/ 108, 110, 113, 116
competition /ˌkɑmpəˈtɪʃən/ 58, 60, 105, 162, 163
complain /kəmˈpleɪn/ 37, 39, 188, 205
complex* /kəmˈplɛks, ˈkɑmplɛks/ 85, 88, 93, 134, 169
concert /ˈkɑnsɚt/ 92, 93, 127, 162
condition /kənˈdɪʃən/ 92, 93, 169, 199, 213
constant* /ˈkɑnstənt/ 197, 199, 211
construction* /kənˈstrʌkʃən/ 161, 162, 169
content /kənˈtɛnt/ 85, 88
contract* /ˈkɑntrækt/ 23, 25
controversial* /ˌkɑntrəˈvɚʃəl◄/ 167, 169, 179
converted* /kənˈvɚtɪd/ 52, 54
convince* /kənˈvɪns/ 203, 204
countryside /ˈkʌntriˌsaɪd/ 141, 143
credit* /ˈkrɛdɪt/ 132, 133
critic /ˈkrɪtɪk/ 69, 70, 110, 116
crowded /ˈkraʊdɪd/ 8, 9, 143, 155
crush /krʌʃ/ 161, 163
customer /ˈkʌstəmɚ/ 31, 33, 70, 79, 104, 180

D

deal with /dil wɪθ, wɪð/ 132, 134, 169
debate* /dɪˈbeɪt/ 178, 180
delivery /dɪˈlɪvəri/ 31, 32, 33
depend on /dɪˈpɛnd ɑn, ən/ 186, 188
deserve /dɪˈzɚv/ 197, 199
desperate /ˈdɛsprɪt, -pərɪt/ 203, 204
detect* /dɪˈtɛkt/ 178, 180
determined /dɪˈtɚmɪnd/ 203, 204
discover /dɪˈskʌvɚ/ 77, 79, 93, 102, 104, 113, 142, 179, 180
dish /dɪʃ/ 69, 70, 104
distinguish /dɪˈstɪŋgwɪʃ/ 92, 93
double /ˈdʌbəl/ 31, 32, 33
doubt /daʊt/ 16, 18, 49, 179

E

economy* /ɪˈkɑnəmi/ 58, 60
embarrassed /ɪmˈbærəst/ 92, 93, 158
empty /ˈɛmpti/ 141, 143, 169
encourage /ɪnˈkɚɪdʒ, -ˈkʌr-/ 141, 143
endure /ɪnˈdʊr/ 197, 199, 211
enemy /ˈɛnəmi/ 161, 162
entertain /ˌɛntɚˈteɪn/ 58, 60, 156, 199
entirely /ɪnˈtaɪɚli/ 52, 54, 93
environment* /ɪnˈvaɪɚnmənt/ 31, 32, 33, 38, 46, 60, 148, 188, 211
equipment* /ɪˈkwɪpmənt/ 203, 204, 211
evidence* /ˈɛvədəns/ 132, 133, 134, 179
exotic /ɪgˈzɑtɪk/ 69, 70, 102
extra /ˈɛkstrə/ 37, 39
extreme /ɪkˈstrim/ 52, 54, 79, 102, 199

F

factor* /ˈfæktɚ/ 115, 117
fade /feɪd/ 167, 168
failure /ˈfeɪlyɚ/ 2, 4, 49
fan /fæn/ 23, 24, 25, 49, 79, 87, 117, 143, 205
festival /ˈfɛstəvəl/ 58, 60
fit in /fɪt ɪn/ 132, 134
floor /flɔr/ 161, 163, 204
focus* /ˈfoʊkəs/ 23, 25, 49, 143, 148
former /ˈfɔrmɚ/ 161, 162, 205
frequently /ˈfrikwəntˌli/ 8, 9, 46, 162, 211
fuel /ˈfyuəl, fyul/ 31, 33, 38, 39

G

generation* /ˌdʒɛnəˈreɪʃən/ 37, 38, 49, 155
genetic /dʒəˈnɛtɪk/ 2, 4
genius /ˈdʒinyəs/ 115, 117
get over /gɛt ˈoʊvɚ/ 2, 4, 9, 134
go on and on /goʊ ɔn, ən ɔn, ənd ɔn, ən/ 147, 148
grades* /greɪdz/ 125, 126
guilt /gɪlt/ 132, 134

H

have trouble /əv, həv ˈtrʌbəl/ 147, 149
head toward /hɛd tɔrd, təˈwɔrd/ 186, 188
height /haɪt/ 161, 162
hero /ˈhɪroʊ/ 16, 18, 49
hit /hɪt/ 115, 116, 148, 204
honor /ˈɑnɚ/ 161, 162
host /hoʊst/ 58, 60, 168, 169

I

ignore* /ɪgˈnɔr/ 132, 134
imaginary /ɪˈmædʒəˌnɛri/ 8, 9
imitate /ˈɪməˌteɪt/ 132, 134, 188, 211, 213
immigration* /ˌɪməˈgreɪʃən/ 69, 70
improve /ɪmˈpruv/ 16, 18, 46, 49
in common /ɪn ˈkɑmən/ 8, 9, 49, 110, 126, 142
in contrast* /ɪn ˈkɑntræst/ 85, 87, 110, 127, 155, 211

in control /ɪn kənˈtroʊl/ 8, 9, 46, 113
increase /ɪnˈkris/ 2, 4, 32, 79, 162
industry /ˈɪndəstri/ 178, 179
influence /ˈɪnfluəns/ 125, 126, 133, 134, 158, 179, 180, 213
insect /ˈɪnsɛkt/ 178, 179, 188, 213
inspiration /ˌɪnspəˈreɪʃən/ 141, 143, 156
instrument /ˈɪnstrəmənt/ 92, 93
insure /ɪnˈʃʊr/ 203, 205
intense* /ɪnˈtɛns/ 161, 162
interact* /ˌɪnt əˈrækt/ 108, 110, 113
invent /ɪnˈvɛnt/ 197, 199
investigate* /ɪnˈvɛstəˌgeɪt/ 203, 205, 211, 213
investment* /ɪnˈvɛstmənt/ 23, 25, 110

J

journey /ˈdʒɚni/ 141, 142, 143, 198

L

lack /læk/ 92, 93
left over /ˈlɛft ˌoʊvɚ/ 85, 88
likely /ˈlaɪkli/ 178, 180
limited /ˈlɪmɪˌtɪd/ 161, 162
local /ˈloʊkəl/ 58, 60, 169, 199
low-budget /loʊ ˈbʌdʒɪt/ 115, 116
luggage /ˈlʌgɪdʒ/ 37, 38, 54

M

made up of /meɪd ʌp əv/ 37, 38
maintenance* /ˈmeɪntˌn-əns/ 167, 169
make a living /meɪk eɪ ˈlɪvɪn/ 125, 127
manager /ˈmænɪdʒɚ/ 167, 168, 169
marketing /ˈmɑrkɪˌtɪŋ/ 115, 116, 117
master /ˈmæstɚ/ 141, 142
materials /məˈtɪriəlz/ 31, 32, 33, 38
mention /ˈmɛnʃən/ 132, 134, 142, 148, 149, 180
mind /maɪnd/ 23, 24, 46, 148, 149, 158, 180
mix /mɪks/ 69, 70, 79, 104
model /ˈmɑdl/ 197, 199
mood /mud/ 147, 149

mud /mʌd/ 58, 60, 104
mystery /ˈmɪstəri/ 203, 205

N

named after /neɪmd ˈæftɚ/ 167, 169
nap /næp/ 147, 149
nevertheless* /ˌnɛvɚðəˈlɛs◄/ 178, 180, 188
note /noʊt/ 85, 87, 93

O

obey /əˈbeɪ/ 125, 126, 127, 156
observe /əbˈzɚv/ 197, 198
occur* /əˈkɚ/ 58, 60, 113, 162
on board /ɔn, ən bɔrd/ 197, 199, 204
on your mind /ɔn, ən yɚ maɪnd/ 147, 149
operation /ˌɑpəˈreɪʃən/ 167, 168
originally /əˈrɪdʒənl-i/ 52, 54, 169
out of business /aʊt əv, ə, bɪznɪs/ 108, 110
overrated /ˌoʊvɚˈreɪtɪd◄/ 141, 143

P

pack /pæk/ 77, 79
pain /peɪn/ 77, 79
passenger /ˈpæsəndʒɚ/ 37, 38, 204
pattern /ˈpætɚn/ 85, 88
peers /pɪrz/ 132, 134
perform /pɚˈfɔrm/ 8, 9, 113
personality /ˌpɚsəˈnælət]i/ 125, 126, 133, 134
pleasure /ˈplɛʒɚ/ 77, 79
poet /ˈpoʊɪt/ 141, 142, 143, 148
poisonous /ˈpɔɪzənəs/ 77, 79, 102, 127
population /ˌpɑpyəˈleɪʃən/ 58, 60, 93
positive* /ˈpɑzətɪv/ 23, 25, 49, 116
post /poʊst/ 23, 25, 87
prison /ˈprɪzən/ 52, 54, 127
process* /ˈprɑsɛs/ 178, 180
profit /ˈprɑfɪt/ 69, 70, 105, 110, 116, 117, 179
proof /pruf/ 178, 180
provide /prəˈvaɪd/ 52, 54, 134
psychologist* /saɪˈkɑlədʒɪst/ 132, 133

Q

quit /kwɪt/ 16, 18, 46, 49, 126, 127

R

race /reɪs/ 161, 162, 168
raise /reɪz/ 125, 127, 133, 134
reach /ritʃ/ 16, 18, 54, 117, 188
rebel /ˈrɛbəl/ 125, 126, 127, 134
reflect /rɪˈflɛkt/ 69, 70, 142
regular /ˈrɛgyələ/ 37, 39, 54, 70, 110, 180
release* /rɪˈlis/ 115, 117, 180, 188, 211, 213
relief /rɪˈlif/ 77, 79
remarkable /rɪˈmɑrkəbəl/ 2, 4, 70, 142
rent /rɛnt/ 167, 169
repair /rɪˈpɛr/ 197, 199
require* /rɪˈkwaɪə/ 31, 33, 38, 46, 60, 180
resemble /rɪˈzɛmbəl/ 85, 87, 102
reserve /rɪˈzɚv/ 52, 54
respond* /rɪˈspɑnd/ 77, 79
review /rɪˈvyu/ 108, 110, 116, 133, 134
robber /ˈrɑbə/ 141, 143
roof /ruf, rʊf/ 167, 169, 211

S

sailor /ˈseɪlə/ 197, 198, 199, 204
salary /ˈsæləri/ 16, 18, 25
satisfied /ˈsæṭɪsˌfaɪd/ 37, 38, 49
sauce /sɔs/ 69, 70
scared /skɛrd/ 8, 9, 46

screen /skrin/ 108, 110
script /skrɪpt/ 108, 110, 113
season /ˈsizən/ 141, 142, 149
seek* /sik/ 58, 60, 105, 204, 211
sell out /sɛl aʊt/ 77, 79, 117
set /sɛt/ 108, 110, 113
set out /sɛt aʊt/ 115, 117, 143, 207
shape /ʃeɪp/ 37, 39, 104, 169, 204, 211
shy /ʃaɪ/ 2, 4, 9
sign /saɪn/ 141, 143
sink /sɪŋk/ 203, 204, 205
skip /skɪp/ 147, 149
species /ˈspiʃiz, -siz/ 186, 188, 213
spicy /ˈspaɪsi/ 69, 70, 79
stage /steɪdʒ/ 186, 188
stand out /stænd aʊt/ 23, 25, 127
star /stɑr/ 8, 9, 25, 49
state /steɪt/ 115, 117
status* /ˈsteɪṭəs, ˈstæ-/ 167, 168
steady /ˈstɛdi/ 125, 127
strict /strɪkt/ 125, 127
succeed /səkˈsid/ 2, 4, 49, 70
surgery /ˈsɚdʒəri/ 178, 179
sweat /swɛt/ 178, 180
syllable /ˈsɪləbəl/ 147, 149
symbol* /ˈsɪmbəl/ 161, 162, 163
system /ˈsɪstəm/ 147, 149

T

take by surprise /teɪk baɪ səˈpraɪz, səˈpraɪz / 115, 116
task* /tæsk/ 203, 204

taste /teɪst/ 69, 70, 79, 102, 104, 105, 180
tend to /tɛnd tə/ 85, 87
the rest /ðə rɛst/ 203, 205
theme* /θim/ 52, 54
theory* /ˈθiəri, ˈθɪri/ 125, 127, 133, 134, 180, 199
ton /tʌn/ 203, 204
tough /tʌf/ 197, 199, 211
tourist /ˈtʊrɪst/ 58, 60, 168
towers /ˈtaʊəz/ 52, 54
trail /treɪl/ 186, 188, 213
trap /træp/ 186, 188, 211
treat /trit/ 16, 18, 213
trust /trʌst/ 115, 116, 156
turn on /tɚn ɔn, ɑn/ 92, 93
turn out /tɚn aʊt/ 125, 127

U

unique* /yuˈnik/ 52, 54, 60, 104, 162
unit /ˈyunɪt/ 147, 149

V

variety /vəˈraɪəṭi/ 77, 79, 104, 149, 213
vision* /ˈvɪʒən/ 186, 188

W

wasteful /ˈweɪstfəl/ 31, 32, 211
weapon /ˈwɛpən/ 186, 188
wish /wɪʃ/ 92, 93
worth it /wɚθ ɪt/ 167, 169

Photo Credits

Page 1 PhotoAlto/Alamy; **p. 2** ROB & SAS/Corbis; **p. 3** Dreamstime.com; **p. 8** (left) Lou-Foto/Alamy, (right) Photos 12/Alamy; **p. 15** Sean Gardner/Reuters/Corbis; p. 16 Melissa Majchrzak/NBAE/Getty Images; **p. 17** Barry Gossage/NBAE/Getty Images; **p. 19** Shutterstock.com; **p. 23** Rich Eaton/AMA/Corbis; **p. 24** Tommy Hindley/Professional Sport/NewSport/Corbis; **p. 26** (1) Shutterstock.com, (2) Shutterstock.com, (3) Shutterstock.com, (4) Shutterstock.com, (5) Shutterstock.com; **p. 30** Andre Kudyusov/Photolibrary; **p. 31** Shutterstock.com; **p. 32** Shutterstock.com; **p. 38** Robert Sorbo/Reuters/Corbis; **p. 51** (left) Shutterstock.com, (middle) Shutterstock.com, (right) Shutterstock.com; **p. 52** (left) Carl & Ann Purcell/Corbis, (middle) Layne Kennedy/Corbis, (right) Richard T. Nowitz/Corbis; **p. 53** Fredrik Sandberg/AFP/Getty Images; **p. 58** Ozimages/Alamy; **p. 60** Juan Jose Pascual/Photolibrary; **p. 62** (1) Shutterstock.com, (2) Shutterstock.com, (3) Shutterstock.com, (4) Shutterstock.com, (5) Shutterstock.com; **p. 65** Shutterstock.com; **p. 68** (left) Shutterstock.com, (middle) Studio Eye/Corbis, (right) Shutterstock.com; **p. 69** (all) Shutterstock.com; **p. 77** Shutterstock.com; **p. 78** Shutterstock.com; **p. 79** Shutterstock.com; **p. 80** (1) Shutterstock.com, (2) Shutterstock.com, (3) Shutterstock.com, (4) Shutterstock.com, (5) Shutterstock.com, (6) Shutterstock.com; **p. 84** Christopher Bigelow/Illustration Works/Corbis; **p. 85** (left) Shutterstock.com, (middle) Shutterstock.com, (right) Shutterstock.com; **p. 86** Shutterstock.com; **p. 87** Shutterstock.com; **p. 92** Shutterstock.com; **p. 98** Shutterstock.com; **p. 107** (left) DreamWorks Pictures/Photofest, (right) Warner Bros./Photofest; **p. 113** Shutterstock.com; **p. 124** Shutterstock.com; **p. 132** Heide Benser/Corbis; **p. 140** John Martin/Images.com; **p. 141** (left) Photos 12/Alamy, (right) Mike Reagan/National Geographic Stock; **p. 142** Shutterstock.com; **p. 147** (left) Moodboard/Alamy, (right) Danita Delimont/Alamy; **p. 148** Werner Forman/Corbis; **p. 154** (left) Shutterstock.com, (right) Shutterstock.com; **p. 157** (top) Shutterstock.com, (bottom) Shutterstock.com; **p. 160** Skyscraper Source Media Inc. SkyscraperPage.com skyscraper diagrams; **p. 161** (left) Shutterstock.com, (middle) Shutterstock.com, (right) Sandra Baker/Alamy; **p. 162** Shutterstock.com; **p. 163** (1) Shutterstock.com, (2) Shutterstock.com, (3) iStockphoto.com, (4) Shutterstock.com; **p. 164** (5) Shutterstock.com, (6) Shutterstock.com; **p. 165** Shutterstock.com; **p. 167** Shutterstock.com; **p. 169** Shutterstock.com; **p. 178** (left) Shutterstock.com, (right) Shutterstock.com; **p. 180** Shutterstock.com; **p. 186** (left) Shutterstock.com, (middle) Shutterstock.com, (right) Shutterstock.com; **p. 187** Arterra Picture Library/Alamy; **p. 196** Shutterstock.com; **p. 197** (left) Horizon International Images Limited/Alamy, (right) National Maritime Museum, London/The Image Works; **p. 198** Pictorial Press Ltd/Alamy; **p. 203** National Maritime Museum, Greenwich, London; **p. 204** Shutterstock.com.

Text Credits

Page 142: "Fallen sick on a journey." From *An Account of Our Master Basho's Last Days* by Takarai Kikaku, translated by Nobuyuki Yuasa in *Springtime in Edo*, 2006, Keisuisha Co. Ltd. Used with permission. "The old-lady cherry." From *Basho and His Interpreters: Selected Haiku with Commentary*, by Makoto Ueda. Copyright © 1992 by the Board of Trustees of the Leland Stanford Jr. University. All rights reserved. Used with the permission of Stanford University Press, www.sup.org. **Pages 143 and 148:** "Having planted a banana tree" from p. 32, How admirable!" from p. 24, and "The old pond." from p. 18 of Haiku by Basho from *The Essential Haiku: Versions of Basho, Buson & Issa*, Edited with an Introduction by Robert Hass. Introduction and selection copyright © 1994 by Robert Hass. Unless otherwise noted, all translations copyright © 1994 by Robert Hass. Reprinted by permission of HarperCollins Publishers. **Page 149:** "To convey one's mood." Used by permission of John Cooper Clarke.

MP3 Audio Tracking Guide

Track	Activity	Page
1	Audio Program Introduction	
2	Chapter 1 Vocabulary	2
3	Chapter 1: Why Are We Shy?	4
4	Chapter 2 Vocabulary	8
5	Chapter 2: It's All an Act	9
6	Chapter 3 Vocabulary	16
7	Chapter 3: A Tall Order	18
8	Chapter 4 Vocabulary	23
9	Chapter 4: Hull City Tigers Discussion Board	24
10	Chapter 5 Vocabulary	31
11	Chapter 5: A Cleaner Way to Shop?	32
12	Chapter 6 Vocabulary	37
13	Chapter 6: Green Airplanes	38
14	Fluency Practice 1: Aquatic Exercise	46
15	Fluency Practice 1: Michael Phelps: Keys to Success	49
16	Chapter 7 Vocabulary	52
17	Chapter 7: The World's Strangest Hotels	54
18	Chapter 8 Vocabulary	58
19	Chapter 8: Small Town, Strange Festival	60
20	Chapter 9 Vocabulary	69
21	Chapter 9: What Is American Food?	70
22	Chapter 10 Vocabulary	77
23	Chapter 10: Why Chilies Are Hot	79
24	Chapter 11 Vocabulary	85
25	Chapter 11: All About Music	87
26	Chapter 12 Vocabulary	92
27	Chapter 12: Can't Name That Tune?	93
28	Fluency Practice 2: Dangerous Dining	102
29	Fluency Practice 2: Wild Treasures	104
30	Chapter 13 Vocabulary	108
31	Chapter 13: Famous Flops	110
32	Chapter 14 Vocabulary	115
33	Chapter 14: Sleeper Hits	116
34	Chapter 15 Vocabulary	125
35	Chapter 15: Rebel with a Cause	126
36	Chapter 16 Vocabulary	132
37	Chapter 16: About *The Nurture Assumption*	133
38	Chapter 17 Vocabulary	141
39	Chapter 17: The Haiku Master	142
40	Chapter 18 Vocabulary	147
41	Chapter 18: So You Want to Write Haiku?	148
42	Fluency Practice 3: Folktales	155
43	Fluency Practice 3: Anansi Tales	158
44	Chapter 19 Vocabulary	161
45	Chapter 19: Race for the Sky	162
46	Chapter 20 Vocabulary	167
47	Chapter 20: Anybody Want to Buy a Stadium?	168
48	Chapter 21 Vocabulary	178
49	Chapter 21: Pheromone Perfume	179
50	Chapter 22 Vocabulary	186
51	Chapter 22: The Language of Pheromones	188
52	Chapter 23 Vocabulary	197
53	Chapter 23: The Chronometer	198
54	Chapter 24 Vocabulary	203
55	Chapter 24: The Treasure of the SS *Central America*	204
56	Fluency Practice 4: BIOMIMICRY: Frequently Asked Questions	211
57	Fluency Practice 4: Swarm Intelligence	213